PROUST AMONG
THE STARS

MALCOLM BOWIE

Proust Among
the Stars

HarperCollins*Publishers*

HarperCollins*Publishers*
77 - 85 Fulham Palace Road,
Hammersmith, London W6 8JB

Published by HarperCollins*Publishers* 1998
1 3 5 7 9 8 6 4 2

A catalogue record for this book
is available from the British Library

ISBN 0 00 255622 7

Set in Postscript Linotype Bulmer
by Rowland Phototypesetting Limited,
Bury St Edmunds, Suffolk

Printed and bound in Great Britain by
Clays Ltd, St Ives plc

Sind *wir* nicht auch ein Weltgebäude, so gut als der Sternenhimmel, und eines das wir besser kennen solten, und besser kennen könnten, sollte man denken, als das dort oben?

GEORG CHRISTOPH LICHTENBERG, *Gedankenbücher*

Are we too not a cosmic system, and one we know better, or at least ought to know better, than we do the heavenly firmament?

Notebooks

It would indeed give me a certain household joy to quit this lofty seeking, this spiritual astronomy, or search of stars, and come down to warm sympathies with you; but then I know well I shall mourn always the vanishing of my mighty gods.

RALPH WALDO EMERSON, 'Friendship'

LET THE MILKY WAY BE SPLIT INTO THE MILKY WAY OF INVENTOR/EXPLORERS AND THE MILKY WAY OF INVESTOR/EXPLOITERS

VELIMIR KHLEBNIKOV, *The Trumpet of the Martians*

CONTENTS

Note on Texts and Translations

My Proust quotations are taken from the new Pléiade edition of *A la recherche du temps perdu* (4 volumes under the general editorship of Jean-Yves Tadié, Paris, Gallimard, 1987–9), and accompanied in my main text by volume number and page. English translations of each passage quoted are taken from C. K. Scott Moncrieff's version as revised by Terence Kilmartin, and further revised, to take account of the additions and corrections made by Tadié and his team, by D. J. Enright (6 volumes, Chatto and Windus, 1992), and again accompanied by volume and number and page. I have silently corrected a number of minor errors in this admirable English version.

The novel itself, and its component volumes, are referred to by their French titles throughout:

A la recherche du temps perdu (*In Search of Lost Time*)
*Du côté de chez Swann** (*Swann's Way*)
A l'ombre des jeunes filles en fleurs (*Within a Budding Grove*)
Le Côté de Guermantes (*The Guermantes Way*)
Sodome et Gomorrhe (*Sodom and Gomorrah*)
La Prisonnière (*The Captive*)
Albertine disparue (*The Fugitive*)
Le Temps retrouvé (*Time Regained*)

* This volume is subdivided into 'Combray', 'Un Amour de Swann' ('Swann in Love'), and 'Noms de pays: le nom' ('Place-Names: The Name').

Sources for all other quotations and references are provided in the Notes section (below, pp. 329–38).

Preface

Le seul véritable voyage, le seul bain de Jouvence, ce ne serait pas d'aller vers de nouveaux paysages, mais d'avoir d'autres yeux, de voir l'univers avec les yeux d'un autre, de cent autres, de voir les cent univers que chacun d'eux voit, que chacun d'eux est; et cela nous le pouvons avec un Elstir, avec un Vinteuil, avec leurs pareils, nous volons vraiment d'étoiles en étoiles.

MARCEL PROUST, *A la recherche du temps perdu*

The only true voyage, the only bath in the Fountain of Youth, would be not to visit strange lands but to possess other eyes, to see the universe through the eyes of another, of a hundred others, to see the hundred universes that each of them sees, that each of them is; and this we can do with an Elstir, with a Vinteuil; with men like these we do really fly from star to star.

In Search of Lost Time

When it comes to the lives and the living quarters of great writers, I have done my share of snooping. Prague beckoned me because it was Kafka's city, and Dublin because it was Joyce's. To Monterey I went, my nostrils ready flared for the fish-stink of Steinbeck's Cannery Row, and to Key West to booze in Hemingway's favourite bars, and to Chawton in Hampshire to run a surreptitious hand across the table at which *Emma* and *Persuasion* were written. I have climbed Skiddaw in the footsteps of Keats, Helvellyn in those of Coleridge, and been driven by bus to the summit of Mont Ventoux, apologising self-importantly to the shade of Petrarch for not repeating the poet's pedestrian ascent of 1336. In Ravenna I have paused before Dante's tomb, and in Stinsford churchyard before the last resting place of Thomas Hardy's heart. Lisbon was Pessoa, Mexico City was Octavio Paz, and Athens became Thucydides for a moment when a taxi-driver spoke of him as if he were a still-living family friend.

I report all this scurrying about of mine without feelings of pride or shame, for tourism has always struck me as a harmless passion, and the literary pilgrimage in particular as the very model of a wholesome leisure pursuit. Besides, my journeys seemed always to enhance rather than damage the pleasures of reading: standing there in yuppified, odourless, modern Monterey, I began to thirst again for the exuberant low life that Steinbeck's writing conjures into being; the very smoothness of Jane Austen's table reminded me of all that was edgy and abrasive in her prose.

Those were my excuses anyway. And they left me ill-prepared for my most recent visit to Cabourg on the Normandy coast. I had known this unremarkable town long ago, and had grown accustomed to the huge hump of its Grand Hotel looming up through the autumn mists. Then as now the hotel was the only peculiarity of the place, but it was of a type that numberless small resorts to the east and west also boasted. I would have shrugged in lofty indifference if I had been told that Cabourg was the main model for Proust's enchanted Balbec, and would have refused to make any practical connection at all between the seaside temple to Eros that appears in his novel and the large commercial establishment perched greyly upon the promenade.

The first mistake I made, coming back to Cabourg after many years, was to order breakfast on the hotel terrace, along-side what was by then already known as the 'promenade Marcel

Proust', and the second was to persuade myself almost successfully that I could see the celebrated 'little band' of young girls
flitting back and forth on the otherwise deserted beach. Here
was perdition indeed for any serious admirer of Proust's *A la
recherche du temps perdu* (1913–27). Here was a world of
would-be Proustian experience that seemed not to require that
the novel be read, a universe parallel to that of Proust's text and
maintained in being by the combined forces of gossip, travelogue
and voyeuristic biographical speculation. Just as no one need see
King Lear performed to find out roughly what goes on in the play,
no one need embark on Proust's long sentences and involved
semantic textures to be charmed by Albertine and her friends, or
by the *petite madeleine*, or by Mme Verdurin's long climb from
the bourgeoisie to the aristocracy. Knowledge of these things is
amply available from commentaries on the novel; and Proust's
life, including his summer holidays, has been turned into such
convincing and accessible near-novels by biographers like André
Maurois and George Painter that the alchemical transformation
he himself performed on that life can easily seem slack and shape-
less in comparison.

I began to know in Cabourg a fear that I had not known at
any other of my literary destinations. This was the fear that I
might lose a supreme work of literature and never get it back;
that I would resign myself to a non-reading knowledge of the
novel, a Proust of tea-parties and table-talk, of selected short
quotations and haunting images that had long ago drifted free
of their original textual moorings. Obvious truths suddenly
needed restating: if Proust's life had been in some respects
mad, his novel was madder; if Proust the man had been both
a snob and an egalitarian, his novel pressed this contradiction
to a point of sublime extremity; if homosexuality had brought
everyday excitement and anxiety to Proust as a biographical
subject, it had become exorbitantly fascinating to the novel's

narrator – a spur to scientific curiosity, an endless adventure of the imagination, an Eleusinian mystery cult. Why settle for an ordinary 'writer's life' when this flagrant fiction was at hand? The little band were not Cabourg summer residents. The only place where Albertine and the others could live their Protean or Mephistophelian lives was on the farther shore of literary invention.

What follows, then, is an introduction to Proust's bulky book, and a tribute to the imaginative energy that propels it page after page. While I have no wish to deprive Cabourg, Illiers-Combray, the boulevard Haussmann or the Père Lachaise cemetery of their status as places of pilgrimage, or as stations on Proust's own journey towards artistic triumph, I shall argue here for the superior magnetism of his writing. My book offers a series of return routes to the dazzling procession of Proust's paragraphs, and a series of modest shrines to plurality, paradox and contradiction. Those paragraphs, to be sure, send the reader outwards to the real world, but to a wide and various world, rather than to the thin thread of Proust's biography.

A majestic respiratory rhythm is at work in *A la recherche du temps perdu*. On the one hand, the narrator of the novel has a mania for multiplicity, wants the world to contain more things rather than fewer, and stands guard over an unstoppable transformational machine. He speaks of the hundreds, thousands and millions of opportunities for new perception that the world affords, and of the novelist as an insatiable traveller in outer and inner space, always on the move and always driven by the demon of imagination to actualise the potential forms of things. How wrong I was, and how dishonest, this narrator cries in *La Prisonnière*, to begin the present volume so schematically and with such a thinned-down sense of what the world has in it: 'ce n'est pas un univers, c'est des millions, presque autant qu'il existe de prunelles et d'intelligences humaines, qui s'éveillent tous les

PREFACE

matins' (III, 696; 'it is not one universe, but millions, almost as
many as the number of human eyes and brains in existence, that
awake every morning' (V, 212)).

On the other hand, everything is connected to everything
else in the remembering or fantasising mind, and the oceanic
swell which seems to bear the voyager onwards to ever-new
destinations can easily bring him home to his habitual tastes
and his over-familiar emotional landmarks. Structure, limitation
and fewness have a way of reasserting themselves even as the
narrator seeks to be convinced that an indefinite plurality of
worlds lies at his feet. In *Le Temps retrouvé* a new parsimony
is discovered on the other side of plenitude. The association
of ideas, having taken the narrator on a long excursion, in due
course brings him back:

> le poète a eu raison de parler des «fils mystérieux» que la
> vie brise. Mais il est encore plus vrai qu'elle en tisse sans
> cesse entre les êtres, entre les événements, qu'elle entre-
> croise ces fils, qu'elle les redouble pour épaissir la trame,
> si bien qu'entre le moindre point de notre passé et tous les
> autres un riche réseau de souvenirs ne laisse que le choix
> des communications.   (IV, 607)

> the poet was right when he spoke of the 'mysterious threads'
> which are broken by life. But the truth, even more, is that
> life is perpetually weaving fresh threads which link one
> individual and one event to another, and that these threads
> are crossed and recrossed, doubled and redoubled to
> thicken the web, so that between any slightest point of our
> past and all the others a rich network of memories gives us
> an almost infinite variety of communicating paths to choose
> from.   (VI, 428)

After the ecstasy of difference without end comes the quiet
satisfaction of a connecting and unifying web.

The narrative breathes out, and the world is many. It

breathes in again, and the world is one. Look at the book from one angle, and it is overflowing with characters and incidents. Look at it from another angle, and the characters begin to merge, while the incidents in which they figure begin to resemble the after-shocks caused by a very small group of primal events. The narrator of the novel, far from being an impersonal manipulator of this rhythm, is himself caught inside it. At one moment, he is a loose compendium of characteristics. His voice contains many voices. He is a magpie and a mimic. He veers this way and that, and takes the colouring of the company he keeps. At the next moment, he seems to stand above the social flux, to be an individual, a singularity, a legislator, the helmsman of an artistic project that is going somewhere and must be kept on course. Proust's narrator is both chorus and soloist, a confusion of appetites and a single long-breathed desire.

Yet the sound of breathing that is to be heard in Proust's book comes not simply from the larger rhythms of its plot or from the periodic concentration and dispersal of the narrator's sense of selfhood, but from a language that is unique within the French literary tradition for its alternating copiousness and restraint. Proust's language now takes risks and now plays safe. It is full of lexical curiosities and of residual deposits left by earlier literary works, but also does many ordinary things in plain words. It cultivates elegance, ornament, obliqueness and *bel canto* and then switches to linguistic rough trade. It speaks of exquisite intimations that can occur only in a half-light and only on the margins of consciousness and then babbles of chamber-pots, leg-irons, aeroplane factories and policemen.

A diction of this kind, especially when it is combined with a literary syntax that seems to offer a working model of speculative thought, has an optimistic underlying message for the reader. Proust's writing – the fantastication of it, the fine-spun

texture of it, the power, pace and percipience of it – is a song
of intellectual gladness and an unwearying tribute to the muse
of comedy. If there were no stubborn philosophical problems
in the world, and no war, famine, disease or torture in it
either, all thinking might resemble a gracious and disinterested
Proustian paragraph. In the present sorry state of the world
we may find ourselves returning to Proust for a new sense
of mental largeness and potentiality. From within our dull,
platitudinous everyday language, we may go back to Proust,
as if to a great poet, to be reminded of the wonders that such
language, under pressure, can still perform. Proust's novel is
a three-thousand-page incantation, an insolently protracted
exercise in word-magic, a tonic, a restorative for any reader
who has gone tired and listless under a late twentieth-century
tide of verbal waste-matter. Perhaps Proust really is Europe's
last great writer, as some of his slogan-prone enthusiasts have
claimed.

Yet Proust's novel has another, less encouraging, story in
it. Seeking to localise this, we might be tempted to say, in the
words of Shakespeare's Troilus, that the narrator's 'desire is
boundless but his act a slave to limit', and there would be
evidence for this view. Proust's protagonist, for all his wishfulness, seems to have limited energy and willpower, and an
ailing sense of purpose. In the course of a very long tale told
about himself, he does not do much. In society, he is immobilised by the spectacle of other people's busy posturings. In the
inner realm, he sees bright futures ahead of him, but often
sinks back into an anxious torpor at the very moment when
decisive action is required to actualise any one of those possible
worlds. He havers. He maunders. He drugs himself with retrospection. Surely the narrator's vision of a boundless, million-
fold, endlessly self-transforming landscape of personal
experience is a compensatory fantasy of precisely the kind that

one would expect from someone who spent too long lazing indoors, refusing to pull himself together, venture forth and seize the day.

Well, yes. This is partly right. Proust's narrator is a comic creation, and he belongs, with Goncharov's Oblomov (1859), a variety of Chekhovian males, the hero of Svevo's *As a Man Grows Older* (1898) and Vladimir and Estragon in Beckett's *Waiting for Godot* (1952), to the company of those who, while seeming merely indolent and indecisive to the impatient observer, are withheld from action by what the connoisseur will recognise as an admirable reticence and *pudeur*. *A la recherche du temps perdu* is a comedy of hypertrophied appetites and shrunken deeds. But Proust is a tragedian, too, and the tragic vision that his novel sets forth is one in which desire itself is a slave to limit. Desire in Proust teases us with the promise of an unceasing plasticity, but underneath the changing array of its objects it is all the while subject to fixation. Early configurations of sexual feeling continue to haunt adult experience. Phobias, obsessions and fetishes keep turning the narrator's prospective, forward-flung imaginings back towards the needs, the injuries and the blighted pleasures of infancy. Desire keeps on repeating itself. It nags and needles, and will not let the past go. And Proust's lengthy book, even while it glitters with fantasy and invention, insists upon this bounded and fixated quality: a desolate pattern of recurrence, a sense of pre-ordained pain and dissatisfaction, governs the procession of its narrative episodes. All love affairs fail, and fail in the same way. All journeys end in disappointment. All satisfactions are too little and too late. Death picks off the narrator's admired mentors one by one, rekindling and reinforcing his childhood feelings of abandonment.

In what follows, then, my travels will take me back and forth inside Proust's novel rather than see me shuttling between my home and Cabourg, or between Cabourg and Balbec. As I travel I shall seek to recreate, in schematic and accessible form, the characteristic rhythms of the novel's unfolding. Proust's great work has 'big' themes, and its path-breaking author has one very old-fashioned way of handling these: his characters will announce a topic, warm to it, and hold forth upon it recklessly. I have chosen a cluster of these topics as my chapter-titles, not so much because Proust's characters have wise things to say about time, sex or death, although they often have, as because the ebb and flow of Proust's attention can be clearly observed against these featureless horizons. Such matters, singled out, have the further advantage of allowing us to look beneath the large tidal movements of the book and to rediscover the cross-currents and counter-rhythms that mark the individual Proust paragraph, and are the hallmark indeed of a speculative style that remains *sui generis*.

Let me not, however, sound too high-minded about the reflections gathered here. I do still long to feel the sand and shingle of the Cabourg shore between my toes, and I have not entirely given up hope of seeing the little band materialised before me as I wander there in the cold, Northern spray. But in the meantime Proust's gritty, breezy and salty book has many wonders, and to these I now turn.

I

Self

mi kirjavaista tähiksi taivaalle,
ne tähiksi taivaalle.

Kalevala

All that in the egg was mottled
Now became the stars in heaven.

The narrator of *A la recherche du temps perdu* is a splendid
example of the human type that Jane Austen called 'the imaginist'. This was her word for the person who spent too much
time fantasising and seemed always to be in flight from real
events and binding obligations. Yet where Emma Woodhouse
and Catherine Morland are gradually cured of their imaginative
excesses and wishful misperceptions, Proust's character is presented not simply as an untreatable case, but as one whose
power of fantasy, even when debilitating, is still essentially a
strength. And while Austen's imaginists devote themselves to
personal relationships, paying special attention to matters of
rank, taste and marriageability, Proust's narrator returns tirelessly to the structure, texture, density, consistency and continuity of the isolated human self. He imagines selfhood lost,
and found, and again lost.

His questions about personal identity sound strict and sol-
uble when they are formulated in philosophical or psychological
terms: is the self one or many, concentrated or dispersed,

1

continuous or fragmented, a rule-governed psycho-physical entity with its own integrative capacities or a side-effect of natural language in daily use? But for all his fluency in the handling of such concepts, the narrator's ruling passion is for images, or for abstractions that have an exposed nerve of imagery running through them. He looks to nature in his search for figurative representations of selfhood, and has a special fondness for the planets and stars. Albertine is a nebula, the little band a constellation; the face of an actress seen in close-up is a Milky Way, and family relationships are the scattered segments of a single exploding star. Whether he looks outwards to his sexual partner or the social group or inwards to the tissue of his own memories and desires, his characteristic task is that of 'modelling nebulae' (III, 874; V, 425). All his heavenly configurations are poised undecidably between coherence and dispersal, just as the real nebulae themselves may contain powerful intimations of structure (here a crab, there a spiral) while continuing to impress us by their sheer nebulosity. Problems posed in these terms can have and need have no solutions. The Proustian imaginist leads a nomadic life. He is at home inside his comet-tail of images.

Modern computational scholarship has revealed that the word *moi*, as noun or pronoun ('self', 'me' or 'myself'), occurs on average 1.1996 times per page in Proust's novel. Few readers, of course, will be surprised by this scrap of statistical information, for the novel is still widely thought of as being concerned above all else with the splendours and miseries of the self-absorbed human individual. Even those who dislike the notion of 'self', and think of it as the sign of a dangerously unhistorical attitude to the study of the human subject, are likely to grant Proust's vast and intricate discussion of the notion an important historical place: the modern, secular, psychological *moi*, launched upon its spectacular European career in the sixteenth century, reaches in Proust a moment of extraordinary power and authority. For a moment, indeed, the human self and its vicissitudes become the essential subject-matter of art. And even if Proust's novel, in its insistent and sometimes deranged talk of the *moi*, contains the seeds of the self's decay, his achievement is none the less a splendid one. The notion of self may seem antiquated, and it may often be used to draw attention away from the interpersonal and social worlds in which the human sense of personal identity is con-structed, but in Proust's account the notion is flexible, hospit-able to experience, thoroughly immersed in society, and obdurately problematic.

The narrator wonders at the beginning of *Le Côté de Guer-mantes* how the human personality acquires its improbable power of endurance. How is it, for example, that, having once fallen into deep sleep, one is able to become again the individual one once was? Why does one not wake up in the morning as someone else?

> On appelle cela un sommeil de plomb, il semble qu'on soit devenu, soi-même, pendant quelques instants après qu'un tel sommeil a cessé, un simple bonhomme de plomb. On n'est plus personne. Comment, alors, cherchant sa pensée, sa personnalité comme on cherche un objet perdu, finit-on par retrouver son propre moi plutôt que tout autre? Pour-quoi, quand on se remet à penser, n'est-ce pas alors une autre personnalité que l'antérieure qui s'incarne en nous? On ne voit pas ce qui dicte le choix et pourquoi, entre les millions d'êtres humains qu'on pourrait être, c'est sur celui qu'on était la veille qu'on met juste la main.   (II, 387)

> We call that a leaden sleep, and it seems as though, even for a few moments after such a sleep is ended, one has oneself become a simple figure of lead. One is no longer a person. How then, searching for one's thoughts, one's

3

personality, as one searches for a lost object, does one
recover one's own self rather than any other? Why, when
one begins again to think, is it not a personality other than
the previous one that becomes incarnate in one? One fails
to see what dictates the choice, or why, among the millions
of human beings one might be, it is on the being one was
the day before that unerringly one lays one's hand.

(III, 93–4)

Seeking the self as one might seek a lost object is here submitted
to one limitation only, but that is a daunting one. The object
cannot not be found. Still baffled by sleep, still dispersed and
nebulous, the newly awake individual homes in upon, and
efficiently reassumes, his accustomed form. He cannot do otherwise. Descriptions of this kind are not unfamiliar in Proust's
book, and they offer an optimistic allegory of its overall ontological project. After battlement, understanding; after dispersal,
concentration and self-knowledge.

Le *Temps retrouvé* fulfils the promise of passages like this.
It sets forth a *tableau vivant* in which the evanescent multitude
of the narrator's previous selves at last finds anchorage; in
which every lost object is found; in which the conflicting dispositions of the human individual, and the endless varieties and
sub-varieties of human passion, are assigned their place in an
inclusive artistic design ('comme une église [. . .] comme un
régime [. . .] comme un monde' (IV, 610); 'like a church [. . .]
like a medical regime [. . .] like a new world' (VI, 431)); and
in which the narrator, speaking on behalf of all men and women
from the vantage-point of that design, can at last affirm as a
source of certainty and clear moral vision the very self that had
previously been so mobile and so scattered. *Le Temps retrouvé*
describes a simple chain reaction: the sudden ecstatic rediscovery of a past that had been thought forever lost reveals the
temporal architecture of the self, the invariant substratum that
until then had been present but unrecognised beneath its fluid

4

and accidental surface forms; this ontological discovery triggers an artistic one, which in turn creates an exhilarating sense of moral purpose. And this culminating sequence of mental events can easily be thought of as providing Proust's plot with its denouement and the reader with a global answer to countless earlier riddles that may have teased her. In the slow unfolding of the book, she will have noticed a bewildering plurality of narrating selves, and may well have wondered what authorisation Proust had, what strange dispensation from the ordinary requirements of verisimilitude, when he brought together, in his portrayal of a supposed single individual, saint and scoundrel, eagle and dove, liar and exemplary truth-teller. The narrator in his last triumphantly stable form becomes a capacious container for all the waywardness, inconsistency and self-division that have marked his passage through the text.

There seems to me something unsatisfactory about any reading of the book that does not resist as well as endorse *Le Temps retrouvé* in the performance of this harmonising and integrating role. Proust's last volume is a guide for the perplexed and does indeed illuminate many corners left dark by earlier volumes. Moreover the supremely accommodating selfhood of *Le Temps retrouvé*, far from merely altering retroactively what has gone before, confirms and blazons forth a notion that has already made many premonitory appearances. We need a guiding, stabilising notion of human individuality with which to battle our way through the intricacies of Proust's text, and, late in the book but also earlier, Proust provides us with one. But what do we lose when we adhere too closely to the ontological *telos* of the book? We lose, I shall be suggesting in what follows, a whole range of paradoxes, dissonances and unusual consonances, and with them a vein of disturbing moral speculation. We lose also the sheer oddity of Proust's final volume. The reader who has felt his or her perplexities dissolve as the general teleological pattern of the book emerges is invited to look again, and more fondly, at certain of its perplexing details. It could be that Proust was in need of a resonant exit-speech when he promoted involuntary memory to its crowning role, and that his narrator's celebrated 'quest' in fact gives no more than a lightweight intellectual superstructure and an air of righteous striving to a mental adventure of a less than public-spirited kind.

The strangeness of this adventure, and the extravagant expenditure of time and ingenuity into which it periodically leads the narrator, may be observed with special clarity in *Le Côté de Guermantes*. Among many passages in which the supposedly overriding ontological programme of the novel is not only absent but unthinkable even as a premonition, I have chosen the scenes of jealousy and recrimination between Saint-Loup and Rachel in which the narrator figures as a singularly elastic *terzo incomodo* (II, 456–81; III, 176–207). The psychological drama here belongs quite as much to the narrator as to the enraged and acrimonious lovers whom he observes. Indeed his monologue is punctuated by silences on the one hand and by cascading repetitions on the other, and in each case displays the symptoms of an urgent undeclared passion. When a chance encounter with two of Rachel's former fellow-prostitutes threatens to reveal to Saint-Loup more of her past than she would care to have him know, it is the anxiously repetitious narrator rather than either of his companions who dominates the scene:

> Il ne fit pas qu'entrevoir cette vie, mais aussi au milieu une Rachel tout autre que celle qu'il connaissait, une Rachel pareille à ces deux petites poules, une Rachel à vingt francs. En somme Rachel s'était un instant dédoublée pour lui, il avait aperçu à quelque distance de sa Rachel la Rachel petite poule, la Rachel réelle, à supposer que la Rachel poule fût plus réelle que l'autre. Robert eut peut-être l'idée alors que

cet enfer où il vivait, avec la perspective et la nécessité
d'un mariage riche, d'une vente de son nom, pour pouvoir
continuer à donner cent mille francs par an à Rachel, il
aurait peut-être pu s'en arracher aisément et avoir les faveurs
de sa maîtresse, comme ces calicots celles de leurs grues,
pour peu de chose. Mais comment faire?   (II, 460)

He not only glimpsed this life, but saw also in the thick of
it a Rachel quite different from the one he knew, a Rachel
like those two little tarts, a twenty-franc Rachel. In short,
Rachel had for the moment duplicated herself in his eyes;
he had seen, at some distance from his own Rachel, the
little tart Rachel, the real Rachel, if it can be said that Rachel
the tart was more real than the other. It may then have
occurred to Robert that from the hell in which he was living,
with the prospect and the necessity of a rich marriage, of
the sale of his name, to enable him to go on giving Rachel
a hundred thousand francs a year, he might easily perhaps
have escaped, and have enjoyed the favours of his mistress,
as the two counter-jumpers enjoyed those of their girls, for
next to nothing. But how was it to be done?   (III, 181)

In a sense, of course, the narrator is simply adopting Saint-
Loup's uncertainties in the act of describing them, and allowing
his own eloquence to be dulled by a passion that can do no
more than impotently repeat the beloved's name. But there is
too much writing of this kind for such an explanation to be
fully satisfactory. The economic dimension of this passage has
already been set forth, and in similarly stammering terms: the
'Rachel . . . Rachel' refrain to be found here continues a lengthy
'vingt francs . . . vingt francs' refrain from a few pages earlier
(II, 457; III, 177–8), and this trifling amount – Rachel's prosti-
tutional price – has been insistently played off against the
excessive amounts that her lover must now expect to pay in
order to keep her, or that he might now be tempted to pay
in order to uncover her secrets. These calculations in francs
proliferate in the text at this point and acquire a fantasmatic

life of their own. And while it is not surprising to be told that passion has a price-structure and is subject to market forces, it is perfectly alarming to find these home truths reiterated and rephrased over several pages. A delirious monetary system has invaded the text and is busily translating its characteristic psychological idiom into cash terms. Why? What was it that worried the narrator so much, once upon a time, and that now so unsettles the telling of his tale?

On the face of it, this is an elaborate Proustian conceit on the familiar themes of duplication and duplicity. Rachel is not what she seems. Or rather, like her namesake in *La Juive* (1835), the Halévy–Scribe opera from which the narrator extracts for her the nickname 'Rachel quand du Seigneur' (I, 567; 'Rachel when from the Lord' (II, 175)), she is two people at once and bears two different prices. Scribe's Rachel is both Jew and Christian; Proust's is both sexual commodity and an idolised lady 'of great price'. But the social and financial *dédoublement* of Rachel prefigures another play of alternating perspectives, and one with which the novel is henceforth to be hugely preoccupied: the play between heterosexuality and homosexuality. And the martyrdom that awaits Scribe's heroine in the closing scene of *La Juive* is to be assumed not by the modern Rachel of *A la recherche* but by the narrator himself, whose path towards knowledge of human sexuality is to be, in its later stages, slow, cruel and disconsolate. The disarray of the narrative during this episode, and its feverish fluctuations of tone, are so marked yet so little explained that we read on 'for the plot', demanding to know more.

The revelation that Saint-Loup is a homosexual prompts, it will be remembered, the long, melancholy coda of *Albertine disparue*. At the end of a volume in which an immitigable sense of loss has become the ground of consciousness – in which Albertine's flight and death bring uncontrollably to the narrator's mind the absences with which she had tormented him when present and alive – the discovery that Saint-Loup is 'comme ça' (IV, 241; 'one of those' (V, 762)) provides consciousness with its culminating loss, its final unthinkable extremity. At the very moment when it was impossible to imagine things worse, worse they became. The vulgar monosyllabic 'comme ça' rings out as a portent and a malediction. And, in a sentence from *Albertine disparue* that in many editions of the novel is used to bring the volume to a close, the narrator's memory of himself, Saint-Loup and Rachel at a restaurant table moves him to tears that the ratiocinative texture of his monologue can do nothing to explain: 'en repensant à ces histoires du lift et du restaurant où j'avais déjeuné avec Saint-Loup et Rachel j'étais obligé de faire un effort pour ne pas pleurer' (IV, 266; 'when I thought about those stories of the lift-boy and of the restaurant in which I had had lunch with Saint-Loup and Rachel, I was obliged to make an effort to restrain my tears' (V, 793)); in a novel that is plotted and paced with astonishing skill throughout, the Saint-Loup sub-plot stands out as a particularly ingenious tale of mystery and suspense. In part, the beauty of its denouement lies simply in the light that the narrator's banal discovery sheds upon earlier incidents in the novel, and in the outrageous expanse of text that separates behavioural effect from psychological cause. Saint-Loup behaves oddly during the restaurant scene and those that follow – he is by turns craven and defiant towards Rachel, and twice resorts to fisticuffs in her company – and it is only after 1,500 pages that this behaviour is at last seen as coherently motivated. This is architectonic plotting of a kind that *Tom Jones* (1749) and *Tristram Shandy* (1759–67) made familiar, although Proust's edifice contains cantilevers, suspensions and buttresses still more audacious than those of Fielding or Sterne.

But this denouement is fine and imposing in another way too. The withheld weeping upon which *Albertine disparue* ends is reminiscent of Tennyson's

> Tears, idle tears, I know not what they mean,
> Tears from the depth of some divine despair
> Rise in the heart, and gather to the eyes,
> In looking on the happy Autumn-fields,
> And thinking of the days that are no more.

The narrator's tears are a symptom without a cause, or with a cause – a 'divine despair', as one might indeed call it – that is much too large to have exact explanatory force. They are *lacrimae rerum* provoked by the memory not of Priam slain but of a tiff and a street brawl. At this level, the ending does not so much solve earlier mysteries as echo and reinforce the narrator's earlier puzzlement. An abiding residue of doubt surrounds the Rachel episode. This has to do not with Saint-Loup's motives but with the narrator's own, and not with a single sexual discovery but with the anxious speculation on sexuality for which the narrator is a perpetual vehicle. In the company of Saint-Loup and Rachel, he cannot say what is going on, for they kindle in him too many disparate desires. And selfhood, if it is here at all, lies not in a stable, adjudicating narrative voice but in the versatile play of appetite that the narrator displays. He is voluble and laconic, intrusive and discreet. He sides with man against woman and woman against man. He aligns himself both with the homosexual desire of the 'promeneur passionné' by whom Saint-Loup is accosted in this scene and with Saint-Loup's seemingly wounded and seemingly heterosexual pride in refusing unwelcome advances. The 'self' on offer here is a vacancy awaiting substance and structure, a mobile force-field in which the desires of others meet and are inflected, a rapid sequence of reactive and imitative gestures.

The relationship between the narrator at the start of *Le Côté de Guermantes* and the narrator at the end of *Albertine disparue* is a strong one and creates a powerful effect of internal cohesion within the novel. But this effect is not produced by recreating at the later point a personality, an identity, a temperament or a pattern of connected psychological motifs that was already present earlier. It comes from the buttressing of one fragmentary psychological portrait against another of the same kind, and from a sense of perplexity and dispossession that becomes more pronounced as the plot unfolds.

What makes Proust's polymorphous narrator such an improbable textual construction in these central volumes of the novel is the cult of scientific precision that he adheres to even as he records his losses and confusions. Not only is the narrator's volatile and almost self-free consciousness not nebulous, but Proust, in describing its characteristic motions and the behaviour in which they issue, repeatedly turns to the exactitude of the exact sciences. When Saint-Loup unleashes blows upon a shabbily dressed sexual opportunist, the narrator reports having seen not fists but a non-human display of matter and kinetic energy:

> tout à coup, comme apparaît au ciel un phénomène astral, je vis des corps ovoïdes prendre avec une rapidité vertigineuse toutes les positions qui leur permettaient de composer, devant Saint-Loup, une instable constellation. Lancés comme par une fronde ils me semblèrent être au moins au nombre de sept. Ce n'étaient pourtant que les deux poings de Saint-Loup, multipliés par leur vitesse à changer de place dans cet ensemble en apparence idéal et décoratif. Mais cette pièce d'artifice n'était qu'une roulée qu'administrait Saint-Loup et dont le caractère agressif au lieu d'esthétique me fut d'abord révélé par l'aspect du monsieur médiocrement habillé, lequel parut perdre à la fois toute contenance, une mâchoire, et beaucoup de sang. (II, 480)

11

suddenly, as an astral phenomenon flashes through the sky, I saw a number of ovoid bodies assume with a dizzy swiftness all the positions necessary for them to compose a flickering constellation in front of Saint-Loup. Flung out like stones from a catapult, they seemed to me to be at the very least seven in number. They were merely, however, Saint-Loup's two fists, multiplied by the speed with which they were changing place in this – to all appearance ideal and decorative – arrangement. But this elaborate display was nothing more than a pummelling which Saint-Loup was administering, the aggressive rather than aesthetic character of which was first revealed to me by the aspect of the shabbily dressed gentleman who appeared to be losing at once his self-possession, his lower jaw and a quantity of blood.

(III, 205 – 6)

The moment of misrecognition is arrested and lingered over, but not because the mental processes involved are complex ones. Indeed the first goal of this description seems to be that of expelling mind from the scene in favour of a pure science of behaviour: wishes, goals and intentions are replaced by the muscular movements of the human body and these then become the professional property of the astronomer, the geometer and the arithmetician.

This holding back of concern for the motivation and moral status of human action is of course a mainspring of much Proustian wit, and is often to be seen at work on a large scale. The social performances of the Guermantes clan become a fencing match, in which their cold, steely gaze turns to real steel (II, 736; III, 513). During the Doncières episode, Saint-Loup retells the history of human warfare as an exquisite tale of bloodless strategic schemes transmitted from age to age (II, 407 – 15; III, 118 – 28). Mme Verdurin, appalled at the mention of a 'bore', is transformed into a lifeless piece of civic sculpture (I, 254; I, 311). Legrandin's sycophancy, as he bows to a local landowner's wife in Combray, is perfectly expressed by, and dissolved into, the 'undulation of pure matter' that passes through his animated rump (I, 148; 'ondulation de pure matière' (I, 123)). In all these cases, the pleasures of scansion, measurement and formal description are rediscovered in the jungle of social life. The narrator removes himself from the savage contest of human desires into a handsomely equipped observatory from which greed, lust, ambition, violence and hatred may be viewed as so much matter extended in space. But Proust's countless sudden excursions into natural science, for all the intellectual clarity that each of them individually displays, do not exert an integrative and centralising force upon his phenomenology of selfhood. His optical expertise is applied in what appears as a conscientiously indiscriminate fashion. This is not Newton's optics, in which the machinery of vision guarantees the intelligibility of the universe, although Proust's scientific phrasing often has an unmistakably Newtonian ring. It is an impatient, desiring optics, intent upon multiplying the opportunities for human sight and enlarging the field of vision, and readily able to accept that each visual constellation is short-lived. Stars become fists, and fists, once recognised as instruments of aggression, trace for a moment a further, more abstract, astronomical pattern. And then the whole contraption is lost from view.

A la recherche contains innumerable moments of intense vision that have no cumulative scientific force and pay no ontological dividend. Proust dramatises the brevity and singularity of these moments with a succession of images, running through the entire book, in which the eye itself becomes an object of sight. Legrandin's eye receives the first of his many wounds when the limits of his social success begin to be revealed:

> je vis au milieu des yeux bleus de notre ami se ficher une
> petite encoche brune comme s'ils venaient d'être percés par
> une pointe invisible, tandis que le reste de la prunelle réagis-
> sait en sécrétant des flots d'azur.   (I, 125–6)

> I saw in the middle of each of our friend's blue eyes a little
> brown nick appear, as though they had been stabbed by
> some invisible pin-point, while the rest of the pupil reacted
> by secreting the azure overflow.   (I, 152)

Later in 'Combray', when the narrator's own worldly ambition
is at stake, his eye undergoes a similar but more pleasurable
violence from the eyes of Mme de Guermantes:

> en même temps, sur cette image que le nez proéminent, les
> yeux perçants, épinglaient dans ma vision (peut-être parce
> que c'était eux qui l'avaient d'abord atteinte, qui y avaient
> fait la première encoche, au moment où je n'avais pas encore
> le temps de songer que la femme qui apparaissait devant
> moi pouvait être Mme de Guermantes), sur cette image toute
> récente, inchangeable, j'essayais d'appliquer l'idée: «C'est
> Mme de Guermantes» sans parvenir qu'à la faire manœuvrer
> en face de l'image, comme deux disques séparés par un
> intervalle.   (I, 173)

> at the same time, I was endeavouring to apply to this image,
> which the prominent nose, the piercing eyes pinned down
> and fixed in my field of vision (perhaps because it was they
> that had first struck it, that had made the first impression
> on its surface, before I had had time to wonder whether the
> woman who thus appeared before me might possibly be
> Madame de Guermantes), to this fresh and unchanging
> image, the idea: 'It's Madame de Guermantes'; but I suc-
> ceeded only in making the idea pass between me and the
> image, as though they were two discs moving in separate
> planes with a space between.   (I, 210)

In the scene with Rachel, Saint-Loup's eyes record his sudden
switches of mood: 'il était tellement rempli par son indignation

contre le danseur, qu'elle venait adhérer exactement à la surface
de ses prunelles [. . .] une zone disponible et souple parut dans
ses yeux [. . .] ses yeux étincelaient encore de colère' (II, 479–
80; 'he was so full of his indignation with the dancer that it
clung to the very surface of his eyeballs [. . .] a zone of accessi-
bility appeared in his eyes [. . .] his eyes were still blazing with
anger' (III, 204–6)). In such cases as these the eyeball is a
transmitter rather than a receiver of information, and a new
set of hallucinatory anatomical and physiological features are
ascribed to it: the eye may release coloured secretions, emit or
receive arrows or pins, contain notches or unsuspected empty
zones, and be coated in an adhesive glaze. The windows of
the soul and the 'speaking' eyes of popular fiction have here
been superseded by an entirely reorganised organ of sight. The
price to be paid for this varied repertory of more-than-ocular
effects, this uncanny ability of the eye to materialise mental
states upon its outer surface, is extreme brevity and discontinuity in the messages it emits. For the eye, like any
other object of sight, is a moving configuration of planes, volumes and textures, and it has almost no retentive power.
Albertine's eyes – 'qui [. . .] semblent faits de plusieurs mor-
ceaux' (III, 599; 'which [. . .] seem to be composed of several
pieces' (V, 96)) – are an unreadable encyclopaedia of fears,
impulses, schemes and deceptions, while those of la princesse
de Nassau – 'yeux stellaires, semblables à une horloge astrono-
mique' (IV, 557; 'stellar eyes, like an astronomical clock' (VI,
363)) – are a flickering chronicle of her remembered and
half-remembered sexual encounters. This dismantling and reassembly of the visual apparatus is a source of pathos at certain
moments in the novel and of creative affirmation at others; the
eye is a miniature world that now slips from the perceiver's
grasp, now offers him a new speculative adventure. But in
either event, Proust's account speaks of perception without a

core, of daily pattern-making that no higher pattern guides.

The narrator's wish to see clearly and to draw reliable infer-ences from what he sees is often outpaced by other emotional demands. His science fails even as he protests its strong-mindedness and rigour. Some obscure yet powerful drive requires the newly achieved explanation or paradigm to fall apart, to return to the 'several pieces' from which it had been made. Science must be present in the book, but without becom-ing cumulative or developing any significant power of predic-tion. He wants coherence, and does not want it.

Such indecision can be intensely disruptive. During his rev-erie on the cries of Paris in *La Prisonnière*, for example, the narrator remarks that the local fruit-and-vegetable seller prob-ably knew nothing of the plainsong that her melodious cries resembled. Although Leo Spitzer, in a celebrated essay, has pointed out that her medieval predecessors are indeed likely to have known certain Gregorian cadences well, it is unreason-able to expect a modern street-trader to have any detailed knowledge of medieval musical theory. Yet this is what the narrator seems for a moment to wish when he speaks of her being ignorant of 'l'antiphonaire et [les] sept tons qui symbo-lisent, quatre les sciences du quadrivium et trois celles du trivium' (III, 625; 'the antiphonary, or of the seven notes that symbolise, four the arts of the quadrivium and three those of the trivium' (V, 127)). Beneath the seeming condescension of this, an urgent Proustian impulse towards exact measurement is finding expression. The cry itself:

> A la tendresse, à la verduresse
> Artichauts tendres et beaux
> Arti-chauts
>
> Tender and green,
> Artichokes tender and sweet,
> Ar . . . tichokes

16

is dizzily overdetermined at this point in the novel. Tenderness has begun to retreat from the human to the vegetable world, and artichokes now possess a freshness that the relationship between Albertine and the narrator does not. The intoned phrases rising from the street connect modern Paris to its medieval past, commerce to religious observance, popular song to elevated musical culture, and eating to the arts and sciences of mankind. This is one of many points at which Proust's text, so richly apparelled in the language-based sciences of the trivium, suddenly becomes aware of the role that the sciences of number and measurement also play in its analytic fabric. His quadrivium is to be found not simply in the scientific imagery of the novel but in the calculating intelligence with which seemingly remote areas of experience are brought into conjunction. But where arithmetic, geometry, music and astronomy were, for the Pythagorean tradition, akin to one another as co-equal and mutually confirming manifestations of Number, for Proust no underlying principle firmer than that of analogy unites them. The 'stellar eyes' of la princesse de Nassau, like Saint-Loup's constellated fists, promise not an ultimate congruence between the minute and the vast but an endless journey from one moment of resemblance, and one relativistic act of measurement, to the next. And this journey in turn promises not a philosophical emancipation from the passions but a new way of measuring their force. Speaking of his infatuation with Mme de Guermantes, the narrator recalls: 'Pour moi ce n'était plus seulement les étoiles et la brise, mais jusqu'aux divisions arithmétiques du temps qui prenaient quelque chose de douloureux et de poétique' (II, 419; 'For me it was no longer the stars and the breeze alone, but the arithmetical divisions of time that assumed a dolorous and poetic aspect' (III, 132)).

Proust's scansions often cross vast distances, and move with an assured step between microcosm and macrocosm. They show him to have been a metaphysical wit possessed of a strong liking for physics, and an 'interdisciplinarist' beyond the dreams of the modern university. In this passage from *Le Temps retrouvé*, for example, a future astronomy of social life is sketched:

> si dans ces périodes de vingt ans les conglomérats de coteries se défaisaient et se reformaient selon l'attraction d'astres nouveaux destinés d'ailleurs eux aussi à s'éloigner, puis à reparaître, des cristallisations puis des émiettements suivis de cristallisations nouvelles avaient lieu dans l'âme des êtres.
>
> (IV, 570)

> If in a period of twenty years [. . .] the conglomerations of social groups had disintegrated and re-formed under the magnetic influence of new stars destined themselves also to fade away and then to reappear, the same sequence of crystallisation followed by dissolution and again by a fresh crystallisation might have been observed to take place within the consciousness of individuals.
>
> (VI, 379)

For a moment the natural and human sciences have become intelligible to each other, and a single dynamism – that of alternating dispersal and concentration – is seen to govern the stars in their courses, the growth of crystals, the structure of the human mind, and Mme Verdurin in her successive salons. This is a vision both of order within the cosmos and of the ungovernable plurality of mental worlds. The self reels between an outer world that is too big for it, and an inwardness that has too many transient shapes.

In *La Prisonnière*, this plurality had already received its loftiest encomium, and had been quite disconnected from any focusing device or principle of order:

18

Des ailes, un autre appareil respiratoire, et qui nous permissent de traverser l'immensité, ne nous serviraient à rien. Car si nous allions dans Mars et dans Vénus en gardant les mêmes sens, ils revêtiraient du même aspect que les choses de la Terre tout ce que nous pourrions voir. Le seul véritable voyage, le seul bain de Jouvence, ce ne serait pas d'aller vers de nouveaux paysages, mais d'avoir d'autres yeux, de voir l'univers avec les yeux d'un autre, de cent autres, de voir les cent univers que chacun d'eux voit, que chacun d'eux est; et cela nous le pouvons avec un Elstir, avec un Vinteuil, avec leurs pareils, nous volons vraiment d'étoiles en étoiles. (III, 762)

A pair of wings, a different respiratory system, which enabled us to travel through space, would in no way help us, for if we visited Mars or Venus while keeping the same senses, they would clothe everything we could see in the same aspect as the things of Earth. The only true voyage, the only bath in the Fountain of Youth, would be not to visit strange lands but to possess other eyes, to see the universe through the eyes of another, of a hundred others, to see the hundred universes that each of them sees, that each of them is; and this we can do with an Elstir, with a Vinteuil; with men like these we do really fly from star to star. (V, 291)

This interlacing of optics, astronomy and music, which is also an indefinite sequence of displacements between small and vast, not only promises no selfhood to the artist and to those who follow his example, it presents selfhood as an impediment to creative perception. The only conception of self that can usefully remain in force is that of a discontinuous itinerary, leading towards but never reaching that moment of plenitude at which the entire range of possible world-forms would stand revealed and realised. When each human being has become a hundred universes, who will then be the gentleman, the liar, the thief or the novelist? Such visions of an ideally dispossessed and characterless human individuality occur often as Proust's novel moves grandly towards the apotheosis of self upon which *Le Temps retrouvé* ends, as if those last moments of potency and moral resolve could be attained only by way of an emptiness within the self resembling that of interstellar space. The '«nous» qui serait sans contenu' (III, 371; 'a *we* that is void of content' (IV, 440)) of which the narrator had spoken in *Sodome et Gomorrhe* has now become an essential precondition for artistic creativity.

What is set out as a credo in *La Prisonnière* has been present from an early stage in the narrator's practical performances both as a social observer and as an introspective. The narrator makes his presence felt by his special habit of removing himself from the scene, becoming weightless, 'without content', *sine materia*. In this as in so many other respects, Swann is his model. Swann passes through social gatherings without leaving his imprint. At the Saint-Euverte *soirée* in 'Un Amour de Swann', he is an all-transforming eye. Grooms become greyhounds as he looks at them, and guests become carp. The domestic staff are a living embodiment of European art history: some of them seem to have emerged three-dimensionally from paintings by Mantegna, Dürer or Goya, and others are animated statues from classical antiquity or from the workshop of Benvenuto Cellini. The assembled males arrange themselves into a procession of highly individualised monocles (I, 317–22; I, 388–94). This vertiginous outward scene is matched by an inconstant inner world thinly disguised as a unified self:

> ce que nous croyons notre amour, notre jalousie, n'est pas une même passion continue, indivisible. Ils se composent d'une infinité d'amours successifs, de jalousies différentes et qui sont éphémères, mais par leur multitude ininterrompue donnent l'impression de la continuité, l'illusion de l'unité. La vie de l'amour de Swann, la fidélité de sa jalousie, étaient

faites de la mort, de l'infidélité, d'innombrables désirs, d'innombrables doutes, qui avaient tous Odette pour objet.

(I, 366)

what we suppose to be our love or our jealousy is never a single, continuous and indivisible passion. It is composed of an infinity of successive loves, of different jealousies, each of which is ephemeral, although by their uninterrupted multiplicity they give us the impression of continuity, the illusion of unity. The life of Swann's love, the fidelity of his jealousy, were formed of the death, the infidelity, of innumerable desires, innumerable doubts, all of which had Odette for their object. (I, 448)

Whether the narrator looks outwards or inwards, he studies hard to become centreless and characterless in this way and to become, in Keats's phrase, 'a thoroughfare for all thoughts'.

The morally resolved artist into whom the narrator is transformed at the end of the novel is himself an improbable construction. He has of course been foreshadowed on numerous earlier occasions, as have the moral principles on which he is to base his critique of social man and woman. That he is eventually to be an altruist, a respecter of individual rights, a truth-teller and a trenchant prosecutor of corruption and folly has already been half-promised by the narrator's elaborately textured social observation. What is more, the narrator has been shown to be capable both of energetic moral commitment and of firm self-criticism for his failures to act virtuously. But as a moralist he has other characteristics too, and these leave us only partially prepared for Proust's exalted final perspectives.

Gilbert Ryle, in his essay on Jane Austen, speaks 'with conscious crudity' of moralists as belonging either to the Calvinist or to the Aristotelian camp. While members of the first group think of human beings 'as either Saved or Damned, either Elect or Reject, either children of Virtue or children of

21

Vice', those of the second pursue distinctions of an altogether
more delicate kind:

> the Aristotelian pattern of ethical ideas represents people as
> differing from one another in degree and not in kind, and
> differing from one another not in respect just of a single
> generic Sunday attribute, Goodness, say, or else Wicked-
> ness, but in respect of a whole spectrum of specific week-day
> attributes. *A* is a bit more irritable and ambitious than *B*,
> but less indolent and less sentimental. *C* is meaner and
> quicker-witted than *D*, and *D* is greedier and more athletic
> than *C*. And so on. A person is not black or white, but
> iridescent with all the colours of the rainbow; and he is not
> a flat plane, but a highly irregular solid.

To some extent this may seem to fit the facts of Proust's
narrator's case well. After all, he possesses to a remarkable
degree the ability to make contrastive moral judgements, and
he deploys his contrasts with such ingenuity that his discourse
often seems dedicated to continuity – 'iridescence' – rather
than discreteness in the handling of moral notions. Besides,
few of Proust's admirers would wish to remove him from the
company of Aristotle and Jane Austen if this meant handing
him over to Ryle's dourly dichotomous Calvin. Yet a crucial
quality of the moral life as lived by Proust's narrator is entirely
missing from Ryle's paradigm. This is the quality that could
be called supererogatory risk-taking; it involves finding limits
and then seeking to transgress them; and it calls for naughtiness
and mischief on a grand scale. In the pursuit of new knowledge,
the narrator must be prepared to traverse uncharted moral
territories and to improvise for himself a value-system commensurate with this or that moment of epistemological zeal or
imaginative extravagance.

At the simplest level, telling the truth to a truth-resistant
audience may involve lying. In *A l'ombre des jeunes filles en*

fleurs, the narrator reports having given his parents an unveri-fied account of the origins and the antiquity of the Swanns' staircase. Without doing so, it would have been impossible for him to persuade them of its true worth: '[m]on amour de la vérité était si grand que je n'aurais pas hésité à leur donner ce renseignement même si j'avais su qu'il était faux' (I, 496; '[my] regard for the truth was so great that I should not have hesitated to give them this information even if I had known it to be false' (II, 89)). In the turbulent world of the child and his family, here is an early intimation of the 'glorious lie' that is art. And once the pursuit of new knowledge has been conceived of as an ethical imperative, lying itself – workaday lying, not the superior mendacities of art – may begin to reveal unsuspected virtues: 'Le mensonge, le mensonge parfait [. . .] est une des seules choses au monde qui puisse nous ouvrir des perspectives sur du nouveau, sur de l'inconnu, puisse ouvrir en nous des sens endormis pour la contemplation d'univers que nous n'aurions jamais connus' (III, 721; 'The lie, the perfect lie [. . .] is one of the few things in the world that can open windows for us on to what is new and unknown, that can awaken in us sleeping senses for the contemplation of uni-verses that otherwise we should never have known' (V, 239)). We must be prepared for the possibility that a new science, which is also a science of newness, may bring with it a new morality.

Closely related to this, there is another form of supererero-gation towards which the narrator is continually drawn. Those who are in pursuit of pleasure – and especially those whose pleasures are familiarly thought of as perverse, aberrant or anti-social – are themselves pursued by the narrator's relent-less, inquisitive gaze. Sado-masochism, for example, which is discussed and theatricalised in numerous ways, from the

Montjouvain episode of 'Combray' (I, 157–63; I, 190–98) to
the scenes in Jupien's brothel in *Le Temps retrouvé* (IV, 388–
419; VI, 147–85), provides an exacting test for the moralist's
powers of discrimination. In each of these extended episodes,
which together place an elaborate frame around the many
plainer accounts of cruel sex that are to be found in the inner
volumes, the narrator's crisp expressions of disapproval free
him to enjoy the pleasures of voyeurism guiltlessly. But the
achievement of pleasure is no more his main goal than is the
defence of rectitude. An ambitious moral experiment is in progress, and the narrator follows a clear experimental principle
in conducting it: let my perception of life in, say, Jupien's
establishment be as delicately calibrated as that which I would
bring to bear upon any other complex scene of social communication and commerce.

His experimental results are presented with relish. Charlus,
emerging in considerable discomfort from the flagellation
chamber, is still able to inspect Jupien's assembled staff with
a discriminating eye and ear:

> Bien que son plaisir fût fini et qu'il n'entrât d'ailleurs que
> pour donner à Maurice l'argent qu'il lui devait, il dirigeait
> en cercle sur tous ces jeunes gens réunis un regard tendre
> et curieux et comptait bien avoir avec chacun le plaisir d'un
> bonjour tout platonique mais amoureusement prolongé [. . .]
> Tous semblaient le connaître et M. de Charlus s'arrêtait
> longuement à chacun, leur parlant ce qu'il croyait leur lan-
> gage, à la fois par une affectation prétentieuse de couleur
> locale et aussi par un plaisir sadique de se mêler à une vie
> crapuleuse.   (IV, 403–4)

Although his pleasure was at an end and he had only come
in to give Maurice the money which he owed him, he
directed at the young men a tender and curious glance which
travelled round the whole circle, promising himself with

each of them the pleasure of a moment's chat, platonic but
amorously prolonged [. . .] Everybody [. . .] seemed to
know him, and M. de Charlus stopped for a long time before
each one, talking to them in what he thought was their
language, both from a pretentious affectation of local colour
and because he got a sadistic pleasure from contact with a
life of depravity.   (VI, 165–6)

The narrator takes his distance from Charlus, but not too much
distance, for he has already described *in propria persona* and
with a similar devotion to piquancy and local colour, the
enlarged field of sexual opportunity that the war had created in
Paris. Canadians were valued for the charm of their ambiguous
accent, but '[à] cause de leur jupon et parce que certains
rêves lacustres s'associent souvent à de tels désirs, les Écossais
faisaient prime' (IV, 402; 'The Scots too, because of their kilts
and because dreams of a landscape with lakes are often associated with these desires, were at a premium' (VI, 164)). But
tracing out this spectrum of libidinal intensities is not a task
for the mere voluptuary or tourist, for an equally differentiated
value-spectrum crosses it at every turn. Although sado-
masochistic transactions of the kind in which Jupien specialises
can scarcely be thought of as possessing, in themselves, a
complex moral content, the larger social world of the brothel
can. Indeed its content is presented as strictly – iridescently –
continuous with that of 'society' itself. In this low-life world
the narrator finds again the hypocrisies, fidelities, betrayals and
occasional unadvertised acts of philanthropy that are the volatile
stuff of salon life, and he also finds ample new material with
which to extend his discussion of such topics as lying, self-
deception and envy. In the moral as in the epistemological
domain, the narrator is a seeker after variety and novelty, and
urges himself forward to the moment of completion – when
the last possible modulation of the moral life will have become

audible. He is not only a pluralising eye, a self constituted from all other selves, but an optimistic surveyor of human conduct – one who expects to discover new notions of virtue and vice at every point of the compass.

Such dreams of plurality and plenitude were of course common among Proust's contemporaries. Busoni – to take a strong but relatively neglected example – lamented in his *Sketch of a New Esthetic of Music* (*c.*1911) that so much in the Western musical tradition, from tonality itself to the standard notational system and the mechanics of keyboard instruments, seemed to want to substitute discreteness for continuity and avoid hearing the true harmony of nature: 'How strictly we divide "consonances" from "dissonances" – *in a sphere where no dissonances can possibly exist!* . . . Nature created an *infinite gradation – infinite!*' Proust hears the true music of moral judgement and takes the risks appropriate to its pursuit. No act of judging can be final, for the continuous gradations of conduct and character flow on. It is not surprising, therefore, that after an adventure so protracted and so full of risk he should wish to stage an apocalypse in the last pages of his book. One could scarcely imagine a better reward at the end of it all than a single choice to make, a single project to execute, a single self to reassume and an overriding moral value to defend.

But where does the novel end? With the narrator's self-discovery, with the death in battle of Saint-Loup, or with the wartime night sky over Paris that each of them contemplates?

Je lui parlai de la beauté des avions qui montaient dans la nuit. «Et peut-être encore plus de ceux qui descendent, me dit-il. Je reconnais que c'est très beau le moment où ils montent, où ils vont *faire constellation*, et obéissent en cela à des lois tout aussi précises que celles qui régissent les constellations car ce qui te semble un spectacle est le ralliement des escadrilles, les commandements qu'on leur donne, leur départ en chasse, etc. Mais est-ce que tu n'aimes pas mieux le moment où, définitivement assimilés aux étoiles, ils s'en détachent pour partir en chasse ou rentrer après la berloque, le moment où ils *font apocalypse*, même les étoiles ne gardant plus leur place? Et ces sirènes, était-ce assez wagnérien, ce qui du reste était bien naturel pour saluer l'arrivée des Allemands, ça faisait très hymne national, avec le Kronprinz et les princesses dans la loge impériale, *Wacht am Rhein*; c'était à se demander si c'était bien des aviateurs et pas plutôt des Walkyries qui montaient.» Il semblait avoir plaisir à cette assimilation des aviateurs et des Walkyries et l'expliqua d'ailleurs par des raisons purement musicales: «Dame, c'est que la musique des sirènes était d'un *Chevauchée*! Il faut décidément l'arrivée des Allemands pour qu'on puisse entendre du Wagner à Paris.» [. . .] à certains points de vue la comparaison n'était pas fausse.   (IV, 337–8)

I spoke of the beauty of the aeroplanes climbing up into the night. 'And perhaps they are even more beautiful when they come down,' he said. 'I grant that it is a magnificent moment when they climb, when they fly off in *constellation*, in obedience to laws as precise as those that govern the constellations of the stars – for what seems to you a mere spectacle is the rallying of the squadrons, then the orders they receive, their departure in pursuit, etc. But don't you prefer the moment, when, just as you have got used to thinking of them as stars, they break away to pursue an enemy or to return to the ground after the all-clear, the moment of *apocalypse*, when even the stars are hurled from their courses? And then the sirens, could they have been more Wagnerian, and what could be more appropriate as a salute to the arrival of the Germans? – it might have been the national anthem, with the Crown Prince and the princesses in the imperial box, the *Wacht am Rhein*; one had to ask oneself whether they were indeed pilots and not Valkyries who were sailing upwards.' He seemed to be delighted with this comparison of the pilots to Valkyries, and went on to explain it on purely musical grounds: 'That's

27

it, the music of the sirens was a "Ride of the Valkyries"! There's no doubt about it, the Germans have to arrive before you can hear Wagner in Paris.' In some ways the simile was not misleading. (VI, 83–4)

In some ways the simile was not misleading, but in others it was. Proust has here transferred from the narrator to Saint-Loup the task of recapitulating, in a burlesque manner, many of the narrator's own metaphorical habits and, in particular, his stargazing, his inventive play with the quadrivium, and his hesitation between explosion and fixity. A sudden new relationship between music and astronomy is glimpsed – one in which measurement and pattern-making are caught up in the machinery of modern warfare. Saint-Loup is continuing to aestheticise violence as he had during the Doncières episode, but he is also prolonging, and recasting in millennial terms, a mode of perception that Proust's narrator has displayed throughout the novel. Aerial combat produces new constellations, new displays of matter and kinetic energy, and these are in direct line of descent from the countless 'astral phenomena' that the narrator had previously recorded. Astral aircraft rise above the mere carnage of war, rather as Halévy's exquisite salon melody in 'Rachel quand du Seigneur' rises above the impending brutality that Scribe's text describes.

In transferring these images to Saint-Loup, Proust is of course preparing the way for the 'real' apocalypse of the book and for the unimpeachable depth and seriousness of artistic perception and moral concern that the narrator, alone among its central characters, is eventually to acquire. Saint-Loup in becoming the supremely witty artist of scattered selfhood, the inventor of momentary geometries and ever-changing optical effects, leaves the way open for the narrator, that nebulous modeller of nebulae, to become a single self at last. But the clarity and complexity that the book's earlier images of dispersal possess cannot simply be removed from the record by the last fortified version of selfhood upon which the narrator reports. On the contrary, those earlier explosions and starbursts have such imaginative authority that they may prove to be the feature of the book that we remember best and cherish most. If so, the centralised and resolved self on which the novel ends may be seen not as a redemption but as one momentary geometry among many others.

II

Time

Wolą fałszywą nutę od muzyki sfer.

WISŁAWA SZYMBORSKA

Out of tune suits them better than the music of the spheres.

From first word to last, Proust's novel is about time. Everyone says so, including Proust himself. Within the dense texture of the narrator's soliloquy, the theme rings out clamorously. Inside his accustomed voice, there is a time voice – urgent, serious, elevated, expansive, and given to sudden bursts of semi-philosophical speculation – whose sound is fashioned, as telephone voices are, by a sense of occasion and a need to impress. The passage of human time is a deadly business, the narrator often reminds his reader, and if the tide of meaning is ever to turn again from ebb to flow the individual must hold himself in readiness to seize time's wonders. Time is no laughing matter. It is the fundamental enigma of living substance, and the artist who solves it has indeed found the philosopher's stone.

The empirical evidence for this view of the novel is irresistible. Where do its principal landmarks come from if not from its temporal obsession? *Le Temps retrouvé* culminates in long passages of impassioned reverie that are doubly devoted to the time dimension: they are essays on time, almost free-standing disquisitions on its alternative registers and intensities, but they are also episodes in the long history of a fictional character's consciousness and closely woven into its characteristic rhythms. What is more, Proust's plot, while having many strands and many denouements, turns upon a central temporal conundrum to which, in the end, after countless diversions and delays, a convincing answer is found. On the first page of the novel, Proust takes aim at a very remote target, and with devastating accuracy he eventually strikes it. In due course, time will be redeemed. A lost past will be recovered, and the dying creature's messianic hopes will be fulfilled.

Time, being highlighted in such ways both by Proust the would-be essayist and by Proust the consummate plotter, has seemed to many admirers of the book to be so clearly its main concern that other candidates for this office have scarcely been worth considering. Time matters to the book precisely because it is a 'big' controlling theme, calls forth an impressive philosophical diction and offers a satisfying overview of Proust's narrative architecture. His last word ('Temps') distils an immutable quintessence from the imperfect world of temporal process to which his first word ('Longtemps') had referred.

Yet there is something not quite right about this view. It answers too many questions, and levitates too obligingly above the restless detail of Proust's writing. *A la recherche du temps perdu* is one of those literary works that spell out at length the terms in which they are to be interpreted and understood. It can be intimidating and coercive when it does this: its author seems to have such clear-cut ideas about his own motives and long-range goals that only a fool or a wilful eccentric would seek other paths to understanding. The problem, however, is that time as presented by the narrator in his abstractly philosophising vein is too big for the ordinary time-bound business of reading Proust. The more instructive time becomes as an overall structuring idea, the more likely it is to disappear from the fabric of individual sentences and paragraphs. Yet it is here, down among Proust's intricate propositional structures with their outrageous embeddings, suspensions and redundancies, that his boldest pieces of temporal architecture are to be found. Already in the second sentence of the book, his grammatical building materials are beginning to acquire a promising elasticity: 'Parfois, à peine ma bougie éteinte, mes yeux se fermaient si vite que je n'avais pas le temps de me dire: «Je m'endors.»' (I, 3; 'Sometimes, the candle barely out, my eyes closed so quickly that I did not have time to tell myself: "I'm falling asleep" ' (I, 1)). Two time-scales are in force at once here, and these set 'real' against 'virtual' time, things that happened against things that might have happened but did not. A proposition belonging to one time-world nests inside a proposition belonging to another, and between them a galvanic spasm passes.

Theodor Adorno, in his 'Short Commentaries on Proust' (1958), wrote with great force about the relationship between the big-time temporality of Proust's novel and spasmodic local time-events such as these. Surely, he began his essay by suggesting, a reader of any work as 'rich and intricate' as Proust's novel must needs retreat from its detail at times and seek to gain an overview. And should not criticism help him in this endeavour? For Adorno, however, this view of criticism was based on a misperception of Proust's work:

> In Proust, however, the relationship of the whole to the detail is not that of an overall architectonic plan to the specifics that fill it in: it is against precisely that, against the brutal untruth of a subsuming form forced on from above, that Proust revolted. Just as the temperament of his work challenges customary notions about the general and the particular and gives aesthetic force to the dictum from Hegel's

Logic that the particular is the general and vice versa, with each mediated through the other, so the whole, resistant to abstract outlines, crystallizes out of intertwined individual presentations. Each of them conceals within itself constellations of what ultimately emerges as the idea of the novel. Great musicians of Proust's era, like Alban Berg, knew that living totality is achieved only through rank vegetal proliferation. The productive force that aims at unity is identical to the passive capacity to lose oneself in details without restraint or reservation. In the inner formal composition of Proust's work, however – and it was not only on account of its long, obscure sentences that Proust's work struck the Frenchmen of his time as so German – there dwells, Proust's primarily optical gifts notwithstanding and with no cheap analogy to composition intended, a musical impulse. It is evidenced most emphatically in the paradox that Proust's great theme, the rescue of the transient, is fulfilled through its own transience, time.

What I shall be proposing is that the 'rank vegetal proliferation' of Proust's text is the most puzzling and rewarding site for his experiments with time, and that the transient materials which Proust accumulates and adroitly manipulates sentence by sentence as his long tale unfolds are pregnant with meaning of a particularly uncomfortable sort. Such details not only make the overview difficult to achieve but tell a story about time that is alarmingly at odds with the official story told by Proust's narrator in his didactic moods.

We must be thankful that it is not necessary to possess time concepts of particular subtlety in order to have time experiences that are complex and moving. Miracles of temporal construction-work can occur in a bar or a bus queue; and one does not need to activate the notions of retrospection and anticipation, and still less their rhetorical counterparts *analepsis* and *prolepsis*, to become aware that the living present of an individual's experience is put together, concocted, from residues of the past and conjectural glimpses of the future. But even 'past' and 'future' sound too conceptual, too thought-about, for the rough-and-tumble of lived time, which can be made from whatever materials are to hand. This is a case in which the sensuous immediacy of art can remind us of something even more immediate-seeming that takes place in ordinary experience. Three brief examples will provide a route back to this feature of daily life, and to Proust as one of its unacclaimed guardians.

In the first movement of the *Eroica* symphony, Beethoven has one of the horns begin the recapitulation prematurely. Some unfathomable eagerness in the ranks of the orchestra, or so it sounds, has produced a solecism, and the listener is obliged to hesitate for a moment between two temporalities, one of them correct, proper and opportune and the other hasty and disjointed. In the closing sequence of *The Spider's Stratagem* (1970), Bertolucci's film adaptation of the Borges story 'Theme of the Traitor and the Hero', a man waits at a deserted railway station: a voice repeatedly announces over the loudspeaker that his train will be delayed, and grass sprouts between the tracks. In Washington, DC, on 13 February 1962, at the height of the North American craze for Brazilian music, Stan Getz plays 'Desafinado': towards the end of his solo he delays the return of Antonio Carlos Jobim's out-of-tune tune by producing ghostly, near-miss alternatives to it. He flirts with his hearers: you can have your tune, but not yet.

What all three cases have in common is that time-effects of considerable complexity are made palpable in the expressive medium of the art form involved. There will be stories in the background, of course, and cunning calculations, and appropriate technical concepts, but the artistry of the artist in each instance lies in his ability to stand clear of all this and treat time as directly manipulable stuff: in the shocking proximity of grass and metal, in the sound of the horn arriving early or of the tenor saxophone arriving late, we rediscover the time of our desires and fears. Artists may choose at moments to confer special privileges on belated or precocious intensities of feeling, but the flexed, syncopated temporal medium that they thereby reveal belongs not to art in particular but to time-dwelling human creatures at large: we live like this, now too early and now too late.

If I insist upon the ordinariness that underlies these exquisite artistic contrivances, it is because I am conscious of an unusual burden that Proust places upon his reader. He expects his reader to proceed slowly, patiently, and with wide-ranging attention. In his characteristic long sentence, with its welter of subordinate material, he obliges us to pursue a number of associative chains at once and expects us all uncomplainingly to accumulate, and then at intervals deploy, large quantities of information. Self-contained propositional events take place against a relatively undifferentiated semantic mass. These qualities of the Proust text seem so clearly to side with contrivance, and against simplicity, that readers may feel themselves summoned to worship in a temple of high art, and somehow required to leave their awkward everyday selves at the door. The presence in the book of a psychology and a metaphysics of time may enhance this impression and suggest that time is an issue in Proust only when his text announces it as such. But 'time-effects', as I have been calling them, are present when the key theoretical ideas are veiled, or absent altogether. And such effects, which belong to the individual sentences of the work long before they are incorporated into any larger narrative scheme, are worth itemising. By doing so, we can begin to see how the 'bottom-up' approach recommended by Adorno might pay special dividends: from the temporality of the individual sentence, through that of the paragraph sequence or the self-contained narrative episode, we may ascend gradually to the temporality of the whole novel as prescribed in its doctrinal passages or enacted in its time-intoxicated plot, and yet not imagine as we rise that this arrangement of levels is a simple hierarchical one. Proust is too venturesome and too perverse to allow us merely to read upwards towards a promised apex.

The following is a sentence from *Du côté de chez Swann* in which the grand temporal design of the book's plot is kept at a safe distance, and in which explicit time-theoretical references are of the thinnest. The narrator describes the Vivonne at the moment when its stream begins to accelerate on emerging from the grounds of a local property:

> Que de fois j'ai vu, j'ai désiré imiter quand je serais libre de vivre à ma guise, un rameur, qui, ayant lâché l'aviron, s'était couché à plat sur le dos, la tête en bas, au fond de sa barque, et la laissant flotter à la dérive, ne pouvant voir que le ciel qui filait lentement au-dessus de lui, portait sur son visage l'avant-goût du bonheur et de la paix.   (I, 168)

> How often have I watched, and longed to imitate when I should be free to live as I chose, a rower who had shipped his oars and lay flat on his back in the bottom of his boat, letting it drift with the current, seeing nothing but the sky gliding slowly by above him, his face aglow with a foretaste of happiness and peace!   (I, 204)

The overall design of the plot may be absent from this sentence, but the underlying emotional teleology of the book is not. The narrator describes his earlier childhood self as driven by an imagined future beatitude. Once the shackles of parental supervision have been untied, he will enjoy the free exercise of his desires and bask negligently in each new-found bliss. Literary ambition already has a part to play in this quest. Just as Dante hastened to rejoin Virgil when he strode on ahead of him in the *Inferno* (XXIII, 145-8), so I, the narrator has just announced, would run to catch up with my parents on the towpath. And Virgil's destiny later in the *Commedia*, we may remember, was to be left behind ... Such references are common in these early stages of the novel, and one happy vision of the future certainly involves a free and self-replenishing literary creativity, to be exercised perhaps on a Dantesque scale. But what is striking about this sentence is not so much its pre-echo of a later outcome as its choice in the here-and-now of a hard path towards 'happiness and peace'.

At least three time-scales are present. The oarsman sinks back languorously after hard work with arms and legs; the narrator enjoys himself when he is finally able to break free from a constraining family; and Proust's sentence arrives at its final visionary affirmation after much syntactic travail. No problem arises from the fact that two futures – 'his' and 'mine' – are being narrated simultaneously, nor from their being consigned to an epoch that is already long past at the moment of narration: we regularly consult other people's hopes in order to understand our own, and will readily own that our past was as future-driven as our present now is. The problem – and the pleasurableness – of sentences on this model lies in their insistent intermixing of past, present and future. Their syntax and tense-pattern deal in prematurity and belatedness to the near-exclusion of linear succession. 'Que de fois j'ai vu ... un rameur, qui ... portait sur son visage l'avant-goût du bonheur et de la paix': such is the straightforward subject-predicate chronology of the sentence if one extracts it from the text, but, left inside the text, this chronology is subject to turbulence and fracture. The narrator blurts out the general import of his fantasy ('quand je serais libre de vivre à ma guise') before the object of his fantasy has been named, and then, having pre-empted his lolling oarsman, holds him back from his moment of abandonment and repose with a series of short staccato phrases.

The temporality of Proust's sentence is insistently heterogeneous: moment by moment, the flow of time is stalled, and unpacked into its backward- and forward-looking ingredients. The reader who does not hesitate is lost: 'j'ai vu', 'j'ai désiré' look as if they are co-ordinated and indeed are; 'filait' and 'portait' look as if they are co-ordinated and are not. Reading forwards involves backtracking, and checking, and measuring one possible syntactic pathway against others; the mutual attraction of 'filait' and 'portait' has first to be felt and then repudiated. The past of such sentences is constantly being revisited and remade. This is an extremely simple case of Proustian time in one of its typical textual incarnations: the reader reaches an anticipated goal, but only after a series of delays and only by an unexpected route. What is happening is that flux and *dérive* are threatening, but not in the end seriously damaging, propositional structure. Indeed, such structure, eventually repossessed and reproclaimed, emerges not just as well-made and obedient to grammatical rule but as the bearer of sensuous satisfaction: completing the syntactic pattern is strictly synchronised with the achievement of ecstasy. Diversion, detour, drift and discontinuity, all the untidy syncopations of lived time, are to be resolved into a sublime timeliness. The force of such writing is not at all in a theory of time, clearly not, but in its power of performance, and its readiness to pass the raw materials of fantasy through a strenuous process of syntactic dismantling and reassembly. By way of such artifice, the narrative rejoins the ordinary panic and disarray that are proper to desire-time.

Musicalised sentences of this kind, in which internal relations multiply, are in some ways especially suited to the rapt, supercharged nature description at which Proust was so adept. The mobile surfaces of the natural world, and the play of light upon them, and the slow, ineluctable processes of organic growth or decay, are themselves a stylistic lesson and may call forth from the writer an imitative tribute. What could be more *natural* than a prose which teemed with inner voices and fluent transformations? Yet Proust is a caustic social observer as well as a devoted dweller among fields and streams, and his syntax does not desert him when his attention turns to the human bestiary of the salon or the seaside hotel.

In this sentence from *Sodome et Gomorrhe*, the narrator begins to explain why he had felt obliged to refuse a tempting invitation from Mme de Cambremer. The invitation had arrived at a time when grief at his grandmother's death had suddenly been revived:

> Et certes il y a seulement deux jours, si fatigué de vie mondaine que je fusse, c'eût été un vrai plaisir pour moi que de la goûter transplantée dans ces jardins où poussaient en pleine terre, grâce à l'exposition de Féterne, les figuiers, les palmiers, les plants de rosiers, jusque dans la mer souvent d'un calme et d'un bleu méditerranéens et sur laquelle le petit yacht des propriétaires allait, avant le commencement de la fête, chercher dans les plages de l'autre côté de la baie, les invités les plus importants, servait, avec ses vélums tendus contre le soleil, quand tout le monde était arrivé, de salle à manger pour goûter, et repartait le soir reconduire ceux qu'il avait amenés. (III, 164)

> And indeed only two days earlier, tired as I was of social life, it would have been a real pleasure to me to taste it, transplanted amid those gardens in which, thanks to the exposure of Féterne, fig trees, palms, rose bushes grew out in the open and stretched down to a sea often as blue and calm as the Mediterranean, upon which the hosts' little yacht would sail across, before the party began, to fetch the most

important guests from the places on the other side of the
bay, would serve, with its awnings spread to shut out the
sun, as an open-air refreshment room after the party had
assembled, and would set sail again in the evening to take
back those whom it had brought.   (IV, 193)

Again, certain of the time-relations here are straightforward:
this is the future I would have enjoyed, in prospect and in
actuality, if I had received the invitation earlier and if the pain
of my bereavement had not returned. Futures, even unrealised
ones, have their history. But the copious elaborations of the
sentence sketch a much more impulsive and diversified passage
of time too. Time is measured by criss-crossing spatial journeys,
held together in a single propositional structure. Two kinds of
transplantation occur at Féterne, the Cambremers' château:
exotic plants have been taken there and flourish thanks to
its favourable position, and exotic social creatures, seasonally
removed from the capital to this seaside neighbourhood, are
gathered up into a shimmering *matinée*. Transport is provided
for guests of appropriate rank or status, and the morning and
evening journeys of the Cambremer yacht trace a thoroughly
socialised map of local space and time. This is the double
portrait of a society and one of its members, and the syntax
of the sentence fuses into a single drama the advance and recoil
of the narrator's sympathy for his would-be hosts. A single
proposition scans, enumerates, explores lateral relationships,
arranges improbable encounters, allows fantasy to take wing,
yet reaches finally a point of narrative and syntactic closure:
the party is over, the yacht bears the privileged guests away,
and a grand amplificatory linguistic mechanism is brought to
rest.

In so far as Proust reconstructs the temporality of daily
living, then, we may already safely say that syntax has a main
role in providing his account with a sense of phenomenological

fullness. The particular ingenuity of his syntax in this respect is that it brings together into one complex pattern a continuous forward-flung intention and a simultaneous host of retrospective or sideways vistas. It seeks stability and finality, celebrates these qualities with its emphatic final cadences, yet leaves the door open too: riddles remain to be solved, curiosity to be satisfied, and a larger narrative syntax to be pursued. A balance must be kept between completion and a necessary provisionality. The reader must be fed, yet kept hungry.

Even during the narrator's lengthy philosophical or psychological discussions of time, even as he deploys his rich vocabulary of chronological terms, his syntax is often quietly performing a quite different and seemingly unauthorised set of tasks. The last of my three single-sentence examples is thoroughly 'time-theoretical' in that it discusses a curious human present largely washed clean of its own past. It is taken from *Le Côté de Guermantes* and concerns Mme de Guermantes's slightly improbable incapacity to bear grudges and nurse grievances:

> Non seulement elle ne s'attardait pas à des explications rétrospectives, à des demi-mots, à des sourires ambigus, à des sous-entendus, non seulement elle avait dans son affabilité actuelle, sans retours en arrière, sans réticences, quelque chose d'aussi fièrement rectiligne que sa majestueuse stature, mais les griefs qu'elle avait pu ressentir contre quelqu'un dans le passé étaient si entièrement réduits en cendres, ces cendres étaient elles-mêmes rejetées si loin de sa mémoire ou tout au moins de sa manière d'être, qu'à regarder son visage chaque fois qu'elle avait à traiter par la plus belle des simplifications ce qui chez tant d'autres eût été prétexte à des restes de froideur, à des récriminations, on avait l'impression d'une sorte de purification. (II, 676)

> Not only did she waste no time in retrospective inquiries, in hints, allusions or ambiguous smiles, not only was there in her present affability, without any harking back to the past, without the slightest reticence, something as proudly rectilinear as her majestic stature, but any resentment which she might have felt against someone in the past was so entirely reduced to ashes, and those ashes were themselves cast so utterly from her memory, or at least from her manner, that on studying her face whenever she had occasion to treat with the most exquisite simplicity what in so many other people would have been a pretext for reviving stale antipathies and recriminations, one had the impression of a sort of purification. (III, 440)

The comedy of this sentence, and the subcutaneous malice which permeates its apparent act of homage, stem from the disproportion between the supposed candour of the duchesse and the hard labour that her virtue seems to entail. Far from being a natural grace of personality, or a fortunate psychological tic, her freedom from grudges is achieved by a triple process of incineration, grinding and scattering, and may even then be an effect of social self-presentation rather than an emotional reality. The narrator puts his syntax to work in the same showily laborious vein: here are all the afterthoughts and retrospective mental retouchings that the duchesse knows nothing of, all deliciously listed at the beginning of the sentence, and wrapped up in an incriminating double negative; and at the end of the sentence, with full cadential force, here is the strange moment of catharsis by which all gritty residues are removed from the scene. It should not be necessary for this region of her soul to be purified over time, for purity is its native condition, but some demon in Proust's writing wants all states, moral or physical, to become transformational processes.

Again, two presentations of time are in play at once in sentences of this kind, and one of them, on the face of it, has a superior claim to generality. Certain mental types enjoy an almost magical ability to forget, just as others are haunted by memories or given to fantastical anticipations of the future, and for a moment Mme de Guermantes has become the emblem of the first group, and a *caractère* almost in the manner of La Bruyère. The narrator's proposition, if we distil it in this way, is simple, self-limiting and cogent. But the second presentation, which belongs to the long, undistilled scansional sentence we in fact possess, has its own general force. It has of course the roughness and waywardness of *temps vécu*. It is assembled from a procession of discrete Janus-faced moments, and the recrudescence inside it of past into present cannot be legislated for or predicted. Yet this presentation has as much of a logic to it as the first: the interplay that it creates between the backwards and forwards glances of the time-bound individual, between his slowness and his precipitation, between spinning a yarn and calling a halt – and especially this interplay as controlled by a single dilated propositional structure – begins indeed to resemble a universal key to the understanding of human time, applicable on terms of strict equality to oarsmen, yachtsmen, noblewomen and novelists.

Proust's novel contains innumerable complex sentences that are built in this way, and many that call for more intensive scanning activity on the reader's part than does any one of these three specimens. His time-drama is in his individual sentences and in the underlying structures they reiterate. But these models of timeliness and epistemic success achieved in the teeth of distraction and anxiety do not simply sit as outliers on the margins of Proust's narrative. They are the carriers of that narrative, and the internal echoes that give certain isolated sentences their combined quality of cohesion and dispersal are to be heard passing between the larger units of the work too. The temporality of propositions is constantly being caught up into larger narrative segments, and retemporalised in the process. Once the reader has penetrated some distance into the book, it begins to acquire its own internal dynamic of past, present and future relationships. The book allows its reader to relive, in the present moment of reading, pasts that it alone has created for him, and to breathe an air of multiple potentiality that is native to this slowly unfolding textual fabric. It is to this larger pattern of recurrences and expectations that I shall now turn, attending principally to a single highly charged nexus of motifs.

Among secrets and enigmas in the Proust world, those that involve sexuality have a special prestige. They are more resistant to the narrator's powers of decipherment than other mysteries of social life, and solutions to them, once discovered, are more likely to falter and decay. Such questions as 'which were his *real* preference, men or women?' or 'what did she *really* do in her younger years?' have a lingering atmosphere of infantile curiosity about them in this novel, yet prompt the narrator to a series of ingenious experimental studies in cognition: Proust echoes Freud's account of the child's wish to know about sex as the prototypical form of all later intellectual endeavour. What is surprising, however, about Proust's handling of sexual secrets is not simply that so much of his plot turns on their solution but that the panic they inspire should be entertained on such a lavish scale. The uncertainties which surround Uncle Toby's wound in Sterne's *Tristram Shandy* (1759–67) or the hero's parentage in Fielding's *Tom Jones* (1749) are positively short-winded in comparison with those surrounding the sexuality and sexual prehistory of Odette, Albertine and Saint-Loup. In simple time-and-motion terms, the quantities of intelligent attention that these investigations require of the narrator are calamitous – when they are not merely farcical. A crucial temporal framework in this book is the one in which sexually driven individuals strive to find things out about each other. And in this pursuit, their expenditure of time is reckless.

I have chosen from among the numerous scenes of sexual enquiry that are to be found in the early volumes of the novel an elaborate intellectual comedy which prefigures much that is to be fully explored later. This is the episode in *A l'ombre des jeunes filles en fleurs* where the narrator discovers a watercolour portrait of 'Miss Sacripant' in Elstir's studio and is thwarted in his desire to be introduced to the 'little band' of young girls (II, 203–20; II, 493–514). At least four currents of feeling are running in parallel here; the narrator wants: to meet the girls, and expects Elstir to help him do so; to find out more about Elstir's art, and about the subject of the portrait; to respect the rhythm of Elstir's working day rather than press his own claims upon the painter's time; and, above all, to seem casual and disengaged in the eyes of the girls themselves. The attempt to achieve some sort of equilibrium between these incompatible wishes involve him in a distended cost-benefit analysis, and a delirium of excuses and explanations. Four stories are being told simultaneously in this episode, which is a tour de force of polyphonic invention, and any one of them may suddenly gather bulk at the expense of the others. Slowness in one narrative may permit a new access of speed in another; opening up a gap in one causal sequence may permit a gap in another to be closed. For example, between the last rekindling of the narrator's hope that an introduction can be arranged and the definitive extinction of that hope, for today at least, Elstir proceeds with tiresome deliberation to complete his own work: he alone has the power to usher the narrator into the force-field of the eternal feminine, but devotes himself instead to the lesser magic that is his painting. The narrator not only describes this delay, but performs a complementary delaying manoeuvre of his own: a long excursus on self-love and altruism, and on the

45

little heroisms of ordinary life, intervenes between Elstir's last brush-stroke and the beginning of their walk together (II, 208-9; II, 499-501). Material that is in itself dignified and serious-minded intrudes hilariously upon the narrator's sentimental adventure; within the unfolding drama, an elaborate moral discussion has the status of a simple accidental misfortune.

By now Proust's narrative architecture has become dangerously elastic. Time may be measured as a connected series of physical events, sense-perceptions, and mental promptings – 'Le soir tombait; il fallut revenir; je ramenais Elstir vers sa villa . . .' (II, 210; 'Dusk was falling; it was time to be turning homewards. I was accompanying Elstir back to his villa' (II, 502)) – or by the key ideas which fuel speculation, rumination or reasoning, or by the inflections of prose discourse itself. In a passage of this kind, Proust moves with gaiety and assured improvisatory skill from one system of measurement to another. Thinking, sensing, acting, writing are given a common pulse, and made into the co-equal modes of a single, encompassing transformational experiment. A sentence which begins with the words 'Le soir tombait' can end well, and with no note of impropriety, upon a supposition enclosed in a hypothesis: '[les jeunes filles qui] avaient l'air de ne pas me voir, mais sans aucun doute n'en étaient pas moins en train de porter sur moi un jugement ironique' (II, 210; '[the girls] who looked as though they had not seen me but were unquestionably engaged in passing a sarcastic judgement on me' (II, 502)). The discrepancy between public time, measurable by events, and mental time, measurable by the development of an individual's ideas or by his changing intensities of feeling, is laid bare by Proust. Dramatic opportunities abound in the disputed territory between outside and inside, and Proust's fluid transpositions between outer and inner time-scales are thoroughly ironic in character. These are the events, the narrator says; this, he adds, is how they look if you change your viewpoint on the scene; and this again is how they look if you remove yourself from the scene altogether and concentrate on the larger tendency of my tale. Yet despite all the attention paid by the narrator to those local repositionings of himself and his addressee, Proust's reader is still encouraged to read 'for the plot', to find things out, and still invited to be seduced by secrets in the footsteps of the hero. And the scale on which this kind of reading occurs is, as I have said, very large indeed. Elstir's painting travels back and forth both in event-time and in mind-time; it is a tight cluster of time-effects, and a time-measuring device for use in the book as a whole.

The image of 'Miss Sacripant' – who, it emerges after a long delay, is the youthful Odette dressed as a boy – is subjected to a barrage of reinterpretations, and gradually becomes a hypnotic sexual icon. The initial description of the portrait already hints at the uncontainable fecundity of the image:

> La blancheur du plastron, d'une finesse de grésil et dont le frivole plissage avait des clochettes comme celles du muguet, s'étoilait des clairs reflets de la chambre, aigus eux-mêmes et finement nuancés comme des bouquets de fleurs qui auraient broché le linge. Et le velours du veston, brillant et nacré, avait çà et là quelque chose de hérissé, de déchiqueté et de velu qui faisait penser à l'ebouriffage des œillets dans le vase. Mais surtout on sentait qu'Elstir, insoucieux de ce que pouvait présenter d'immoral ce travesti d'une jeune actrice pour qui le talent avec lequel elle jouerait son rôle avait sans doute moins d'importance que l'attrait irritant qu'elle allait offrir aux sens blasés ou dépravés de certains spectateurs, s'était au contraire attaché à ces traits d'ambiguïté comme à un élément esthétique qui valait d'être mis en relief et qu'il avait tout fait pour souligner.   (II, 204–5)

The whiteness of the shirt-front, as fine as soft hail, with its gay pleats gathered into little bells like lilies of the valley, was spangled with bright gleams of light from the room, themselves sharply etched and subtly shaded as if they were flowers stitched into the linen. And the velvet of the jacket, with its brilliant sheen, had something rough, frayed and shaggy about it here and there that recalled the crumpled brightness of the carnations in the vase. But above all one felt that Elstir, heedless of any impression of immorality that might be given by this transvestite costume worn by a young actress for whom the talent she would bring to the role was doubtless of less importance than the titillation she would offer to the jaded or depraved senses of some of her audience, had on the contrary fastened upon this equivocal aspect as on an aesthetic element which deserved to be brought into prominence, and which he had done everything in his power to emphasise.   (II, 495)

Elstir was particularly attracted, the narrator suggests, by the undecidability of this girl-boy, but he has prepared the way for the exquisite indecision that his figure provokes in the spectator by sexualising the entire space of his picture. Light itself has two separate pictorial roles. On the one hand it is a uniform radiance emanating from objects, or an elucidating flow of energy passing across their surface and removing disparities as it goes. On the other hand, here and on numerous occasions elsewhere in the novel, light plays upon surfaces and inscribes them with its momentary messages: the outside world survives into the domestic interior as a series of ghostly reflections; a wide roomful of light is concentrated into a pattern of dancing flecks upon a bodice. Then again, Elstir's brush has located tangles and raggedness where other artists, less daring and less ingenious in their sexual explorations, would have settled for a simple sheen: inside the close-cropped fabric of a jacket, or between smoothly enfolded carnation-petals, secret places with an unkempt covering of hair have been found. The figure of 'Miss Sacripant', so exhaustively boyish and girlish at the same time, and by way of the same sequence of brush-strokes, reclaims for the human body and for the arts of couture, an eroticism that is everywhere anyway, as readily available as light and air in the natural world.

Proust turns an imaginary painting into a *tableau vivant*; the central image and its accompanying furniture are motionless yet constantly reanimated by the narrator's observing eye. He tells stories as he looks. He free-associates and, from a purely iconographical viewpoint, behaves badly: the art object is casu-ally folded back into the 'ordinary life' of the narrator's nascent sexual desires, and then abandoned with equal nonchalance for a semi-theoretical reverie on questions of artistic method. Yet what is remarkable in all this seeming flouting of the rules – whether of story-telling, or art history, or inferential argument – is that something strict and rule-governed is still going on sentence by sentence. Distinctions have to be clear if a coherent play of ambiguity, as distinct from mere semantic havering or fuss, is to be sustained. The machinery for making such distinctions is to be found in the bifurcating syntax of the long Proustian sentence, and it is the peculiar property of these sentences, placed end to end and seemingly so autonomous, to organise long stretches of text around relatively few underlying structural schemes. The sentences do many unruly things, of course: their syntax ramifies and proliferates; their meanings are sometimes amplified and embellished to the point of distrac-tion. Yet they studiously repeat, almost in the manner of intel-lectual home truths, certain characteristic patterns of thought. Antithetical qualities are held against each other in equipoise. The alternative potentialities of a single situation are expounded. Surprising details yield large insights, and large insights, once they have been naturalised, seize upon the further surprising details they require to remain credible. Expectations are now confounded and now confirmed. Attention is dispersed and reconcentrated; increasing speed of perception leads to a plateau of immobilised absorption. And so forth.

The typical thought-shapes that Proust's long sentences endlessly mobilise provide secure bridges between the markedly different kinds of writing that his novel yokes together. By the time we reach the following passage, for example, the secret of Miss Sacripant's identity and of her former relations with Elstir have been revealed, and reflections on the perceptual rather than the sexual dealings between artist and model are apparently in order:

> Mais d'ailleurs le portrait eût-il été, non pas antérieur, comme la photographie préférée de Swann, à la systématisation des traits d'Odette en un type nouveau, majestueux et charmant, mais postérieur, qu'il eût suffi de la vision d'Elstir pour désorganiser ce type. Le génie artistique agit à la façon de ces températures extrêmement élevées qui ont le pouvoir de dissocier les combinaisons d'atomes et de grouper ceux-ci suivant un ordre absolument contraire, répondant à un autre type. Toute cette harmonie factice que la femme a imposée à ses traits et dont chaque jour avant de sortir elle surveille la persistance dans sa glace, chargeant l'inclinaison du chapeau, le lissage des cheveux, l'enjouement du regard, d'en assurer la continuité, cette harmonie, le coup d'œil du grand peintre la détruit en une seconde, et à sa place il fait un regroupement des traits de la femme, de manière à donner satisfaction à un certain idéal féminin et pictural qu'il porte en lui. (II, 216)

But in any case, even if the portrait had been, not anterior, like Swann's favourite photograph, to the systematisation of Odette's features into a new type, majestic and charming, but subsequent to it, Elstir's vision would have sufficed to discompose that type. Artistic genius acts in a similar way to those extremely high temperatures which have the power to split up combinations of atoms which they proceed to combine afresh in a diametrically opposite order, corresponding to another type. All that artificial harmony which a woman has succeeded in imposing upon her features, the maintenance of which she oversees in her mirror every day before going out, relying on the angle of her hat, the smoothness of her hair, the vivacity of her expression, to ensure its continuity, that harmony the keen eye of the great painter instantly destroys, substituting for it a rearrangement of the woman's features such as will satisfy a certain pictorial ideal of femininity which he carries in his head.   (II, 509)

Artist and model are both masters of artifice, but where the model's first move is to quell the disorder of her past conduct and present appearance by constructing a smooth social persona, the artist's is to introduce disorder into the unreally tranquillised scene offered by the model's face, hair and clothes. His aggression, however, comes not from a simple preference for the wild over the tame, or for energy over repose, but from a wish to install on the canvas a smooth construction of his own. One fabrication must be dismantled and cleared away to make room for another, and the newcomer is still more obsessionally preserved from ruin than the original: where the woman simply checks herself in the mirror to make sure that each effect of art is in place, the artist, we are soon to be told, pursues his 'pictorial ideal of femininity' with crazed consistency from one model to the next.

On the face of it, this passage simply moves discussion of the artist's passions from the sensuous to the conceptual plane and begins to speak of new things. We now read of systematisation, dissociation, harmony and continuity where before we were offered velvet, mother-of-pearl, bristles and tousled heads. But the relation between the two paragraphs is in fact much closer than their divergences of diction would suggest. The second remembers and reinflects exactly the interplay between orderliness and an exciting, irruptive disorder that had given the first its clarity and strength. There is a rhythm here, or a thought-shape, or a paradigmatic tension, that is preserved from one occasion to the next. The special virtuosity that Proust ascribes to his narrator allows him to begin his own thinking with hair and prickles, to pursue it with cognitive concepts and to give both dimensions the same underlying structure of articulate hesitation. Inside the sentence we are currently reading earlier sentences continue to sound. Present reading time is haunted by reading times past.

Two new features of Proust's temporality begin to emerge, then, when we look beyond the retrospective and prospective dispositions of the individual complex sentence. First, within paragraphs, the propulsive energy of the writing, the living sense of futurity that drives the narration on, comes from an astonishing power of recapitulation. An ambiguity in sexual identity refashions earlier ambiguous relations – between, say, light that shines and light that dances, or between smooth and rough in the painterly representation of fabrics. The way forward into a clear new future always involves revisiting the past. Secondly, within extended episodes, continuities of this sort are at work even when the narration insists upon irreversible change. Uncovering Elstir's secret, or meeting the little band face to face for the first time, changes for ever the way the world looks. The whole map has to be redrawn. But the text carries along, from the before of unknowing into the afterwards of knowledge, not just a lively memory of key events and their affective colouring but the imprint of mental structures that have already proved themselves and can be expected to see active service again. The appetite to know survives the moment of its own satiation, and the instruments by which the world is made intelligible, far from being thrown away after use, remain importunately in place and demand further exercise. Whatever the 'open' future holds, its broad contours have already been foretold.

Yet when the large-scale temporal patterning of Proust's text is described solely in these terms an important quality is still missing from the overall picture. For although recapitulation and recurrence give the narrative a range of captivating refrains – here in *La Prisonnière* are the tribulations of jealousy, as acute now, in the narrator's manhood, as they were before his birth, and here in *Albertine disparue* is Legrandin being Legrandin, unchanged after all these years and pages – the past is not always treated as kindly as this, and simply revisited or revived at the narrator's leisure. Retroaction rather than simple retrospection sometimes occurs. The past is not just subjected to an indefinite process of reinterpretation, but can be materially altered by the desiring intelligence of the narrator: armed with new information and switching the direction of his gaze, he can give the past new contents. That Miss Sacripant should be Odette rather than an anonymous actress for ever lost behind the name of a stage character, that she should be Odette rather than a fantasy figure in one of Elstir's youthful caprices, changes the way the light had fallen, moments ago, in Elstir's studio. In the wake of the narrator's discovery, new sexual predilections spring into being for Elstir, Swann, and Odette herself, and a new element is added to the already troubled prehistory of the Swann–Odette marriage. A catalytic reaction spreads backwards from the very recent past of the narrator himself into the barely recoverable recesses of other people's lives. All is altered.

We rewrite the history of our lives from moment to moment, of course, even those of us who cling steadfastly to an 'official' autobiography, and our retroactive inventions are for the most part tiny and unremarkable. They are certainly not the stuff of which great literary plots are made. Proust turns a banal psychological mechanism into a major source of dramatic interest and energy, however, by concentrating the attention of his narrator on only a limited number of cases and by giving large-scale structural importance only to those cases involving the sexuality of his characters. The most celebrated of these is perhaps the episode of the 'lady in pink', seen briefly by the narrator in the home of his great-uncle Adolphe in the early pages of the novel (I, 75; I, 89) and still continuing to fascinate him at the very end (IV, 607; VI, 427). The 'lady in pink', like Miss Sacripant, is Odette during the heyday of her career as a courtesan, but the unveiling of her identity takes an inordinately long time, during which the narrator reveals to the reader what his earlier, narrated self still does not know. A respectable woman has had an enticingly disreputable past, and knowing this, when he eventually does know it, changes the adult narrator's childhood, especially as Odette's sexual magnetism had played upon a member of his otherwise harmonious and upright family circle.

Much more remarkable, however, is the case of Saint-Loup's homosexuality, which is first intimated in gossip, and then firmly attested as fact, at the end of *Albertine disparue* (IV, 241; V, 762). As we saw in the preceding chapter, this discovery prompts in the narrator an elegy to lost friendship – built on the bizarre assumption that friends who come out or are 'outed' are automatically lost – and a protracted examination, cog by cog, of the machinery of retroactive remembering. So many aspects of Saint-Loup's past behaviour that had previously seemed obscure now make a familiar and dispiriting kind of sense. His relationship with Rachel in particular is summoned up as a procession of episodes all demanding to be reconstrued. The evidence was all there long ago, but the narrator had no eyes with which to see it. Once the knowledge is out that Saint-Loup is 'comme ça', he, Rachel, and the narrator himself take up their positions in a new narrative sequence, and the switching of the narrator's emotional investments from an old story to a new is a hugely laborious and painful affair.

Retroaction is not only a feature of Proust's sentences and of his plot, but serves also to characterise one aspect of the narrator's personality: his combined strength and vulnerability. At certain watershed moments in the novel he is withheld from decision-making and from action; his personal history seems to rewrite itself spontaneously, and to turn him into the plaything of an inscrutable impersonal force. This can happen benignly, when a new access of happiness removes pain and doubt from the remembered past, as in this passage, which contains a perfect dictionary illustration of the unusual intransitive verb *rétroagir* ('to retroact') in use:

> la pensée ne peut même pas reconstituer l'état ancien pour le confronter au nouveau, car elle n'a plus le champ libre: la connaissance que nous avons faite, le souvenir des premières minutes inespérées, les propos que nous avons entendus, sont là qui obstruent l'entrée de notre conscience et commandent beaucoup plus les issues de notre mémoire que celles de notre imagination, ils rétroagissent davantage sur notre passé que nous ne sommes plus maîtres de voir sans tenir compte d'eux, que sur la forme, restée libre, de notre avenir.   (I, 528)

> our thoughts cannot even reconstruct the old state in order to compare it with the new, for it has no longer a clear field: the acquaintance we have made, the memory of those first, unhoped-for moments, the talk we have heard, are there now to block the passage of our consciousness, and as they control the outlets of our memory far more than those of our imagination, they react more forcibly upon our past, which we are no longer able to visualise without taking them

into account, than upon the form, still unshaped, of our future. (II, 128)

Or it can happen in the manner of a nightmare, when ever more pretexts for pain begin to assail the jealous mind:

> On n'a pas besoin d'être deux, il suffit d'être seul dans sa chambre à penser pour que de nouvelles trahisons de votre maîtresse se produisent, fût-elle morte. Aussi il ne faut pas ne redouter dans l'amour, comme dans la vie habituelle, que l'avenir, mais même le passé qui ne se réalise pour nous souvent qu'après l'avenir, et nous ne parlons pas seulement du passé que nous apprenons après coup, mais de celui que nous avons conservé depuis longtemps en nous et que tout d'un coup nous apprenons à lire. (III, 595)

> There is no need for there to be two of you, it is enough to be alone in your room, thinking, for fresh betrayals by your mistress to come to light, even if she is dead. And so we ought not to fear in love, as in everyday life, the future alone, but even the past, which often comes to life for us only when the future has come and gone – and not only the past which we discover after the event but the past which we have long kept stored within ourselves and suddenly learn how to interpret. (V, 91)

What these passages have in common, the one taken from *A l'ombre des jeunes filles en fleurs* and involving Gilberte and the other from *La Prisonnière* and involving Albertine, is the extraordinary assurance with which the analysis is conducted. This recreation of the past is a mental automatism which the narrator reportedly merely underwent in his experience of love, but it is one which he takes in hand and magisterially dissects in the elaboration of his text. There is little to be done about a mechanism as powerful as this, apart from rediscovering one's strength in writing about it. Constructing sentences is already a form of retroactive play for Proust, and constructing sentences like these allows him to create an eerie match between suspended syntax and being in love: both involve an incessant remaking of the past; and both allow, in the words of the apparent paradox on which the first of these quotations ends, retroaction to be carried forward into a 'free' future.

But even if the Proust time-map is extended in this way, to include the backwash of the present into the past as well as the irresistible encroachments of an unquiet past into the onwards flow of present time, a last element in the workaday complexity that Proust's reader has to cope with is still missing. In living our lives forwards, hurling ourselves headlong into an ever-receding future, we take our reminiscences with us. Sometimes as obliging friends, and sometimes as demons. And these reminiscences have only to be hardened somewhat into a pattern to acquire considerable prefigurative force: they not only accompany later events but can help them to happen. A 'certain slant of light', in the words of a great poem by Emily Dickinson, can bring an unanswerable intimation of death into an ordinary winter afternoon. But that same light, made memorable by who knows what conjunction of place, mood and memory, can tell us how to inhabit later afternoons, visited by different rays, differently slanted. A sudden savage word from Albertine, finding its way into an otherwise even-tempered conversation, can bring anxiety and suspicion into the narrator's later social encounters. An anonymous actress, alive with erotic provocation, can become the very model of the temptress and the tease and begin strangely to determine an apprentice lover's later choice of partner.

Templates are being created, and futures foretold, throughout the first two volumes of the novel. The scene of voyeurism at Montjouvain, the episode of the withheld goodnight kiss, the first ecstatic experience of involuntary memory, together with the entire forensic reconstruction in 'Un Amour de Swann' of the early relationship between Swann and Odette, are the embryonic forms from which complex later narratives are to spring. In some early episodes of this kind, including the decipherment of Miss Sacripant, Proust uses a special compressed form of dramatic irony. Rather than allow the reader to glimpse a future state of affairs and then oblige him or her to wait patiently for this to be actualised at an appointed later moment, he interconnects two parallel stories and allows one to illuminate the other. Odette as Miss Sacripant prefigures Albertine, just as Swann in the guise of jealous lover prefigures the adult narrator. But by this stage in the development of the plot, Albertine, still only fitfully distinguishable from her companions on the Balbec shore, is already an object of desire. The failed encounter with her occurs within the larger drama of Elstir's watercolour portrait, between the announcement of its enigma and the discovery of a key. All the materials from which the narrator's future affair with Albertine is to be fashioned, even down to the tremor of indecision which her sexuality is to prompt and the artifice which she is to employ in constructing an innocuous social persona, are already to hand in this more than prophetic scene. There is no need to wait for the future, for the future is already here.

Anticipation as manipulated in the ingenious plotting of Proust's novel enlarges and dramatises a far commoner range of mental activities. We invent futures from residues of the past. When we are not sunk in torpor or blocked by external circumstances, we strive to pre-empt the future rather than have it thrust upon us. We model our future selves on the predecessors we admire. Proust's narrator is a tireless psychologising commentator on such matters. He sets against his lively account of the 'open' or still-to-be-invented future a gloomy picture of the future as biologically or culturally pre-ordained. The individual becomes what he or she already is:

Les traits de notre visage ne sont guère que des gestes devenus, par l'habitude, définitifs. La nature, comme la catastrophe de Pompéi, comme une métamorphose de nymphe, nous a immobilisés dans le mouvement accoutumé. De même nos intonations contiennent notre philosophie de la vie, ce que la personne se dit à tout moment sur les choses.

(II, 262)

The features of our face are hardly more than gestures which force of habit has made permanent. Nature, like the destruction of Pompeii, like the metamorphosis of a nymph, has arrested us in an accustomed movement. Similarly, our intonation embodies our philosophy of life, what a person invariably says to himself about things. (II, 565)

Excessively strong or pre-emptive anticipation of this kind is in its turn set against the retroactive tricks of the remembering mind: Proust attends minutely to the whorls and vortices that the joint action of these mechanisms produces in the here and now. Whether you are writing a novel, painting a portrait, or living a life from hand to mouth, the task is always to turn the past-and-future-haunted present moment to account and to shake off its air of fatedness. A terrifying powerlessness is never far away. In both directions the exits are closed, and only by a mad wager and an inspired suspension of temporal law can we ever expect them to open again.

What I have been describing here are time mechanisms that can be observed in miniature in individual sentences and on a grand scale in the unfolding of the novel as a whole. There is perhaps, nevertheless, too much symmetry in this account, and too much regularity in the flow of Proustian time pictured in this way. What about suddenness and surprise? What about all the swerves, short-cuts and 'transversal threads' (I, 490; 'ligne [. . .] transversale' (I, 400)), as Proust calls them, that create improbable connections within the textual fabric? Time in this novel surely needs to be seized in its zig-zags and *pointilliste* stipplings as well as in the orderly inter-looping of its alternative zones.

The later destinies of the 'Miss Sacripant' motif are played out in a bewildering network of lateral connections and implied time-frames. Whereas in *A l'ombre des jeunes filles en fleurs*, the portrait was rapidly stabilised into an emblem, a potent and portable representation of sexual allure, in *Le Côté de Guermantes* it becomes fluid and fuzzy-edged again. A photograph of the portrait is sent to the narrator by the *valet de chambre* of his great-uncle Adolphe, who is now dead. The servant had judged this image, and a number of others from his employer's collection of souvenirs, more likely to appeal to a young man than to older members of the family, and had sent his own son – one Charles Morel – to deliver it:

> Comme j'avais été très étonné de trouver parmi les photographies que m'envoyait son père une du portrait de Miss Sacripant (c'est-à-dire Odette) par Elstir, je dis à Charles Morel, en l'accompagnant jusqu'à la porte cochère: «Je crains que vous ne puissiez me renseigner. Est-ce que mon oncle connaissait beaucoup cette dame? [. . .]»   (II, 563)

> As I had been greatly surprised to find among the photographs which his father had sent me one of the portrait of Miss Sacripant (otherwise Odette) by Elstir, I said to Charles Morel as I accompanied him to the carriage gateway: 'I don't suppose you can tell me, but did my uncle know this lady well? [. . .]'   (III, 305)

It is in the course of this episode that the reader is first introduced to Morel, who is to be a major presence in the remainder of the book, and there is more than a hint of prophecy in his being the bearer of the photograph: like Odette herself, and like the figure in Elstir's watercolour, Morel is sexually ambiguous. Indeed he is Proust's fullest representation of carefree bisexuality, and it is fitting that he should be given responsibility for the transportation of an icon that knits together his divergent sexual tastes. But the photograph has moved in quite different circles too: it served an aged libertine as a titillating reminder of his adventures in the *demi-monde* and, as we already know, was Swann's favourite depiction of his wife. Miss Sacripant, during her momentary reappearance in *Le Côté de Guermantes*, connects narrative past to narrative future straightforwardly enough, but she also sends echoes racing through Proust's socio-sexual labyrinth. Her *travesti* connects her to countless other characters trapped inside an unstoppable masked ball.

Towards the end of *La Prisonnière*, this aspect of Miss Sacripant reaches its apotheosis. She no longer circulates in photographic form, as a mere image caught at a third remove from the 'real' Odette, but still more impalpably as a figment of other people's gossip. Charlus, in the course of his long harangue on the history and sociology of homosexuality, begins to speak about Swann's sexual character, and, prompted by Brichot, about Swann's wife:

> Mais voyons, c'est par moi qu'il l'a connue. Je l'avais trouvée charmante dans son demi-travesti, un soir qu'elle jouait Miss Sacripant; j'étais avec des camarades de club, nous avions tous ramené une femme, et bien que je n'eusse envie que de dormir, les mauvaises langues avaient prétendu, car c'est affreux ce que le monde est méchant, que j'avais couché avec Odette. Seulement, elle en avait profité pour venir m'embêter, et j'avais cru m'en débarrasser en la présentant à Swann. De ce jour-là elle ne cessa plus de me cramponner, elle ne savait pas un mot d'orthographe, c'est moi qui faisais les lettres. (III, 803)

> Why, it was through me that he came to know her. I had thought her charming in her boyish get-up one evening when she played Miss Sacripant; I was with some club-mates, and

61

each of us took a woman home with him, and although all
I wanted was to go to sleep, slanderous tongues alleged –
it's terrible how malicious people are – that I went to bed
with Odette. In any case she took advantage of the slanders
to come and bother me, and I thought I might get rid of
her by introducing her to Swann. From that moment on
she never let me go. She couldn't spell the simplest word,
it was I who wrote all her letters for her.   (V, 339–40)

Odette is a woman about whom tongues wag. She flits from
anecdote to anecdote, and the chronicle of her lovers, which
Charlus proceeds to rehearse, enhances this sense of multiform-
ity. She is a creature called into being by other people's desires,
fantasies and projections. The renaming of Miss Sacripant at
this point in the novel makes her into a passing effect of speech
inside an indefinitely loquacious community.

The temporality of these later references and allusions is
in one sense very simple. They are chronological markers
within the overall teleology of the book. *A la recherche du
temps perdu* is not only 'about' time but about the linear
process of uncovering new time-truths: the plot leads slowly
towards a grandly orchestrated redemptive view, and time
envisaged in these terms is emphatically distinguished from
the dimension in which hours and days are merely spent,
lost or frittered away. The declared direction of the book,
until the threshold of its final revelations is reached, is
downhill into darkness. It is entirely fitting that the image of
Odette should be fuzzied and frittered as the narrative proceeds,
and that its repeated appearances should mark out the graduated stages of a much more general decline, for such is the
worldly lesson that Proust seeks to impose: things fall apart
and the clockwork runs down. The narrator's journey takes
him to an extreme limit, at which decay is visible on every
human face and nullity speaks from behind every eye, and it
is only when this limit has been reached and its intolerable

pain felt that an apocalyptic arrest of time becomes possible.

Yet the book would be a very thin affair if its long, ruminative unfolding were readable only in this way. Proust does of course handle linear time supremely well: the stations on the narrator's journey provide the book with huge, unmistakable calibrations; questions that need answers in due course find them; causes precede effects; and although the flow of time may almost congeal during a protracted *soirée*, or be accelerated mercilessly by a sudden recital of marriages and deaths, it is for the most part reliably unidirectional. Events that occur latterly occur only because former events have prepared the way for them. Within subsequence consequence is to be found. The final apocalypse itself is fully motivated by what has gone before, and the build-up to it is presented as a sub-divisible process, a phased dawning of new awareness. Yet the broad intentional structure of the book catches up within itself a dancing array of materials that are not subduable to any overall project. Proust offers his reader a simultaneous web of associations, as well as the undeflected flight of time's arrow. Across the canvas of the book points of special intensity are scattered, and we are invited by the narrator, who is a virtuoso in such matters, to scan back and forth between them, making improbable connections as we go. Proust's text rebels against the smooth linear temporality to which his narrator for the most part adheres in the telling of his tale, and incorporates into itself not just the vibrant internal reflections that typify Elstir's art but its raggedness and its rough patches.

The webs, the tangles and the improvised cross-stitchings that Proust's writing contains speak not of timeliness or timelessness but of an alternative and glaringly familiar temporality. And, although it would no doubt require topological schemata of great subtlety to model this temporality satisfactorily, its main features can be enumerated with ease. It ordains that past, present and future are composites rather than simples; that recapitulations of the past are projections into the future too; that synchronicity comprises, and may be broken down into, myriad diachronic sequences; that certain time-effects are intelligible only if spatially extended; that parallel universes may be conflated into a single newly conceived space–time continuum; and that any temporally extended system of differences may collapse into an undifferentiated flux. This is the time of human desire, and the time that Proust's book inhabits sentence by sentence. It is defiantly non-linear, and runs counter both to the plot of the book, and to much of its 'theory'. If we place Miss Sacripant, or any other elaborately recurring motif, within this alternative temporality we discover not a disconsolate ebbing away of meaning as time passes but a restoration of meaning within a temporal manifold. Odette *en travesti* becomes not just a static emblem of the desirable woman, but an intersection point in a moving network of desiring pathways. Against the pessimism of linear time and its losses, the book provides us – and not just in its ending, but all through and even in its darkest hours – with an optimistic view of time as connection-making and irrepressible potentiality. This time is not a concept, or a connected series of points, or a fixed scale against which geological epochs or human life-spans can be measured. It is a stuff and there for the handling.

A significant advantage is to be had from thinking of Proust as an artful manipulator of ordinary time rather than as the harbinger of an unusual, specialised or occult temporal vision. By this route more of his text remains readable, and its overall account of time becomes richer and more provoking. Involuntary memory, which is the gateway to Proust's apocalypse – to his time of redemption – is ordinary enough, of course. The phrase itself would scarcely have enjoyed its remarkably successful career if it had not encapsulated a common experience, and 'Proustian moments', like 'Freudian slips', would not have entered the vernacular if their import had been in any way obscure. But when it comes to the experience of reading the successive pages of Proust's novel and taking time over them, involuntary memory is oddly inert and unhelpful. Applying it as a key to the understanding of Proustian time is rather like looking at the working day from the viewpoint of weekends and holidays, or at the lives of plain-dwellers from the neighbouring mountain-tops. The time that is proper to Proust's long sentences, however, and to his extended episodes and to the long-range patterns of expectation and remembrance which organise the novel as a whole, is both ordinary and extremely complex. Ordinary in that it belongs to the everyday world of mortal, desire-driven creatures, and complex in that its many criss-crossing dimensions are mobile and difficult to construe. Past, present and future are intricately conjoined within sentences, and reconjoined still more intricately during extended narrative sequences. Sentences come to rest upon a recovered sense of propositional fullness and completion, only to have certain of their elements wrested from them and driven into new associative configurations by what follows. The temporality of a narrative which is made from unstable building blocks of this kind is one of continuous scattering and concentration. Temporality is retemporalised endlessly, and time-features that are awkward and obtuse are given special prominence in the fabrication of the text. Snags, discrepancies, prematurities, belatednesses, prophetic glimpses, misrecognitions, and blocked or incongruous memories – these tragi-comical indignities are the mainspring of Proust's vast fictional contrivance. He finds the plenitude of his book in this epic catalogue of unsatisfactory moments.

Such impure and unsimple ordinary time accompanies the narrator, enfolds him, to the very end of his narrative. When he recounts his culminating discoveries, during which he discerned a celestial exit from loss and waste at last coming into view, Proust's writing has an enhanced rather than a diminished sense of temporal pulsation:

> L'être qui était rené en moi [. . .] languit dans l'observation du présent où les sens ne peuvent la [l'essence des choses] lui apporter, dans la considération d'un passé que l'intelligence lui dessèche, dans l'attente d'un avenir que la volonté construit avec des fragments du présent et du passé auxquels elle retire encore de leur réalité en ne conservant d'eux que ce qui convient à la fin utilitaire, étroitement humaine, qu'elle leur assigne. Mais qu'un bruit, qu'une odeur, déjà entendu ou respirée jadis, le soient de nouveau, à la fois dans le présent et dans le passé, réels sans être actuels, idéaux sans être abstraits, aussitôt l'essence permanente et habituellement cachée des choses se trouve libérée, et notre vrai moi qui, parfois depuis longtemps, semblait mort, mais ne l'était pas entièrement, s'éveille, s'anime en recevant la céleste nourriture qui lui est apportée.   (IV, 451)

The being which had been reborn in me [languishes in] the observation of the present, where the senses cannot feed it [the essence of things] with this food [. . .] as it does in the consideration of a past made arid by the intellect or in the anticipation of a future which the will constructs with fragments of the present and the past, fragments whose reality it still further reduces by preserving of them only what is suitable for the utilitarian, narrowly human purpose for which it intends them. But let a noise or a scent, once heard or once smelt, be heard or smelt again in the present and at the same time in the past, real without being actual, ideal without being abstract, and immediately the permanent and habitually concealed essence of things is liberated and our true self, which seemed – had perhaps for long years seemed – to be dead but was not altogether dead, is awakened and reanimated as it receives the celestial nourishment that is brought to it.   (VI, 224)

Proust sings of redeemed time in a language that is still restless and unsubdued. In the first of these sentences a familiar music is to be heard: the syntax continues to interconnect past, present and future, to manipulate memory and expectation, to tease out the paradoxes of desire-time and to pursue a broken path towards propositional fullness. We could almost be back, with the narrator, in the Swanns' drawing room, or on the Cambremers' yacht, or in the grievance-free mental half-light of the duchesse de Guermantes. But in the second sentence, which speaks of a past and a present ecstatically dissolved into each other and of a future which promises further increments of delight, this music also sounds. Here too the path is broken, and long. Both sentences end well, with their syntactic pattern closed and completed, and both are hungry for a future: beyond utility a new joy remains to be found; beyond the administering of 'celestial food' a new life of wakeful and risk-filled animation remains to be explored. Nothing in these closing pages of the novel shrinks away from the exactions of ordinary time, or of 'embodied time' as the narrator now calls it (VI, 449; 'temps incorporé' (IV, 623)). Indeed the last cadence of the book, its last well-made proposition, is a call back to the unredeemable temporal process which makes writing possible. At the close, closure is most to be resisted.

There is of course a temporal hierarchy in Proust's book. The time-patterning that holds the whole novel together is more impressive and does more work than the patterning that holds the individual sentences together, whatever the structural similarities the two orders display. 'Ordinary time' is much more ordinary on certain occasions than on others. And there are mountain-tops from which the pains and penalties which beset time-dwellers do seem to disappear. But Proust weaves between levels, distrusts summits, and has a special fondness for the small temporal effects that are to be found within the 'rank vegetal proliferation' of a literary text.

III

Art

The whole universe takes part in the dancing.
The Acts of John

Mary McCarthy once memorably rebelled against the residual cult of 'art for art's sake' in prose fiction by pointing out that novels were often lumpy with undisguised 'fact' and could be put to use for all manner of everyday purposes: 'you can learn how to make strawberry jam from *Anna Karenina* and how to reap a field and hunt ducks'. For some of Proust's admirers such an idea will seem impious. They will see in *A la recherche du temps perdu* a triumph of the aesthetic over the merely useful, and wish to protect Proust's good name from the taint of commerce or cookery. There is something about the transforming energy of Proust's style, they will perhaps claim, that belongs unashamedly to high art. They might even murmur, remembering the dithyramb upon which Walter Pater's *The Renaissance* (1873) ends, that Proust in his style has achieved the aesthete's dream par excellence: 'To burn always with this hard, gem-like flame, to maintain this ecstasy, is success in life.' No jam, no ducks.

Proust's narrator sees things very differently. Although he is repeatedly drawn back, mothlike, to the Pateresque aesthetic flame, he is also fascinated by art-objects as commodities, and by the changing valuations that are placed upon them as they circulate in social space. When Bergotte dies, his afterlife of literary fame is firmly anchored to the spending power of individual consumers:

> On l'enterra, mais toute la nuit funèbre, aux vitrines éclairées, ses livres, disposés trois par trois, veillaient comme des anges aux ailes éployées et semblaient pour celui qui n'était plus, le symbole de sa résurrection. (III, 693)

> They buried him, but all through that night of mourning, in the lighted shop-windows, his books, arranged three by three, kept vigil like angels with outspread wings and seemed, for him who was no more, the symbol of his resurrection. (V, 209)

In due course, Bergotte's books may begin to resemble Rilkean angels, winged messengers from a transcendent sphere provisionally called Art, but for the time being they remain caught inside a system of trading arrangements: their angelic look is the product of a window-dresser's artistry, and has a solid commercial motive behind it. Bergotte is dead, and already immaterially resurrected in the minds of his admirers, but the booksellers are still alive and need to earn a living. Throughout the novel Proust dwells on the socio-economic conditions of artistic production: works of art are prized and have prices, and the mechanisms by which they are bought and sold are for practical purposes quite separate from the labour of hand and brain which produces them. The art-work may have a glorious public career while its producer lives and dies in destitution. The market forces which govern the lives and the posthumous standing of artists operate on a broad front, generically, and have little respect for individual merit or distinctiveness: 'Comme à la Bourse, quand un mouvement de hausse se produit, tout un compartiment de valeurs en profitent' (III, 210; 'As on the Stock Exchange, when a rise occurs, a whole group of securities profit by it' (IV, 248)).

Proust's narrator distinguishes firmly between the use value and the exchange value of artistic commodities, and gives a personal twist to the teachings of classical political economy. Art has use value in so far as it procures delight, joy, intellectual certainty or a general sense of emotional well-being for its consumer or its proprietor, and exchange value when its characteristic products move around in the fickle world of opinion. Individual works are valued highly because they are capable of serving human wants and producing pleasurable sensation, but any moment during which they are successfully used for these purposes is hedged about by stubborn questions of social status and prestige. Art is a weapon in the salon wars. Mme Verdurin enacts rapture for the benefit of her 'little clan', drives herself towards the extremes of aesthetic sensitivity which will identify her as a charismatic personage in their eyes, and presents her own artistic experience as a special form of suffering nobly and altruistically borne. Listening to a sonata or a septet is always a social act in Proust, and extravagantly so when Mme Verdurin buries her head in her hands in seeming retreat from her fellow hearers.

Although this stage management of artistic response runs as a comic leitmotif throughout the novel, Proust extracts a more complex poetry from the rise and fall of entire artistic reputations. 'Poussin' or 'Chopin' are commodities like rubber, copper or coffee, and a diffuse but effective international machinery regulates their prices. Among many satirical set-pieces on this theme none more completely overreaches the task of correcting human folly than the episode in *Sodome et Gomorrhe* where the narrator brings news of Chopin's revived market fortunes to Mme de Cambremer, who has paid him a visit at Balbec. The full extent of Chopin's rehabilitation is revealed to the narrator's victim not directly but, 'as in a game of billiards', by bouncing the latest state of informed opinion off her mother-in-law, the aged, music-loving marquise de Cambremer, who has accompanied her:

> Ses yeux brillèrent comme ceux de Latude dans la pièce appelée *Latude ou trente-cinq ans de captivité* et sa poitrine huma l'air de la mer avec cette dilatation que Beethoven a si bien marquée dans *Fidelio*, quand ses prisonniers respirent enfin «cet air qui vivifie». Je crus qu'elle allait poser sur ma joue ses lèvres moustachues. «Comment, vous aimez Chopin? Il aime Chopin, il aime Chopin», s'écria-t-elle dans un nasonnement passionné, comme elle aurait dit: «Comment, vous connaissez aussi Mme de Francquetot?» avec cette différence que mes relations avec Mme de Francquetot lui eussent étés profondément indifférentes, tandis que ma connaissance de Chopin la jeta dans une sorte de délire artistique. L'hypersécrétion salivaire ne suffit plus. N'ayant même pas essayé de comprendre le rôle de Debussy dans la réinvention de Chopin, elle sentit seulement que mon jugement était favorable. L'enthousiasme musical la saisit. «Élodie! Élodie! il aime Chopin.» Ses seins se soulevèrent et elle battit l'air de ses bras. «Ah! j'avais bien senti que vous étiez musicien, s'écria-t-elle. Je comprends, hhartiste comme vous êtes, que vous aimiez cela. C'est si beau!» Et sa voix était aussi caillouteuse que si, pour m'exprimer son ardeur pour Chopin, elle eût, imitant Démosthène, rempli sa bouche avec tous les galets de la plage. Enfin le reflux vint, atteignant jusqu'à la voilette qu'elle n'eut pas le temps de mettre à l'abri et qui fut transpercée, enfin la marquise essuya avec son mouchoir brodé la bave d'écume dont le souvenir de Chopin venait de tremper ses moustaches. (III, 212–13)

Her eyes shone like the eyes of Latude in the play entitled *Latude, or Thirty-five Years in Captivity*, and her bosom inhaled the sea air with that dilatation which Beethoven has depicted so well in *Fidelio*, at the point where his prisoners at last breathe again 'this life-giving air'. I thought that she

71

was going to press her hirsute lips to my cheek. 'What, you like Chopin? He likes Chopin, he likes Chopin,' she cried in an impassioned nasal twang, as she might have said: 'What, you know Mme de Francquetot too?', with this difference, that my relations with Mme de Francquetot would have been a matter of profound indifference to her, whereas my knowledge of Chopin plunged her into a sort of artistic delirium. Her salivary hyper-secretion no longer sufficed. Not having even attempted to understand the part played by Debussy in the rediscovery of Chopin, she felt only that my judgment of him was favourable. Her musical enthusiasm overpowered her. 'Elodie! Elodie! He likes Chopin!' Her bosom rose and she beat the air with her arms. 'Ah! I knew at once that you were a musician,' she cried, 'I can quite understand your liking his work, *hhartistic* as you are. It's so beautiful!' And her voice was as pebbly as if, to express her ardour for Chopin, she had imitated Demosthenes and filled her mouth with all the shingle on the beach. Then came the ebb-tide, reaching as far as her veil which she had not time to lift out of harm's way and which was drenched, and finally the Marquise wiped away with her embroidered handkerchief the tidemark of foam in which the memory of Chopin had steeped her moustaches.

(IV, 250)

Debussy's favourable opinion of Chopin, funnelled downwards by the narrator into the dimly lit world of the Cambremers, triggers a violent physical reaction: the throat, the nasal membranes and the salivary ducts of the old marquise, which have already been sketched at some length, are now so energised by the narrator's announcement that she begins to resemble an impersonal natural force. She secretes, but in the manner of the ocean nearby. The pebbled shore, the incoming tide, the foaming waves, remove her from a mere social encounter and give her a place in the conversation of the elements. From the viewpoint of breeding and decorum, her reaction to a risen-again composer is as grotesque and uncomely as her moustache.

This is caricature reaching towards sublimity. The excellence of Beethoven's music and of Demosthenes's oratorical style are by stealth co-opted into the narrator's portrait of incontinent old age. High art, represented by Chopin, Debussy and the great chorus, 'O welche Lust!' which opens the Act I finale of *Fidelio*, is brought into alignment with the very low art of a sensational boulevard melodrama, and the expressive power of art itself with embarrassing bodily functions. A revolutionary hymn to freedom is interwoven with the free growth of facial hair and the free expression of spit. Writing of this kind passes beyond simple vitriol and disgust and moves towards a lofty vision of art as necessarily inclusive, heterogeneous and impure. From within a malicious account of exchange value a new usefulness is discovered for the artistic commodity: it produces delight from the most improbable raw materials. An abject beauty is born.

Proust's account of the art market is as much a celebration as a critique. Commercial motives and financial transactions are 'low' materials, but ones upon which the high-toned Proustian novel thrives. The narrator keeps on reminding himself of these, reserving a special place in his own prospective novel for getting and spending, and the exploitation of art for other than artistic ends. *A la recherche du temps perdu* thus anticipates in detail one of the destinies to which it has been subject since its publication. The novel has been pressed into service as a source-book for the social history of late nineteenth-century France, and has acted as an informal guide to the sensibilities, manners, tastes and fashions of the period. It has come to resemble the *Voyage artistique à Bayreuth* (1897) that was so popular in Proust's own day. This volume, by Albert Lavignac, was the complete *vade mecum* for those setting out on their Wagnerian pilgrimage, and combined operatic plot-summaries and music-examples with advice on travel, including railway ticket prices and journey times, hotel accommodation and local dishes. Proust's novel is regularly treated as a voyage in space and time to a lost Faubourg Saint-Germain, and valued because it tells us what books its inhabitants were reading, what plays they were seeing and what coiffures and evening gowns they wore:

le visage d'Odette paraissait plus maigre et plus proéminent parce que le front et le haut des joues, cette surface unie et plus plane était recouverte par la masse de cheveux qu'on portait alors prolongés en «devants», soulevés en «crêpés», répandus en mèches folles le long des oreilles; et quant à son corps qui était admirablement fait, il était difficile d'en apercevoir la continuité (à cause des modes de l'époque et quoiqu'elle fût une des femmes de Paris qui s'habillaient le mieux), tant le corsage, s'avançant en saillie comme sur un ventre imaginaire et finissant brusquement en pointe pendant que par en dessous commençait à s'enfler le ballon des doubles jupes, donnait à la femme l'air d'être composée de pièces différentes mal emmanchées les unes dans les autres; tant les ruchés, les volants, le gilet suivaient en toute indépendance, selon la fantaisie de leur dessin ou la consistance de leur étoffe, la ligne qui les conduisait aux nœuds, aux bouillons de dentelle, aux effilés de jais perpendiculaires, ou qui les dirigeait le long du busc, mais ne s'attachaient nullement à l'être vivant, qui selon que l'architecture de ces fanfreluches se rapprochait ou s'écartait trop de la sienne s'y trouvait engoncé ou perdu.   (I, 194)

Odette's face appeared thinner and sharper than it actually was, because the forehead and the upper part of the cheeks, that smooth and almost plane surface, were covered by the masses of hair which women wore at that period drawn forward in a fringe, raised in crimped waves and falling in stray locks over the ears; while as for her figure – and she was admirably built – it was impossible to make out its continuity (on account of the fashion then prevailing, and

in spite of her being one of the best-dressed women in Paris)
so much did the corsage, jutting out as though over an
imaginary stomach and ending in a sharp point, beneath
which bulged out the balloon of her double skirts, give a
woman the appearance of being composed of different sections badly fitted together; to such an extent did the frills,
the flounces, the inner bodice follow quite independently,
according to the whim of their designer or the consistency
of their material, the line which led them to the bows, the
festoons of lace, the fringes of dangling jet beads, or carried
them along the busk, but nowhere attached themselves to
the living creature, who, according as the architecture of
these fripperies drew them towards or away from her own,
found herself either strait-laced to suffocation or else completely buried.   (I, 236)

This portrait of the young Odette from the beginning of 'Un
Amour de Swann' already speaks of her as a construction,
an unstable precipitate of other people's desires, and artfully
suggests, in its cascading three-item lists of detachable decorative elements, the difficulty that Swann is soon to experience
in his attempts to immobilise and control her. But even if we
train ourselves to be suspicious of such descriptions, and
remind ourselves of the ways in which their brilliant literary
art overlays and obscures the art of the hairdresser or the
couturier, they do still have enough of the documentary record
about them to serve at least as corroborative evidence for the
professional social historian. For the amateur, Proust's dresses
will of course be close enough to the real thing for no pedantic
questions about their evidential status to be asked. Indeed
Proust's novel tells us so crisply about so many aspects of
social life – from bicycles and telephone exchanges to modes
of address and hotel accommodation – that most modern
readers will be happy to treat its curious lore as simple fact.
Why shrink away from the novel's utilitarian role as an encyclopaedia of its times?

This posthumous treatment of Proust's novel really does seem to have been authorised by Proust himself, for whom prose fiction should no more be shorn of fact and utility than the marquise de Cambremer's upper lip should be depilated. Just as the narrator of *Le Temps retrouvé* is propelled towards creative action by the unevenness of paving stones or the rigidity and roughness of a table-napkin (IV, 446–7; VI, 218–19), so the book in which he figures seems to crave a constant contact with the recalcitrant particularity of material things. In order to produce new knowledge, the human sensorium needs to be goaded, stung, taken aback. From a moment's disequilibrium between the writer's sense-fields, from a snag, a discrepancy or an overload, comes first a new power of vision, and then writing. 'Please handle me roughly' is the writer's request to the world.

When Proust inserts imaginary works of art, minutely described, into the fabric of his narration, these are at one and the same time disruptive, in that they slow the plot down, and facilitating, in that they tell the reader in the form of a self-contained allegory what manner of plot the book as a whole has. In recounting his experience of Elstir's painting 'Le port de Carquethuit' in *A l'ombre des jeunes filles en fleurs* (II, 192–4; II, 480–82) or of the Vinteuil septet posthumously performed at a Verdurin soirée in *La Prisonnière* (III, 752–69; V, 279–300), for example, the narrator pays tribute to the integrative power of artistic imagination as it exercises itself on a mass of unruly and short-lived particulars. Whatever sensations of grace or ease the work of art may eventually cause, it is not allowed to forget that it is the product of hard work upon resistant stuff and that the artist can properly feed on the hard work of others when he comes to choose his subject matter:

Des hommes qui poussaient des bateaux à la mer couraient aussi bien dans les flots que sur le sable, lequel, mouillé, réfléchissait déjà les coques comme s'il avait été de l'eau [. . .] des femmes qui ramassaient des crevettes dans les rochers, avaient l'air, parce qu'elles étaient entourées d'eau et à cause de la dépression qui, après la barrière circulaire des roches, abaissait la plage (des deux côtés les plus rapprochés des terres) au niveau de la mer, d'être dans une grotte marine surplombée de barques et de vagues, ouverte et protégée au milieu des flots écartés miraculeusement. Si tout le tableau donnait cette impression des ports où la mer entre dans la terre, où la terre est déjà marine et la population amphibie, la force de l'élément marin éclatait partout; et près des rochers, à l'entrée de la jetée, où la mer était agitée, on sentait, aux efforts des matelots et à l'obliquité des barques couchées à angle aigu devant la calme verticalité de l'entrepôt, de l'église, des maisons de la ville, où les uns rentraient, d'où les autres partaient pour la pêche, qu'ils trottaient rudement sur l'eau comme sur un animal fougueux et rapide dont les soubresauts, sans leur adresse, les eussent jetés à terre.   (II, 193)

The men who were pushing down their boats into the sea were running as much through the waves as along the sand, which, being wet, reflected the hulls as if they were already in the water [. . .] women gathering shrimps among the rocks had the appearance, because they were surrounded by water and because of the depression which, beyond the circular barrier of rocks, brought the beach (on the two sides nearest the land) down to sea-level, of being in a marine grotto overhung by ships and waves, open yet protected in the midst of miraculously parted waters. If the whole picture gave this impression of harbours in which the sea penetrated the land, in which the land was already subaqueous and the population amphibian, the strength of the marine element was everywhere apparent; and round about the rocks, at the mouth of the harbour where the sea was rough, one sensed, from the muscular efforts of the fishermen and the slant of the boats leaning over at an acute angle, compared with the calm erectness of the warehouse, the church, the houses in

the town to which some of the figures were returning and
from which others were setting out to fish, that they were
riding bareback on the water as though on a swift and fiery
animal whose rearing, but for their skill, must have unseated
them.   (II, 480–81)

The muscular efforts of fishermen and shrimp-collecting
women are echoed in the transpositional labour of Elstir's
brush, which moves land-features seawards and sea-features
landwards, and re-echoed in the animation and bustle of the
narrator's prose. Writing immerses itself in the interplay of
natural forces and human trades, and improves upon the art
of the painter in one essential respect: by way of its syntax,
writing offers not a still effigy of movement but movement itself.
It inhabits time, and in its goal-driven effortfulness rejoins the
time-bound seafarers as they push out their boats or steer them
among the waves. A novel in headlong motion towards a distant
goal offers the reader a sudden model of itself in its completed
state, and of the navigational prowess required to get it there.

Proust's prefigurative sketches of his own finished book
reach their culmination in the episode of Vinteuil's septet,
which is a large double portrait of art and labour. What is so
remarkable about this celebrated scene is that it brings together,
and interconnects, a pure strain of Pateresque aesthetic ecstasy
on the one hand and a prosy view of the artisan's workshop
on the other. The septet is repeatedly differentiated from
the earlier violin sonata by Vinteuil, which had supplied
Odette and Swann with the 'national anthem of their love'
(I, 262; 'l'air national de leur amour' (I, 215)), as if the contrast
between the two works contained a clue to the enigma of all
artistic perception. First of all the main difference is stated in
the empurpled language that a programme-note writer might
use to endow abstract music with an accessible content of
images:

Tandis que la sonate s'ouvrait sur une aube liliale et cham-
pêtre, divisant sa candeur légère mais pour se suspendre
à l'emmêlement léger et pourtant consistant d'un berceau
rustique de chèvrefeuilles sur des géraniums blancs, c'était
sur des surfaces unies et planes commes celles de la mer
que, par un matin d'orage, commençait au milieu d'un aigre
silence, dans un vide infini, l'œuvre nouvelle, et c'est dans
un rose d'aurore que, pour se construire progressivement
devant moi, cet univers inconnu était tiré du silence et de
la nuit. Ce rouge si nouveau, si absent de la tendre, champê-
tre et candide sonate, teignait tout le ciel, comme l'aurore,
d'un espoir mystérieux. Et un chant perçait déjà l'air, chant
de sept notes, mais le plus inconnu, le plus différent de tout
ce que j'eusse jamais imaginé, à la fois ineffable et criard,
non plus roucoulement de colombe comme dans la sonate,
mais déchirant l'air, aussi vif que la nuance écarlate dans
laquelle le début était noyé, quelque chose comme un mys-
tique chant du coq, un appel ineffable mais suraigu, de
l'éternel matin.   (III, 754)

Whereas the sonata opened upon a lily-white pastoral dawn,
dividing its fragile purity only to hover in the delicate yet
compact entanglement of a rustic bower of honeysuckle
against white geraniums, it was upon flat, unbroken surfaces
like those of the sea on a morning that threatens storm, in
the midst of an eerie silence, in an infinite void, that this
new work began, and it was into a rose-red daybreak that
this unknown universe was drawn from the silence and the
night to build up gradually before me. This redness, so
new, so absent from the tender, pastoral, unadorned sonata,
tinged all the sky, as dawn does, with a mysterious hope.
And a song already pierced the air, a song on seven notes,
but the strangest, the most remote from anything I had ever
imagined, at once ineffable and strident, no longer the cooing
of a dove as in the sonata, but rending the air, as vivid as
the scarlet tint in which the opening bars had been bathed,
something like a mystical cock-crow, the ineffable but ear-
piercing call of eternal morning.   (V, 282–3)

This is supercharged 'programmatic' description in that it offers a battery of special effects – sunrises, flower arrangements and a transcendentalised farmyard – in lieu of musical analysis proper, but it is also, by the very floridity and excess of its language, something more. The gap between the pale dawn of a violin sonata and the red dawn of a septet is rediscovered endlessly and everywhere: between repose and action, cooing and shrieking, doves and cocks, pastoralism and farming, the ordinary calendrical procession of days and a new apocalypse. The paragraph continues lengthily in the same vein, and spawns further alternative versions of what seems to be a single underlying difference. Difference itself, the fact and principle of it, has become the mystery of mysteries and sends the writing in mad pursuit of its key.

This rapturous recreation of musical hearing is interrupted by social reportage of one kind or another – Mme Verdurin is restaging her martyrdom to art, and Charlus is negotiating for sexual favours with members of the domestic staff – but when music itself returns the binary pair 'sonata *v.* septet' is again given a central expressive role. So many other pairs are available from within the language of Western music – melody *v.* harmony, major *v.* minor, treble *v.* bass, homophony *v.* polyphony, sonata form *v.* baroque ritornello form – but none has the strange undeserved prestige of two instruments *v.* seven. At the climactic moment of this episode, music is drained of all sensuous content and its entire thrust and dynamic are handed over to a group of almost synonymous abstract terms. The play of difference and similarity, which had previously been embodied in music, heard, touched and visualised as note followed note, is now reinvented in the bare alternation of the terms *difference* and *similarity*, and their synonyms:

c'était justement quand [Vinteuil] cherchait puissamment
à être nouveau, qu'on reconnaissait, sous les différences
apparentes, les similitudes profondes et les ressemblances
voulues qu'il y avait au sein d'une œuvre, quand Vinteuil
reprenait à diverses reprises une même phrase, la diversifiait,
s'amusait à changer son rythme, à la faire reparaître sous sa
forme première, ces ressemblances-là, voulues, œuvre de
l'intelligence, forcément superficielles, n'arrivaient jamais à
être aussi frappantes que ces ressemblances dissimulées,
involontaires, qui éclataient sous des couleurs différentes,
entre les deux chefs-d'œuvre distincts; car alors Vinteuil,
cherchant puissamment à être nouveau, s'interrogeait lui-
même, de toute la puissance de son effort créateur atteignait
sa propre essence à ces profondeurs où, quelque question
qu'on lui pose, c'est du même accent, le sien propre, qu'elle
répond. (III, 760)

it was precisely when [Vinteuil] was striving with all his
might to create something new that one recognised, beneath
the apparent differences, the profound similarities and the
deliberate resemblances that existed in the body of a work;
when Vinteuil took up the same phrase again and again,
diversified it, amused himself by altering its rhythm, by
making it reappear in its original form, those deliberate
resemblances, the work of his intellect, necessarily superficial, never succeeded in being as striking as the disguised,
involuntary resemblances, which broke out in different
colours, between the two separate masterpieces; for then
Vinteuil, striving to do something new, interrogated himself,
with all the power of his creative energy, reached down to
his essential self at those depths where, whatever the question asked, it is in the same accent, that is to say its own,
that it replies. (V, 289)

Again, this is only part of a long careering paragraph in which
a single polarity is tirelessly recast. Beneath a phenomenal
surface in which difference reigns supreme, an underlying similarity or self-identity gathers force. Although the later work is

unassimilable to the earlier, and boasts about its own stridencies and its refusal to blend voice smoothly into voice, an uncontrollable, non-volitional Vinteuil manner speaks up for sameness even as difference has its day. But this is not the end of the story, for the more Vinteuil becomes an individual and the more recognisable his stylistic fingerprints prove to be, the more he removes himself from those with whom he shares a mere period style. No sooner is difference lost from view inside an individual corpus of creative works than it re-emerges within a larger community of artists: a great composer sounds like himself and no one else. An abstract language which talks insistently of difference has been given propulsive force and become the vehicle of an unquenchable Dionysian vision. Music overspills the page, the stave and the recital room, and floods the entire scene of thought and action; it seizes everything in its path and becomes, in Pater's words, 'the focus where the greatest number of vital forces unite in their purest energy'.

The air of excitement and uplift that Proust confers upon these descriptions of Vinteuil's late work may at first seem to sit oddly with his accompanying emphasis on the labour that art requires of its creators and recreative performers. But their co-ordinated efforts of mind and muscle, far from being noted in passing, are incorporated bodily in the narrator's trance; the texture of his reverie on art is woven not only from a generalising speculative language but from memories of other people at work, menially applying themselves to the materials of their craft or trade:

> Le violoncelliste dominait l'instrument qu'il serrait entre ses genoux, inclinant sa tête à laquelle des traits vulgaires donnaient, dans les instants de maniérisme, une expression involontaire de dégoût; il se penchait sur sa contrebasse, la palpait avec la même patience domestique que s'il eût épluché un chou, tandis que près de lui la harpiste, encore

enfant, en jupe courte, dépassée de tous côtés par les rayons horizontaux du quadrilatère d'or, pareil à ceux qui, dans la chambre magique d'une sibylle, figureraient arbitrairement l'éther, selon les formes consacrées, semblait aller y chercher çà et là, au point assigné, un son délicieux, de la même manière que, petite déesse allégorique, dressée devant le treillage d'or de la voûte céleste, elle y aurait cueilli, une à une, des étoiles. (III, 755–6)

The cellist was hunched over the instrument which he clutched between his knees, his head bowed forward, his coarse features assuming an involuntary expression of disgust at the more mannerist moments; he leaned over his double bass, fingering it with the same domestic patience with which he might have peeled a cabbage, while by his side the harpist, a mere child in a short skirt, framed behind the diagonal rays of her golden quadrilateral, recalling those which, in the magic chamber of a sibyl, arbitrarily denote the ether according to the traditional forms, seemed to be picking out exquisite sounds here and there at designated points, just as though, a tiny allegorical goddess poised before the golden trellis of the heavenly vault, she were gathering, one by one, its stars. (V, 283–4)

Proust has arranged a delicious reversal of conventional musical values in this passage: the cellist, whose instrument – oddly called a *contrebasse* ('double bass') in the original French – has serious melodic and harmonic responsibilities in the instrumental music of the time, is consigned to the kitchen as a rude cabbage-stripper, while the harpist escapes from her customary supporting role to become a goddess plucking stars from the heavenly vault. Blessed are the meek, and those who merely tweak. But both instrumentalists are workers, practical folk, appliers of instrumental reason. From their scraping and twanging, from their devoted coaxing of wood, wire and gut, comes other people's joy:

Enfin le motif joyeux resta triomphant, ce n'était plus un appel presque inquiet lancé derrière un ciel vide, c'était une joie ineffable qui semblait venir du Paradis; une joie aussi différente de celle de la sonate que, d'un ange doux et grave de Bellini, jouant du théorbe, pourrait être, vêtu d'une robe d'écarlate, quelque archange de Mantegna sonnant dans un buccin. Je savais que cette nuance nouvelle de la joie, cet appel vers une joie supraterrestre, je ne l'oublierais jamais. Masi serait-elle jamais réalisable pour moi?   (III, 764–5)

In the end the joyous motif was left triumphant; it was no longer an almost anxious appeal addressed to an empty sky, it was an ineffable joy which seemed to come from paradise, a joy as different from that of the sonata as some scarlet-clad Mantegna archangel sounding a trumpet from a grave and gentle Bellini seraph strumming a theorbo. I knew that this new tone of joy, this summons to a supraterrestrial joy, was a thing that I would never forget. But would it ever be attainable to me?   (V, 294)

The narrator's plaintive question provides the cue for a further exorbitant disquisition on the sheer long-haul laboriousness that art may require of its disciples. It would of course be gratifying to find that artistic joys were there for the plucking, requiring little or nothing by way of training, preparatory study or technical address, but mostly they are not there in advance of the human appetite for them. They have to be elicited, and slowly. The writer, the painter, the composer, and the performing musician too, have to spend long hours in what Roland Barthes aptly called 'the kitchen of meaning' ('la cuisine du sens'), sweating away to create a richly interfused semantic broth.

At this point in this extraordinary episode, the narrator, seeking an answer to his question, makes a bold sideways move, and speaks not about the writing of music but about its editing, and about the skills and temperamental qualities that successful editors typically require. Vinteuil had died before completing his septet, and the task of producing a performable score had been hampered by the confused state in which the sketches had been left. The task had been taken on and brought to fruition by a woman who had, much earlier in the novel, figured with the composer's daughter in a primal scene of perverse sexual play:

> en passant des années à débrouiller le grimoire laissé par Vinteuil, en établissant la lecture certaine de ces hiéro-glyphes inconnus, l'amie de Mlle Vinteuil eut la consolation d'assurer au musicien dont elle avait assombri les dernières années, une gloire immortelle et compensatrice [. . .] Comme dans les illisibles carnets où un chimiste de génie, qui ne sait pas la mort si proche, a noté des découvertes qui resteront peut-être à jamais ignorées, elle avait dégagé, de papiers plus illisibles que des papyrus ponctués d'écriture cunéiforme, la formule éternellement vraie, à jamais féconde, de cette joie inconnue, l'espérance mystique de l'ange écar-late du matin. (III, 766–7)

> by spending years unravelling the scribblings left by him, by establishing the correct readings of those secret hiero-glyphs, she had the consolation of ensuring an immortal and compensatory glory for the composer over whose last years she had cast such a shadow [. . .] As in the illegible note-books in which a chemist of genius, who does not know that death is at hand, jots down discoveries which will perhaps remain for ever unknown, Mlle Vinteuil's friend had disentangled, from papers more illegible than strips of papyrus dotted with a cuneiform script, the formula, eter-nally true and for ever fertile, of this unknown joy, the mystic hope of the crimson Angel of the Dawn. (V, 295–6)

The cruel passions of the woman have been magically trans-muted into the patient, public-spirited, scholarly toil without which the red dawn of Vinteuil's last work would have remained invisible, and its cock-crow unheard.

With his constant stress on the undecipherability of Vinteuil's manuscripts, and on the co-responsibility of the composer and editor for the joy that the completed work can produce in its hearers, the narrator seems at first to be describing a hierarchical division of artistic labour. Editors are like cellists and harpists in that their efforts help to bring the art-work to birth as organised sound, but the composer himself still retains his major privileges, for the ideational and affective contents of the work are his alone. Inspiration belongs to him, and perspiration to useful lesser beings. It would have suited one of the narrator's self-images well to leave matters there. Let other people do the work, get their hands dirty, have sexual eccentricities and other signs of character, and let the artist have brilliant ideas and a capacity to delegate. Yet the narrator does not settle for invisibility, or aloofness from mere work, during this, his supreme hymn to the potency of Art. On the contrary, he comes alive as a character precisely in his greed for work, and for eccentricity, and for other people's specialised skills. The clarion-call that his writing sounds, its noisy dawn-song and its forward-rushing clamour, are born of a will-to-include that thrives equally on eloquence and babble, ecstasies and exertions, cabbages and stars. For a moment, even Mme Verdurin's snoring dog is caught up in the enlarged acoustic space of Vinteuil's work, and writing has a similar opportunistic power of absorption. These pages are a gloriously impure, lumber-filled rhapsody. In them Proust's art reveals art, lays bare its inner workings, comes clean about its insecurities and low motives, and pins snapshots of the production-process on to the finished product. This combined description and reinvention has unparalleled summative force: it is an allegorical representation both of what the narrator's book will eventually be like and of what Proust's book has already been like from its first page.

While one tendency of the narrator's voice throughout the novel takes him towards the seemingly disembodied labour of speculative thought, another, almost as insistent, moves him back into the company of full-time handworkers. Electricians, motor mechanics, porcelain repairers, dressmakers and switchboard operators are all caught up in the reflective texture of the narrator's monologue, and their specialist skills are sometimes characterised at length:

> Dans une boucherie, où à gauche était une auréole de soleil et à droite un bœuf entier pendu, un garçon boucher très grand et très mince, aux cheveux blonds, son cou sortant d'un col bleu ciel, mettait une rapidité vertigineuse et une religieuse conscience à mettre d'un côté les filets de bœuf exquis, de l'autre de la culotte de dernier ordre, les plaçait dans d'éblouissantes balances surmontées d'une croix, d'où retombaient de belles chaînettes, et – bien qu'il ne fît ensuite que disposer pour l'étalage, des rognons, des tournedos, des entrecôtes – donnait en réalité beaucoup plus l'impression d'un bel ange qui au jour du Jugement dernier préparera pour Dieu, selon leurs qualités, la séparation des Bons et des Méchants et la pesée des âmes.   (III, 644–5)

> In a butcher's shop, between an aureole of sunshine on the left and a whole ox suspended from a hook on the right, a young assistant, very tall and slender, with fair hair and a long neck emerging from a sky-blue collar, was displaying a lightning speed and a religious conscientiousness in putting on one side the most exquisite fillets of beef, on the other the coarsest parts of the rump, and placing them on glittering scales surmounted by a cross from which there dangled a set of beautiful chains, and – although he did nothing afterwards but arrange in the window a display of kidneys, steaks and ribs – was really far more reminiscent of a handsome angel who, on the Day of Judgement, will organise for God,

according to their quality, the separation of the good and
the wicked and the weighing of souls.   (V, 150)

Like the dyer's hand in one of Shakespeare's sonnets, the nature
of this butcher's boy is 'subdued to what it works in'. Raw
meat is his expressive medium, and within this world of cuts
and joints he is able to achieve an inventive patterning that is
for a moment strictly comparable to the painter's work with
pigment or the composer's with notes. (The handsome angel
weighing souls is likely to have been borrowed from Rogier
van der Weyden's great 'Last Judgement' altarpiece in the
Hôtel-Dieu at Beaune.) The narrator's gentle humour in passages like this is based on a real sense of fraternity in toil, and
the angelic cadence on which the sentence comes to rest speaks
entirely of a this-worldly pride in a job well done. As if to
reinforce the point that heavenly beings belong to the real
world, the angels in Giotto's Arena chapel are presented, later
in the novel, as working messengers, expending their loco-
motive energy in robust contact with the oxygen-rich earthly
air:

Avec tant de ferveur céleste, ou au moins de sagesse et
d'application enfantines, qu'ils rapprochent leurs petites
mains, les anges sont représentés à l'Arena, mais comme
des volatiles d'une espèce particulière ayant existé réelle-
ment, ayant dû figurer dans l'histoire naturelle des temps
bibliques et évangéliques. Ce sont de petits êtres qui ne
manquent pas de voltiger devant les saints quand ceux-ci
se promènent; il y en a toujours quelques-uns de lâchés
au-dessus d'eux, et comme ce sont des créatures réelles et
effectivement volantes, on les voit s'élevant, décrivant des
courbes, mettant la plus grande aisance à exécuter des loop-
ings, fondant vers le sol la tête en bas à grand renfort d'ailes
qui leur permettent de se maintenir dans des positions con-
traires aux lois de la pesanteur, et ils font beaucoup plutôt

penser à une variété disparue d'oiseaux ou à de jeunes élèves
de Garros s'exerçant au vol plané, qu'aux anges de l'art de
la Renaissance.   (IV, 227)

For all the celestial fervour, or at least the childlike obedience
and application, with which their minuscule hands are
joined, they are represented in the Arena chapel as winged
creatures of a particular species that had really existed, that
must have figured in the natural history of biblical and
apostolic times. Constantly flitting about above the saints
whenever the latter walk abroad, these little beings, since
they are real creatures with a genuine power of flight, can
be seen soaring upwards, describing curves, 'looping the
loop', diving earthwards head first, with the aid of wings
which enable them to support themselves in positions that
defy the laws of gravity, and are far more reminiscent of an
extinct species of bird, or of young pupils of Garros practis-
ing gliding, than of the angels of the Renaissance. (V, 744)

The 'reality' of these winged creatures is repeatedly reinforced
here, rather as if the stubborn rumour of their heavenly origin
had to be scotched once and for all. They are a lost breed of
bird, or trainee pilots under the supervision of the French
air-ace Roland Garros (1888–1918), and the aerobatic adventures of these assembled air-workers belong unmistakably to
the modern day. *Looping* in the sense of 'looping the loop' is
recorded by Paul Robert's dictionary as making its first appearance in French in 1911, and both examples given are from
Proust's novel. One trembles slightly at the thought of these
very early aerial exploits, yet can only admire the speed with
which both languages found an appropriate term for the most
dangerous of them. No sooner had English adopted a vigorous
expression from a fairground attraction of the day, than French
had borrowed it in an abbreviated form. Proust, with characteristic historical long-sightedness, traces the gravity-defying insolence of the gesture back to the iconography of the Middle

Ages, and, beyond that, to the bird-life of biblical times.

The work of art, according to the narrator's prescription, must commemorate the labour from which it springs, or at the very least acknowledge within itself the comparable labours of those who, caring little or nothing for art, nevertheless contribute distinctively to the common good. The sculptural decoration of Laon cathedral contains a perfect emblem of this relationship: the narrator reminds us of 'les tours où des bœufs, se promenant paisiblement sur la toiture, regardent de haut les plaines de Champagne' (II, 313–14; 'the towers, between which oxen grazing calmly on the roof look down over the plains of Champagne' (III, 6)), and in so doing gives these working animals an afterlife of action. They had hauled stone blocks to the top of the knoll on which the cathedral was to be built, and now move around freely at their perpetual pasture. They have become part of the beauty which they helped to create. Similarly, Proust sweeps a workforce of modern fabricators into the fabric of his novel, naming them, specifying their crafts, keeping them in motion, and finding endless uncondescending ways of associating their skills with his.

One group of artisans has a special role in the long slow narrative of *A la recherche du temps perdu*: writers. Great writers, from Homer to Flaubert, modern men of letters, journalists, letter writers, lapidary inscription carvers and librettists crowd the scene. Real writers rub shoulders with imaginary ones, Mme de Sévigné with Mme de Beausergent, Anatole France, Pierre Loti and Edmond Rostand with the magnificent forename-shorn Bergotte. There is of course nothing surprising in the fact that the narrator should have chosen to populate his tale with authors, for reading books or claiming to have read them is a prominent feature of contemporary middle-class and aristocratic manners. Just as Freud's patients had bookish dreams, which they reported to a clinician who was himself well-read and willing to put literature to work for the purposes of dream interpretation, so Proust's characters use literary references and allusions as a versatile common currency in social exchange. Proust's novel redreams European literature, giving a further lease of imaginative life to favourite characters from fiction and drama and new pungency to the memorable sayings of essayists. The monumental weight of a centuries-old literary tradition dissolves into the light-limbed dance of the narrator's fantasies and talk.

While there is scarcely a page of Proust's novel that is without its literary reference, the pressure exerted by earlier writers on his own literary technique is subject to wide variation. At one extreme, the narrative may be given over, for pages on end, to extempore critical effusions. Plot, character and dialogue are swallowed into a loosely associative essay form. Towards the end of *La Prisonnière*, for example, the narrator, who is beginning to wish himself free of his weighty captive, unleashes for her benefit a tirade of literary impressions. The roll-call is impressive: Barbey d'Aurevilly, Hardy, Stendhal, Dostoevsky, Mme de Sévigné, Gogol, Paul de Kock, Laclos, Mme de Genlis, Baudelaire and Tolstoy. Two of these – Barbey d'Aurevilly and Hardy – are treated very much in the manner of an ingratiating reference work: first 'Le rideau cramoisi' from *Les Diaboliques* (1874), *Une vieille maîtresse* (1851) and *L'Ensorcelée* (1854), and then *Jude the Obscure* (1895), *The Well-Beloved* (1897) and *A Pair of Blue Eyes* (1873), are listed with lively comments on each. Later the narrator's attention switches to *The Idiot* (1868) and *The Brothers Karamazov* (1880) and to an enthusiastic enumeration of their characters. Vermeer, Rembrandt, Carpaccio and the nameless sculptors who decorated Orvieto cathedral are enlisted in supporting roles.

The narrator is making a serious point, as one might say,

in so far as he is again sketching the family resemblances between scenes and between entire works that create an overall sense of imaginative coherence and individuality for each of his great artists in turn. There is a Hardy tone of voice and an obsessional core of Hardy images. While disclaiming for the time being any personal wish to become a novelist, the narrator is setting out an artistic programme for himself, continuing to reflect upon the double pull towards difference and sameness that he had earlier discovered in the music of Vinteuil, and recreating exactly that tension in his own rampaging spoken exercises in criticism and aesthetic theory. But for every 'serious' strain in Proust's plot there is a comic descant. Proustian opera is *seria* and *buffa* at the same time. There is a massive failure of tact in the narrator's erudite assault upon his partner. 'Lock up your daughters when a literary critic comes wooing', the muse of comedy seems to say as these speeches reach their airless cruising altitude. Albertine is a conversational foil in the manner of a docile minor participant in one of Plato's dialogues:

> Je n'avais pas voulu vous interrompre, mais puisque je vois que vous quittez Dostoïevski, j'aurais peur d'oublier. Mon petit, qu'est-ce que vous avez voulu dire l'autre jour quand vous m'avez dit: «C'est comme le côté Dostoïevski de Mme de Sévigné.» Je vous avoue que je n'ai pas compris. Cela me semble tellement différent. – Venez, petite fille, que je vous embrasse pour vous remercier de vous rappeler si bien ce que je dis, vous retournerez au pianola après. Et j'avoue que ce que j'avais dit là était assez bête. Mais je l'avais dit pour deux raisons. La première est une raison particulière. Il est arrivé que Mme de Sévigné, comme Elstir, comme Dostoïevski, au lieu de présenter les choses dans l'ordre logique, c'est-à-dire en commençant par la cause, nous montre d'abord l'effet, l'illusion qui nous frappe. C'est ainsi que Dostoïevski présente ses personnages. (III, 880)

'I didn't want to interrupt you, but now that I see that you're leaving Dostoievsky, I'm afraid I might forget. My sweet, what was it you meant the other day when you said: "It's like the Dostoievsky side of Mme de Sévigné." I must confess that I didn't understand. It seems to me so different.' 'Come, little girl, let me give you a kiss to thank you for remembering so well what I say. You shall go back to the pianola afterwards. And I must admit that what I said was rather stupid. But I said it for two reasons. The first is a special reason. What I meant was that Mme de Sévigné, like Elstir, like Dostoievsky, instead of presenting things in their logical sequence, that is to say beginning with the cause, shows us first of all the effect, the illusion that strikes us. That is how Dostoievsky presents his characters.'

(V, 432)

The narrator's unforgettable *mot* on Mme de Sévigné and Dostoevsky, which is a pre-echo of the Borges story in which Céline and Joyce are imagined as the authors of the *Imitation of Christ*, leads him into an implicit self-description: he too, like his distinguished predecessors, will produce a literary work in which effects precede causes and illusions are entertained at length before being dispelled. But although the narrator is still composing a manifesto during his reply to Albertine, he is also, by the conceited virtuosity with which he addresses her on assorted literary topics, helping to provoke the catastrophe on which *La Prisonnière* ends. An affair must be nearing its end when it begins to be conducted as an academic seminar on the Russian novel. Love of literature has reached crisis level, and behaves like a predator or an asset-stripper towards love between persons.

At the other extreme from these highly exposed essays, lectures or seminars on literature is the power of implication or of irradiation that certain literary works possess. Such works go underground for long periods and, stored in the reader's memory, continue to have an active, shaping role in the procession of key episodes. The most remarkable case of this kind is George Sand's *François le Champi* (1850), for this short novel of country life and incestuous passion occupies a main buttressing position in the architecture of Proust's plot yet at the same time speaks quietly, as a diffuse reminiscence. Sand's novel is named and discussed in 'Combray' and rediscovered in the Guermantes library, and discussed again, in *Le Temps retrouvé* (I, 41–3, IV, 462–5; I, 47–9, VI, 239–43). It is the work with which the narrator's mother had soothed him during the childhood incident involving a withheld goodnight kiss, and the work which, stumbled upon in adulthood, triggers one of his culminating involuntary memories. *François le Champi* is a slender and even, in the narrator's judgement, a slightly derisory book, yet it sends a mighty echo from one end to the other of Proust's voluminous edifice. Time is regained as the narrator holds the Guermantes copy of Sand's novel in his hands.

Sand tells an Oedipal success story: a foundling is adopted by a miller's wife, Madeleine Blanchet, leaves home, returns to support his adoptive mother when she is widowed and in due course marries her. As a child Proust's narrator had not understood these events, for his mind had wandered during his mother's reading and she had in any case omitted all the love-scenes. Yet without grasping the changing relationship between Madeleine and François, he was already experiencing in his own person the driving force of the foundling's no longer simply filial devotion. For a moment, on that distant night, his main rival for his mother's affection had been removed, and he had enjoyed his own intense sensation of amatory success:

Mes remords étaient calmés, je me laissais aller à la douceur de cette nuit où j'avais ma mère auprès de moi. Je savais qu'une telle nuit ne pourrait se renouveler; que le plus grand désir que j'eusse au monde, garder ma mère dans ma chambre pendant ces tristes heures nocturnes, était trop en opposition avec les nécessités de la vie et le vœu de tous, pour que l'accomplissement qu'on lui avait accordé ce soir pût être autre chose que factice et exceptionnel.   (I, 42)

My aching heart was soothed; I let myself be borne upon the current of this gentle night on which I had my mother by my side. I knew that such a night could not be repeated; that the strongest desire I had in the world, namely, to keep my mother in my room through the sad hours of darkness, ran too much counter to general requirements and to the wishes of others for such a concession as had been granted me this evening to be anything but a rare and artificial exception.   (I, 49)

This brief consummation of a male child's love for his mother is overseen by a literary work, but a work which has the status of a bare mythical story rather than that of a full social or psychological canvas. *François le Champi* is the foundation myth, or the 'national anthem', for the entire Oedipal dimension of Proust's book, and it resonates, without being named, throughout the love-scenes of the central volumes. The adult narrator changes his position within the family triangle: sometimes he desires as a child might, and sometimes, identifying with the maternal figure, he desires as a mother might; at moments he occupies the place of the absent third party, relegated to the margins of an amorous exchange. Allusions to Racine's incestuously desiring Phèdre abound. Albertine is now a surrogate mother and now a substitute child, but even in the aftermath of their affair the narrator's real mother continues to figure. The energy with which the narrator attributes possessiveness and desire to his mother during the Venice episode in *Albertine disparue* is a projective expression of his own still childlike feelings:

ne m'ayant pas reconnu tout de suite, dès que de la gondole
je l'appelais elle envoyait vers moi, du fond de son cœur,
son amour qui ne s'arrêtait que là où il n'y avait plus de
matière pour le soutenir, à la surface de son regard passionné
qu'elle faisait aussi proche de moi que possible, qu'elle
cherchait à exhausser, à l'avancée de ses lèvres, en un sourire
qui semblait m'embrasser, dans le cadre et sous le dais du
sourire plus discret de l'ogive illuminée par le soleil de midi.

(IV, 204)

not having recognised me at first, as soon as I called to her
from the gondola, she sent out to me, from the bottom of
her heart, a love which stopped only where there was no
longer any corporeal matter to sustain it, on the surface of
her impassioned gaze which she brought as close to me as
possible, which she tried to thrust forward to the advanced
post of her lips, in a smile which seemed to be kissing me,
within the frame and beneath the canopy of the more discreet
smile of the arched window lit up by the midday sun.

(V, 717)

The narrator goes on to say that this maternal passion, displaying itself so fulsomely in Venice, left for ever its imprint on
his memory of the local architectural style. The pointed Gothic
arch becomes, one might say, a topological diagram of the
Oedipal threesome. What is elaborated and reworked in such
passages has already been stated in its primitive, kernel form
during the earlier Combray episode. *François le Champi* has
become the invisible schema from which all such later Oedipal
fantasies derive. The 'country matters' of which Sand's novel
speaks underlie the metropolitan complications of modern
love.

Between these extremes of explicitness and implicitness lies
a broad middle territory where Proust grazes at leisure on the
work of his predecessors. In this field he is to a large extent
free from the demands of plot-making, and can enjoy fortuitous

textual encounters without being cramped or coerced by his own emerging grand scheme. Virgil's *Eclogues*, *Georgics* and *Aeneid* are all here, and are joined, in a spirit of time-travelling literary festivity, by the Bible, the *Divine Comedy*, the tragedies of Corneille and Racine and the new epics in verse and prose of nineteenth-century France. The overall effect is one of benignly scattered literary enthusiasm, the more engaging because the narrator shares with an entire range of other characters, including the bores and the buffoons, the minor social art of surprise citation. The bores cite clumsily, while the narrator, Saint-Loup, Swann, Charlus and the duchesse de Guermantes do so with urbane dexterity, but they are all players in the same bantering and bartering textual game.

Proust's Homer is a particularly fertile contributor to the novel's allusive chorus, for although memories of the *Iliad* and the *Odyssey* seem often to be sprinkled as an archaising spice across the surface of the text, references to the supreme epic poems of Europe have by the end acquired their own logic and power of summation. Brief moments of poetic sarcasm abound. In *Le Côté de Guermantes* Mme de Villeparisis, whose intelligence is 'almost that of a second-rate writer' and whose memoirs seem likely to set her apart from rival hostesses, is already eligible to enter the company of the immortals:

> c'est le salon de Mme de Villeparisis [. . .] qui sera considéré comme un des plus brillants du XIXe siècle par cette postérité qui n'a pas changé depuis les temps d'Homère et de Pindare, et pour qui le rang enviable c'est la haute naissance, royale ou quasi royale, l'amitié des rois, des chefs du peuple, des hommes illustres.   (II, 492)

> it is the salon of Mme de Villeparisis [. . .] which will be regarded as one of the most brilliant of the nineteenth century by that posterity which has not changed since the days

97

c'est le salon de Mme de Villeparisis [. . .] qui sera considéré comme un des plus brillants du XIXe siècle par cette postérité

of Homer and Pindar, and for which the enviable things are exalted birth, royal or quasi-royal, and the friendship of kings, of leaders of the people and other eminent men.

(III, 219)

The composite name borne by le prince de Faffenheim-Munsterburg-Weinigen reminds the narrator of vineyards whose products have a similar polysyllabic grandeur about them and are in their turn reminiscent of the conjoined epithets that Homer gave his heroes (II, 553; III, 293). A specialist visiting the narrator's dying grandmother arrives 'avec sa trousse chargée de tous les rhumes de ses clients, comme l'outre d'Eole (II, 620; 'his bag packed with all the colds and coughs of his other patients, like Aeolus's goatskin' (III, 372)). Aeolus, in Book X of the *Odyssey* was

the master of all the winds
with power to calm them down or rouse them as he pleased.

Once opened, this pouch in which his winds were kept brought Odysseus and his crew close to drowning. The narrator's warning about modern medicine is clear.

Homeric quotation is a dangerous weapon, as the narrator has already made plain, and can bring those responsible for it close to absurdity. Legrandin, declaiming to the narrator and his family upon the delights of the Normandy coast in 'Combray' had spoken of it as a true 'land of the Cimmerians' (I, 156; 'le véritable pays des Cimmériens' (I, 129)), and, by his reference to the opening of Book XI of the *Odyssey*, had provided a culminating instance of empty verbal embellishment and ostentation. Clearly, the narrator is in depraved company when he himself plays the quoting game. Yet poor, blustering, pretentious Legrandin has stumbled upon a precious fragment of true poetry in this speech, and Homer's Cimmerians, 'their realm and city shrouded in mist and cloud', are to reappear in *A l'ombre des jeunes filles en fleurs* as a leitmotif within the narrator's own reverie. He travels to Balbec as if into a land of myth and retains his sense of poetry and magic against considerable odds:

> je m'efforçais, pour penser que j'étais dans l'antique royaume des Cimmériens, dans la patrie peut-être du roi Mark ou sur l'emplacement de la forêt de Brocéliande, de ne pas regarder le luxe de pacotille des constructions qui se développaient devant moi et entre lesquelles la villa d'Elstir était peut-être la plus somptueusement laide.   (II, 190)

> I endeavoured, in order to persuade myself that I was in the ancient realm of the Cimmerians, in the country, perhaps, of King Mark, or on the site of the Forest of Broceliande, not to look at the gimcrack splendour of the buildings that extended on either hand, among which Elstir's villa was perhaps the most sumptuously hideous.   (II, 477)

Somewhere between the eighteenth-century mock epic – perfectly embodied in Pope's *Rape of the Lock* (1714) or *Dunciad* (1728) – and the failed or imploding epic of the modern age, a new genre seems to be coming into being in Proust's appropriation of Homer. *A la recherche du temps perdu* is a work which worries about its own claims to epic status and in its ever-renewed hesitancy on the matter seems to acquire a strange tough-mindedness. A constant play of distance and recognition takes place between modern people, including writers, and the gods and heroes of antiquity, as in this passage from *Le Côté de Guermantes*:

> Les gens des temps passés nous semblent infiniment loin de nous. Nous n'osons pas leur supposer d'intentions profondes au-delà de ce qu'ils expriment formellement; nous sommes étonnés quand nous rencontrons un sentiment à peu près pareil à ceux que nous éprouvons chez un héros d'Homère.   (II, 710)

> The people of bygone ages seem infinitely remote from us.
> We do not feel justified in ascribing to them any underlying
> intentions beyond those they formally express; we are
> amazed when we come upon a sentiment more or less akin
> to what we feel today in a Homeric hero. (III, 481)

The current of fellow feeling is blocked but then, without
warning, it passes. The courtesy of the Guermantes seems at
one moment to be part of an ancestral code, handed down
from generation to generation, and, at the next, to be a fraudu-
lent disguise for the disreputable conduct of their caste. In this
antiquity or an artful sham? The narrator, thinking that he has
made contact with Homer, may in fact have discovered the
mock-antiquity of Ossian.

In *Sodome et Gomorrhe* a new version of the same anxiety
is visible: the narrator discusses the modern fashion for cor-
rectness in the spelling of Homeric names, and a new preference
for the original Greek names over their more familiar Latin
equivalents (III, 230–31; IV, 272); on the slenderest of pretexts, he incorporates into his narrative a joyful catalogue of
Greek names, plundered for the purpose from Leconte de
Lisle's translation (1869) of the Orphic hymns (III, 234; IV,
276). Can there be a prose epic of the contemporary world?
The narrator puts the question in a variety of forms, and finds
one convincing answer not in a nostalgic return to antiquity
but in a militant espousal of the lowly, the transient and the
topical. Zola had perhaps achieved something of the sort, he
suggests, half-sharing Mme de Guermantes's view that Zola is
more a poet than a mere novelist of the realist school, and that:
'il grandit tout ce qu'il touche [. . .] il en fait quelque chose
d'immense; il a le fumier épique. C'est l'Homère de la vidange!'
(II, 789; 'he magnifies everything he touches [. . .] he makes
it into something colossal. His is the epic dungheap! He is the
Homer of the sewers!' (III, 576–7)).

It is in *Le Temps retrouvé* that the narrator comes closest to a realisable vision of a new epic style, to an *Iliad* that would be appropriate to the squalor and dishonourable carnage of modern warfare and to an *Odyssey* tailor-made for a bourgeois wanderer in aristocratic salons. The route he takes towards his new Homer is an improbable one. His further references to Book XI of the *Odyssey*, for example, have a poignancy almost worthy of Ronsard and Du Bellay in their learned imitation of Classical models. The narrator moves about at the final *matinée* of the work as a new Odysseus greeting ghost upon ghost during his journey to Hell. Odette seems in some respects to have been rejuvenated by the passing years, but there are signs on her person of an altogether different destiny: 'Et pourtant, de même que ses yeux avaient l'air de me regarder d'un rivage lointain, sa voix était triste, presque suppliante, comme celle des morts dans l'*Odyssée*' (IV, 528; 'and yet, just as her eyes appeared to be looking at me from a distant shore, her voice was sad, almost suppliant, like the voice of the shades in the *Odyssey*' (VI, 323)). The pathos of this is, however, a partial one. Odette's voice speaks not only from the timeless realm of the already dead but from inside a lively local scene: it still has a hint of an English accent about it, and Odette still lards her talk with English expressions. Elsewhere, Homer brings not just the social manners of the contemporary world but a self-conscious technological modernity in his wake. The narrator had recognised, but not recognised, an old friend earlier in the same scene:

> j'aurais bien voulu reconnaître mon ami mais, comme dans l'*Odyssée* Ulysse s'élançant sur sa mère morte, comme un spirite essayant en vain d'obtenir d'une apparition une réponse qui l'identifie, comme le visiteur d'une exposition d'électricité qui ne peut croire que la voix que le phonographe restitue inaltérée soit tout de même spontanément émise par une personne, je cessai de reconnaître mon ami. (IV, 523)

I should have liked to recognise my friend, but, like Ulysses in the *Odyssey* when he rushes forward to embrace his dead mother, like the spiritualist who tries in vain to elicit from a ghost an answer which will reveal its identity, like the visitor at an exhibition of electricity who cannot believe that the voice which the gramophone restores unaltered to life is a voice spontaneously emitted by a human being, I was obliged to give up the attempt.   (VI, 315)

In remembering these lines from the *Odyssey*:

> And I, my mind in turmoil, how I longed
> to embrace my mother's spirit, dead as she was!
> Three times I rushed toward her, desperate to hold her,
> three times she fluttered through my fingers, sifting away
> like a shadow, dissolving like a dream, and each time
> the grief cut to the heart

the narrator sounds again his familiar maternal theme, and allows a dead mother, as distinct from a dead grandmother, into his ceremony of remembrance. His description of Carpaccio paintings had allowed him the same momentary licence in *Albertine disparue* (IV, 225; V, 742–3): in both cases an art-work prompts him to picture a still-living mother as dead. The switch from such solemnity to a trade fair of the present day is abrupt and unpitying. A common humanity links Odysseus facing his mother's ghost to the overawed user of a new electrical gadget, but there are no shortcuts for the literary artist seeking solidarity with his pre-eminent predecessor. The distance separating them must itself be dramatised.

This distance yawns terrifyingly during the narrator's second return visit to Paris at the beginning of *Le Temps retrouvé*. He meets Charlus, who is in disgrace in certain quarters for his apparent pro-German sympathies, and receives from him a series of characteristic conversational broadsides. Charlus upbraids his former allies for their simplistic views on the mind and temper of the German people, and singles out the new-found patriotism of Brichot for special blame:

> J'avoue que je partage son admiration pour certaines gran-
> deurs de la guerre actuelle. Tout au plus est-il étrange qu'un
> partisan aveugle de l'Antiquité comme Brichot, qui n'avait
> pas assez de sarcasmes pour Zola trouvant plus de poésie
> dans un ménage d'ouvriers, dans la mine, que dans les
> palais historiques, ou pour Goncourt mettant Diderot
> au-dessus d'Homère et Watteau au-dessus de Raphaël, ne
> cesse de nous répéter que les Thermopyles, qu'Austerlitz
> même, ce n'était rien à côté de Vauquois. Cette fois du reste,
> le public qui avait résisté aux modernistes de la littérature et
> de l'art suit ceux de la guerre, parce que c'est une mode
> adoptée de penser ainsi et puis que les petits esprits sont
> écrasés, non par la beauté, mais par l'énormité de l'action.
>
> (IV, 358)

> I admit that I share his admiration for certain elements of
> greatness in the present war. I do, however, find it strange
> that a blind partisan of antiquity like Brichot, who could
> not be sarcastic enough about Zola for discovering more
> poetry in a working-class home or a coal-mine than in the
> famous palaces of history, or about Goncourt for elevating
> Diderot above Homer and Watteau above Raphael, should
> incessantly drum into our ears that Thermopylae and even
> Austerlitz were nothing compared with Vauquois. And this
> time, to make things worse, the public, after resisting the
> modernists of literature and art, is falling into line with the
> modernists of war, because it is an accepted fashion to think
> like this and also because little minds are crushed, not by
> the beauty, but by the hugeness of the action.   (VI, 110)

Homer has become a tiny spot on a remote horizon, and is
visible only through a series of distorting lenses. This passage
is the narrator's transcript of Charlus on Brichot on the Goncourts on Homer. Layer upon layer of uncrossable distance
separates the modern novelist from the monuments of antiquity.

Homer has indeed fallen on hard times when Charlus, of all unlikely custodians of the European cultural archive, steps forward to defend him. Why, such treatment is almost as offensive as being quoted with approval by Legrandin.

But yet these speeches, for all Charlus's conceit, self-interest and opportunism, have their own monumental quality, and their own contribution to make to the structure of Proust's novel. Charlus brings the reader up to date with the fortunes of other characters, and circles back in a series of large retrospective loops into the detail of the preceding narrative. The narrator is soon to do the same thing in his own voice. The novel is becoming indefinitely aware of its own past. We may find ourselves remembering, and not incongruously, the penultimate book of the *Odyssey*, in which Odysseus recounts his adventures to Penelope. The suitors have been killed; husband and wife have been to bed; Odysseus tells his tale. While he spoke, Penelope

> listened on, enchanted . . .
> Sleep never sealed her eyes till all was told.

All through the poem the telling of tales has been an essential part of the tale being told, but towards the end the activity has a splendid closural power. While so much else in the closing stages of the existing Homeric epic suggests that the Odyssean adventure can never truly end, this long moment of recapitulation, this story made of stories, strives towards completeness and rest. Charlus's retrospect contains no memorable exploits, and no heroic virtue or valour. On the contrary, it thrives on low motives, selfish deeds and an all-consuming *mondain* shallowness, and in it, adding fuel to the debate on Zola that had been sketched much earlier in the plot, Charlus simultaneously rules against all such baseness as subject matter for literature. Proust himself, at this stage of the novel, seems to be siding more plainly than before with Mme de Guermantes on the question of the 'modern epic', and to be envisaging if not a 'Homer of sewage' in the manner of Zola himself at the very least a grand work through which would run a tide of verbal waste bearing a silt of silliness and pomposity. High art, in Proust's formula, must always begin low, be prepared to plunge from its summits back into the trivial and the everyday, and do this even as it reaches its moment of epic culmination. *A la recherche du temps perdu* is a self-deflating epic, but Homer, together with Virgil, Dante and Hugo, is an unexorcisable phantom within it. Great writers like these remind the reader of a heroism that has been lost, and of the new heroism from which Proust's own novel sprang.

Proust devotes himself, then, for large tracts of time to opinions about art, and to the manipulation of artistic knowledge for worldly ends. As our gaze passes from the characters who hold forth about their aesthetic preferences, to those who smuggle their views into the conversation of society with a complicit nod or grimace, to the narrator's own insinuating use of quotation and allusion, we find ourselves entering an artistically saturated space. Mme de Guermantes is a caricatural embodiment of a general tendency to art-talk among the characters of the novel, and is pursued by the narrator until the very end, lest the last fluctuation of her changing tastes remain unrecorded:

> Ce style Empire, Mme de Guermantes déclarait l'avoir tou- jours détesté; cela voulait dire qu'elle le détestait maintenant, ce qui était vrai car elle suivait la mode, bien qu'avec quelque retard. Sans compliquer en parlant de David qu'elle connais- sait peu, toute jeune elle avait cru M. Ingres le plus ennuyeux des poncifs, puis brusquement le plus savoureux des maîtres de l'Art nouveau, jusqu'à détester Delacroix. Par quels degrés elle était revenue de ce culte à la réprobation importe

peu, puisque ce sont là nuances de goût que le critique d'art
reflète dix ans avant la conversation des femmes supérieures.

(IV, 602)

Mme de Guermantes declared that she had always detested
[the Empire style], a remark which meant merely that she
detested it now, which was true, for she followed the fashion,
even if she did not succeed in keeping up with it. To say
nothing of David, whose work she hardly knew, when she
was quite young she had thought M. Ingres the most boring
and academic of painters, then, by a brusque reversal – which
caused her also to loathe Delacroix – the most delectable of
the masters revered by *art nouveau*. By what gradations she
had subsequently passed from this cult to a renewal of her
early contempt matters little, since these are shades of taste
which the writings of an art critic reflect ten years before
the conversation of clever women.   (VI, 421)

David, Ingres and Delacroix have become painters without
characteristics. Their names are a rudimentary scansional
system, designed to plot a specimen graph of the enthusiasms
and antipathies of a social lioness, and nothing at all remains
to be said about their brushwork or their handling of colour
and line. Artists exist in order to become murmurings on the
breeze of salon conversation. Opinion smothers judgement.
True learning, insight and discernment, together with artistic
rapture itself, disappear behind a barrage of affectations, snob-
beries and schemes.

   What I have been saying so far about the use-value and
exchange-value of artistic commodities in Proust places him
firmly in the company of those whom Aldous Huxley in *Music
at Night* called 'Whole Truth' artists. These were to be distinguished from artists who sought after chemically pure distil-
lations of experience. Apostles of the Whole Truth had no
qualms about impurity, and indeed were eager to accommodate
din, fisticuffs, bad teeth, bad taste and street life into their

works. A contemporary of Proust's who fits Huxley's description particularly well is Mahler, whose symphonic arguments contain a clutter and a clatter of extra-musical references. Sleigh-bells, cow-bells, posthorns, bugles and hurdy-gurdies, whether recruited into the orchestra or imitated by its standard instruments, speak out of turn. By the simplest association of ideas, travel, the farmyard, the postal services and military drills intrude upon the rarefied colloquy of strings, woodwind and brass. Proust, whom Huxley mentions in his essay as an exemplary figure, is magnificently impure in the same way. He could have been immaculate either as an introspective psychologist, or as a comedian of manners. He could have distilled a tragedy from his own unhappiness in love. But instead he infuses his book with tittle-tattle and its obnoxious sub-species title-tattle. Noises off are brought on to the stage. Air-aces are ushered into the Arena Chapel. Homer is passed from hand to hand as a blemished consumer durable.

Proust's wittiest Whole-Truth account of the artistic imagination at work is to be found in a long excursus on Wagner's *Tristan* in *La Prisonnière*. The narrator plays excerpts from the opera on the piano, and imagines, in the thick of his own work at the keyboard, the work that Wagner himself had performed during the act of composition:

> j'entendais redoubler le rire immortellement jeune et les coups de marteau de Siegfried, en qui du reste, plus merveilleusement frappées étaient ces phrases, l'habileté technique de l'ouvrier ne servait qu'à leur faire plus librement quitter la terre, oiseaux pareils non au cygne de Lohengrin mais à cet aéroplane que j'avais vu à Balbec changer son énergie en élévation, planer au-dessus des flots, et se perdre dans le ciel. Peut-être, comme les oiseaux qui montent le plus haut, qui volent le plus vite, ont une aile plus puissante, fallait-il de ces appareils vraiment matériels pour explorer

l'infini, de ces cent vingt chevaux marque Mystère, où pourtant, si haut qu'on plane, on est un peu empêché de goûter
le silence des espaces par le puissant ronflement du moteur!

(III, 667–8)

I could hear the immortally youthful laughter and the ham-
merblows of Siegfried ring out with redoubled vigour; but
the more marvellously those phrases were struck, the technical skill of the craftsman served merely to make it easier for
them to leave the earth, birds akin not to Lohengrin's swan
but to that aeroplane which I had seen at Balbec convert
its energy into vertical motion, glide over the sea and vanish
in the sky. Perhaps, as the birds that soar highest and fly
most swiftly have more powerful wings, one of these frankly
material vehicles was needed to explore the infinite, one of
these 120 horse-power machines – the Mystère model – in
which nevertheless, however high one flies, one is prevented
to some extent from enjoying the silence of space by the
overpowering roar of the engine! (V, 178)

There is no such thing as an immaterial art, the narrator pro-
claims, and the aviation industry provides him with an instructive, up-to-the-minute parable on this theme. Just as it takes
the work of plane-makers and mechanics to send us soaring
into the upper air, and the work of engines to keep us there,
so the sublime intimations that art may bring are dependent
upon tools and tackle, and a laborious production process.
And the aeroplane of Art and Mystery hangs in space very
much as Bergotte's angelic books are soon to sit in the shop-
windows – as a commodity with its price-tag attached. Proust
writes all this into his own book with great glee, invents a
prose which draws attention to the noise of its own engine, and
finds ever-new ways of bringing the otherworldly pretensions of
artists back down to earth.

Yet Proust's novel has within it an ambitious alternative view
of art. In this other dimension the material world is not forgot-

ten and there is no idle talk of transcendence, but the impalpable construction work of intelligence and imagination is accorded its own mode of action and its own glamour. Proust, like Wagner and Vinteuil, is an artist who has specialist skills in chromatic modulation and the transformation of leitmotifs or thematic cells, and the movement between a matter-based and a mind-based view of art provides skills of this kind with vigorous exercise throughout the novel.

At the end of his 'An Ordinary Evening in New Haven', Wallace Stevens's last cadence can stand as a paradigm-case of such a transition. New Haven is full of particulars; Stevens's verse brims over with peculiarities of diction; the 'edgings and inchings of final form', the definitive self-subsistent power of the art-work, seem destined to emerge within a real world that produces sense-events in humans. Nevertheless, Stevens concludes:

> It is not in the premise that reality
> Is a solid. It may be a shade that traverses
> A dust, a force that traverses a shade.

Take away the convenient bedrock afforded by solid material entities, and you are left with another world-ground, which may possibly be that of energy diffusing itself through dusty interstellar space but which is primarily that of shadowy, deathbound humankind exercising its capacity for thought. Thought is the necessary modulator or transformer of matter without which there is no New Haven, no *Tristan*, no aeroplane poised on the runway; its characteristic motions, for Proust as for Stevens, must be declared, and their drama seized, inside the work of art. In assembling his alternative, thought-suffused view of art, Proust uses a language that is still often artisanal – the composer thinking in timbres is as much a craftsman as the carpenter thinking in timbers, or the butcher in meat – but that has at the same time a vast store of psychodynamic concepts at its disposal. This is not at all a homogenous or 'chemically pure' philosophical diction, but an array of abstract terms in which the travail and creativity of mind can be experimentally recreated.

From a very early stage in the novel, works of art are essential aids to the narrator's self-analysis. They are mental concentrates, devices whereby the mind's self-revelation can be accomplished in conditions of urgency and intensity. The young narrator in the second part of 'Combray', for example, discovers in the prose of Bergotte a new sense of his own mental capacities. A Bergotte novel seems to objectify for him the very process of self-discovery:

> Un de ces passages de Bergotte, le troisième ou le quatrième que j'eusse isolé du reste, me donna une joie incomparable à celle que j'avais trouvée au premier, une joie que je me sentis éprouver en une région plus profonde de moi-même, plus unie, plus vaste, d'où les obstacles et les séparations semblaient avoir été enlevés. C'est que, reconnaissant alors ce même goût pour les expressions rares, cette même effusion musicale, cette même philosophie idéaliste qui avait déjà été les autres fois, sans que je m'en rendisse compte, la cause de mon plaisir, je n'eus plus l'impression d'être en présence d'un morceau particulier d'un certain livre de Bergotte, traçant à la surface de ma pensée une figure purement linéaire, mais plutôt du «morceau idéal» de Bergotte, commun à tous ses livres et auquel tous les passages analogues qui venaient se confondre avec lui, auraient donné une sorte d'épaisseur, de volume, dont mon esprit semblait agrandi. (I, 93)

One of these passages of Bergotte, the third or the fourth which I had detached from the rest, filled me with a joy to which the meagre joy I had tasted in the first passage bore no comparison, a joy that I felt I was experiencing in a deeper, vaster, more integral part of myself, from which all obstacles and partitions seemed to have been swept away. For what had happened was that, while I recognised in this passage the same taste for uncommon phrases, the same musical outpouring, the same idealist philosophy which had been present in the earlier passages without my having recognised them as being the source of my pleasure, I now had the impression of being confronted not by a particular passage in one of Bergotte's works, tracing a purely bi-dimensional figure upon the surface of my mind, but rather by the 'ideal passage' of Bergotte, common to every one of his books, to which all the earlier, similar passages, now becoming merged in it, had added a kind of density and volume by which my own understanding seemed to be enlarged. (I, 111)

There are two two-dimensional models of the mind here: the explorer can descend through its strata to reach its deepest level and then, having reached that level, discover a vast obstacle-free interior landscape. Bergotte's writing offers both a cross-section of the mind and a map of one of its regions. The experience of reading him is then shrunk to a single dimension – that of a unilinear figure traced 'on the surface of thought' – and finally expanded in triumph to three: the work now being read suddenly begins to summon up other works from the same pen; the volume in hand produces a sense of mental volume. A book helps the mind to a new sense of its own size and capacity, and the fourth dimension, that of time, provides an envelope for the entire discussion. Mind is at work, and time-dwelling change is its native condition.

Throughout the novel, real, imaginary, and real but entirely reimagined works of art are pressed into the service of the narrator's voluminous introspective programme. But however concentrated and informative such works are they have no secure boundaries or watertight seals separating them from other mental products, and the programme itself, as we have seen, is a greedily inclusive one. The elementary structures of the mental life may become newly visible under the glare of Bergotte or Wagner or Virgil, but they do not have to wait upon a dignified prompting of this kind to declare themselves. The Verdurins will do. And the tone in which the mind speaks of its own deep structures does not have to be elevated or serious. Frivolity and sarcasm are illuminating too. In this passage from *La Prisonnière* the gifts bestowed upon the Verdurins by their grateful followers pass from one domicile to the next and provide all concerned with a sense of well-being:

> encombrement joli, désordre des cadeaux de fidèles qui a suivi partout la maîtresse de la maison et a fini par prendre l'empreinte et la fixité d'un trait de caractère, d'une ligne de la destinée; profusion des bouquets de fleurs, des boîtes de chocolat qui systématisait, ici comme là-bas, son épanouissement suivant un mode de floraison identique [. . .] tous ces objets enfin qu'on ne saurait isoler des autres, mais qui pour Brichot, vieil habitué des fêtes des Verdurin, avaient cette patine, ce velouté des choses auxquelles, leur donnant une sorte de profondeur, vient s'ajouter leur double spirituel; tout cela, éparpillé, faisait chanter devant lui comme autant de touches sonores qui éveillaient dans son cœur des ressemblances aimées, des réminiscences confuses et qui, à même le salon tout actuel, qu'elles marquetaient çà et là, découpaient, délimitaient, comme fait par un beau jour un cadre de soleil sectionnant l'atmosphère, les meubles et les tapis, poursuivant d'un coussin à un porte-bouquets, d'un tabouret au relent d'un parfum, d'un mode d'éclairage à une prédominance de couleurs, sculptaient, évoquaient, spiritualisaient, faisaient vivre une forme qui était comme la figure idéale, immanente à leurs logis successifs, du salon des Verdurin.   (III, 789-90)

the attractively disordered clutter of the presents from the faithful which had followed the lady of the house from place

to place and had come in time to assume the fixity of a trait
of character, of a line of destiny; the profusion of cut flowers,
of chocolate-boxes, which here as in the country system-
atised their efflorescence in accordance with an identical
mode of blossoming [. . .] all those things, in short, which
one could not have isolated from the rest but which for
Brichot, an old habitué of Verdurin festivities, had that
patina, that velvety bloom of things to which, giving them
a sort of depth, a spiritual *Doppelgänger* has come to be
attached – all this sent echoing round him so many scattered
chords, as it were, awakening in his heart cherished resemblances, confused reminiscences which, here in this actual
drawing-room that was speckled with them, cut out, defined,
delimited – as on a fine day a shaft of sunlight cuts a section
in the atmosphere – the furniture and carpets, pursued, from
a cushion to a flower-stand, from a footstool to a lingering
scent, from a lighting arrangement to a colour scheme,
sculpted, evoked, spiritualised, called to life, a form which
was as it were the idealisation, immanent in each of their
successive homes, of the Verdurin drawing-room. (V, 323)

But the accidental furniture of the Verdurin habitat speaks of
something far more deeply interfused lying beneath the social
and domestic scene, and of something resembling necessity in
the activities of the mental apparatus. Two dimensions yield
to three, as in Bergotte's prose or Vinteuil's music, and the
surveying of physical space, with its discriminating professionalised vocabulary – *marqueter*, *découper*, *délimiter*, *sec-
tionner* – gives way to a comedy of mental system-building.
The Verdurins' successive salons are a mindscape extended in
time, and to that extent, despite their accumulated trinkets and
baubles, they are strictly indistinguishable from works of art.

Proust navigates back and forth with tireless invention
between art proper and an ordinary world lightly touched and
animated by thought. In doing this he relies upon a special
vocabulary of what might be called 'switch-words' or
'crossover-terms'. These often originate in a localised semantic

field, and seem in some cases to belong to the jargon of a single art, craft or intellectual pursuit, but their role is a mobile and diplomatic one. They make disparate fields of human activity intelligible to one another. Such negotiation has its own Proustian lexicon: *transition*, *transposition*, *transmutation*, *substitution*, *transformation*, *transmigration*, *modulation*, *traduction* ('translation'). But the quicksilver of Proust's writing on mental action and transaction is supplied by his cognitive terms: *mesurer* ('measure'), *calculer* ('calculate'), *comprendre* ('understand'), *constater* ('register'), *induire* ('induce'), *déduire* ('deduce'), *scander* ('punctuate'), *superposer* ('superimpose'), *distinguer* ('distinguish'), *deviner* ('guess'), *établir* ('establish') and countless others, with their cognates, are overseen by the ubiquitous *connaître* ('know') itself. Equally rich storehouses exist for sense-impressions, ideational constructs, memories and for the spasmodic world of feeling, desire and intention in which all such productions of the human mind bathe. The work of art triggers in the narrator as exemplary reader, hearer or beholder a sensuously enlivened process of construal and interpretation, but then so does sunlight falling on walls, the noise of gossip, the blossoming of shrubs, or the inscrutable behaviour of a lover, as in this passage from *Sodome et Gomorrhe* on the divergent desires prompted in him by Albertine:

> Cet effort de l'ancien sentiment pour se combiner et ne faire qu'un élément unique avec l'autre, plus récent, et qui, lui, n'avait pour voluptueux objet que la surface colorée, la rose carnation d'une fleur de plage, cet effort aboutit souvent à ne faire (au sens chimique) qu'un corps nouveau, qui peut ne durer que quelques instants. Ce soir-là, du moins, et pour longtemps encore, les deux éléments restèrent dissociés. Mais déjà aux derniers mots entendus au téléphone, je commençai à comprendre que la vie d'Albertine était située (non pas matériellement sans doute) à une telle dis-

tance de moi qu'il m'eût fallu toujours de fatigantes explorations pour mettre la main sur elle, mais de plus, organisée
comme des fortifications de campagne et, pour plus de sûr-
eté, de l'espèce de celles que l'on a pris plus tard l'habitude
d'appeler «camouflées».   (III, 130 – 31)

This effort on the part of the old feeling to combine and
form a single element with the other, more recent, which
had for its voluptuous object only the coloured surface, the
flesh-pink bloom of a flower of the sea-shore, was one that
often results simply in creating (in the chemical sense) a new
body, which may last only a few moments. That evening, at
any rate, and for long afterwards, the two elements remained
apart. But already, from the last words that had reached me
over the telephone, I was beginning to understand that
Albertine's life was situated (not in a physical sense, of
course) at so great a distance from mine that I should always
have to make exhausting explorations in order to seize hold
of it, and moreover was organised like a system of earthworks
which, for greater security, were of the kind that at a later
period we learned to call 'camouflaged.'   (IV, 153 – 4)

The desire for knowledge of the beloved, or of art, or of the
photon-stream shedding a sudden radiance on brickwork, turns
unfailingly into the would-be knower's desire for knowledge of
his own cognitive skills and disabilities. Unification, dissociation, organisation, exploration, combination . . . the quest
for knowledge has many names and many aliases in this passage,
and in numerous others resembling it, but the narrator's emphasis is always on the process itself, on the dynamic interplay
between alternative shapes and intensities, rather than on any
form of finality or closure. Each happy intellectual outcome
envisaged in the text is a transient hypothesis rather than a
consummation of the will to know.

Although works of art thought about in this mentalising way
are indefinitely porous, and always likely to be engulfed by what
looks like a generalised phenomenology of thinking, Proust's

narrator does come to have decided views on the qualities that considerable works of art might be expected to possess. He plans the novel he is eventually to write by looking closely at the work of the artists with whom he already identifies, and sketches an ideal fictional work in the margins of his always alert and never disinterested critical commentaries. The species-specific characteristics of this still-to-be-realised novel are easily isolated. It will be dense, associative, contrapuntally layered, flecked with allusions. It will alternate between diffuseness and concentration, and be marked by long-range refrains and echo-effects. It will take chances, create discomfort for its reader by its combined levity and gravity, and set particular store by coincidences and other improbabilities. The bizarre, the startling and the excessive will have special rights within it. It will hesitate endlessly between unilinear development and a compacted motivic interlace. It will be all of a piece, close-woven all through, yet have passages of singular intensity that seem to gather into themselves pre-emptively the meanings of the emerging whole.

Listed in this way, these features of an imagined book seem unexceptionable, and many of them are indeed part of the copper-coinage of modern literature in Europe and the Americas. Yet the aesthetic discussions of Proust's self-educating narrator can be signally disruptive within the novel itself, and can resonate outwards in astonishing ways from the art-works he discusses to the art-work we ourselves as readers are holding in our hands. In the celebrated death-scene of Bergotte, for example, intensity, layering, close-wovenness and long-range recall all figure prominently, but to whom do they belong? To Bergotte, to Vermeer, to the narrator, or to Proust himself? Prompted by a critic, Bergotte goes to an exhibition of Dutch painting in search of a detail he had not previously noticed in Vermeer's *View of Delft*:

Enfin il fut devant le Ver Meer qu'il se rappelait plus éclatant, plus différent de tout ce qu'il connaissait, mais où, grâce à l'article du critique, il remarqua pour la première fois des petits personnages en bleu, que le sable était rose, et enfin la précieuse matière du tout petit pan de mur jaune. Ses étourdissements augmentaient; il attachait son regard, comme un enfant à un papillon jaune qu'il veut saisir, au précieux petit pan de mur. «C'est ainsi que j'aurais dû écrire, disait-il. Mes derniers livres sont trop secs, il aurait fallu passer plusieurs couches de couleur, rendre ma phrase en elle-même précieuse, comme ce petit pan de mur jaune.» Cependant la gravité de ses étourdissements ne lui échappait pas. Dans une céleste balance lui apparaissait, chargeant l'un des plateaux, sa propre vie, tandis que l'autre contenait le petit pan de mur si bien peint en jaune. Il sentait qu'il avait imprudemment donné la première pour le second. «Je ne voudrais pourtant pas, se dit-il, être pour les journaux du soir le fait divers de cette exposition.» Il se répétait: «Petit pan de mur jaune avec un auvent, petit pan de mur jaune.»

(III, 692)

At last he came to the Vermeer which he remembered as more striking, more different from anything else he knew, but in which, thanks to the critic's article, he noticed for the first time some small figures in blue, that the sand was pink, and finally, the precious substance of the tiny patch of yellow wall. His dizziness increased; he fixed his gaze, like a child upon a yellow butterfly that it wants to catch, on the precious little patch of wall. 'That's how I ought to have written,' he said. 'My last books are too dry, I ought to have gone over them with a few layers of colour, made my language precious in itself, like this little patch of yellow wall.' Meanwhile he was not unconscious of the gravity of his condition. In a celestial pair of scales there appeared to him, weighing down one of the pans, his own life, while the other contained the little patch of wall so beautifully painted in yellow. He felt that he had rashly sacrificed the

117

former for the latter. 'All the same,' he said to himself, 'I
shouldn't like to be the headline news of this exhibition for
the evening papers.' He repeated to himself: 'Little patch of
yellow wall, with a sloping roof, little patch of yellow wall.'

(V, 207–8)

Bergotte discovers in Vermeer's exquisite detail what the narrator had already found in Bergotte's prose: a flat surface that
is suddenly stratified and opened up into the dimension of
depth. A small segment of a complex work suddenly begins to
have more affective power than the work in its entirety. The
Delft townscape is lost to this one fragment of illuminated wall.
Proust's novel is testing our powers of recall, telling us how
to handle its fierce local intensities, and drawing our attention
to its counterpoint. We are given a beautiful singularity that
takes us back into the labyrinth of the text we have been reading
but at the same time issues a warning of mortal danger. This
layered beauty was the last thing Bergotte saw.

This sense of danger creates the strangest link between the
book the narrator sketches and the book Proust actually wrote.
In all other respects we could say that the link is a straightforward one: Proust kept his narrator's promises and assembled
his grand edifice in accordance with the narrator's blueprint.
A la recherche du temps perdu does indeed, as we have been
invited to surmise, resemble an Elstir painting, a Vinteuil septet,
a Gothic cathedral, a Wagnerian opera, an *Odyssey*, a Giotto
interior or a Venetian townscape; the great novel teems with
allegories of itself, contains within itself a shimmering population of homunculus novels, each claiming to speak for the
gigantic whole. Its diffuseness, its gossip, its manic flights of
verbal invention are controlled and eventually brought to rest
by a solid pattern of refrains that seem to grow spontaneously
from the people and places of the tale. Swann's soul trans-
migrates into the narrator, and Odette's into Albertine. The

Méséglise and Guermantes worlds, having seemed originally to be so far apart, are in due course brought together and fused. Venice replicates certain features of Balbec, and Jupien's Parisian brothel certain features of rural Montjouvain. Counterpoint, incongruity and dense associative textures are similarly present in Proust's book in ways that have been prefigured by the narrator's artistic commentaries. But Bergotte's last gaze, and the painted surface that is lodged as an after-image inside his dying brain, create a different sort of complicity between author and character.

They become fellow artists in speaking of the unspeakable. If they are artisans still, their craft is of the most spectral. They look beyond the mind-forged art-work towards the grain and texture of its ceasing to be. Not walls but exits are their speciality. A shade traverses the dust that they are to become. Into *Sodome et Gomorrhe* the narrator slips one of those sudden cameos in which the novel abounds, but this is the self-portrait of a ghost: 'moi l'étrange humain qui, en attendant que la mort le délivre, vit les volets clos, ne sait rien du monde, reste immobile comme un hibou et comme celui-ci, ne voit un peu clair que dans les ténèbres' (III, 371; 'I, the strange human who, while he waits for death to release him, lives behind closed shutters, knows nothing of the world, sits motionless as an owl, and like that bird can only see things at all clearly in the darkness' (IV, 440–41)). Such are the burdens that the mind-based view of art imposes upon its practitioners: the whole wondrously proficient transformational device that the human mind is, and the unbroken fabric of meaning that it sometimes seems destined to produce for ever, is fragile and drawn towards its own breakdown. Proust himself and the would-be writer he places as a controlling intelligence at the centre of his fiction are alike in their appetite for negation and night. Each insists on placing destructiveness as well as creativity at the centre of his mindscape, and on infiltrating into his optimistic knowledge-seeking programme a demon of unknowing for whom the shutters are already closed and the outside world is invisible. This creature comes to know more about mental processes than about the rest of nature, and, knowing that minds in the end wane and die, rejoices in the impermanence of their constructions: image melts into image, and each new hypothesis or theorem requires that an earlier one be destroyed. The work of art that such an artist creates has an extreme kind of porosity. It is open pore by pore to its own extinction.

The artist trapped inside a death-shadowed mind-world of this kind seems at first to have two mutually exclusive futures: he can seek death, hasten its coming by obliterating the real world, or he can seek to rejoin that world as an object among objects. The creative process itself can begin to seem unsatisfactory and enervating precisely because it keeps him in an undecidable in-between-world: consciousness is caught between its futures, unable to make a definitive choice between two different forms of extinction. On the one hand it could wane away into emptiness, and on the other it could yield before the fullness and the self-evidence of nature newly revealed. But an artist of the kind that Proust's narrator wants to become, and that Proust himself proudly is, cannot do more than imagine these exits, and bring the sensation of them, and of their incompatibility, back into the commotion of his text.

Stevens imagines them in lines from his 'The Man on the Dump' that combine doctrinal statement with a vertigo of the senses:

> Now, in the time of spring (azaleas, trilliums,
> Myrtle, viburnums, daffodils, blue phlox),
> Between that disgust and this, between the things
> That are on the dump (azaleas and so on)

And those that will be (azaleas and so on)
One feels the purifying change.

The 'purifying change' taking place between a real world that blooms and flourishes and a real world that dies and decays has been brought about by a mere act of mind. This act is at once a simple apprehension and an elaborate recreation: there, boxed in by their brackets, are the emblems of a North American spring, and there also, trilling, vibrating, alliterating, rushing in flocks from *a* to *z*, are the inventive energies of a literary text spilling out from their confinement, performing the change that the Stevens aesthetic doctrine calls for. Stevens imagines the creative mental act taking place and simultaneously imagines it failing or being retracted.

On the last page of *Du côté de chez Swann*, Proust performs a similar feat of imagination, and again in a small space. The narrator revisits the Bois de Boulogne as an adult and sees women resembling the female figures who had peopled his childhood fantasies:

Hélas! dans l'avenue des Acacias – l'allée de Myrtes – j'en revis quelques-unes, vieilles, et qui n'étaient plus que les ombres terribles de ce qu'elles avaient été, errant, cherchant désespérément on ne sait quoi dans les bosquets virgiliens. Elles avaient fui depuis longtemps que j'étais encore à interroger vainement les chemins désertés. Le soleil s'était caché. La nature recommençait à régner sur le Bois d'où s'était envolée l'idée qu'il était le Jardin élyséen de la Femme; au-dessus du moulin factice le vrai ciel était gris; le vent ridait le Grand Lac de petites vaguelettes, comme un lac; de gros oiseaux parcouraient rapidement le Bois, comme un bois, et poussant des cris aigus se posaient l'un après l'autre sur les grands chênes qui sous leur couronne druidique et avec une majesté dodonéenne semblaient proclamer le vide inhumain de la forêt désaffectée.   (I, 419)

Alas! in the acacia-avenue – the myrtle-alley – I did see some
of them again, grown old, no more now than grim spectres
of what they had once been, wandering, desperately searching for heaven knew what, through the Virgilian groves.
They had long since fled, and still I stood vainly questioning
the deserted paths. The sun had gone. Nature was resuming
its reign over the Bois, from which had vanished all trace
of the idea that it was the Elysian Garden of Woman; above
the gimcrack windmill the real sky was grey; the wind
wrinkled the surface of the Grand Lac in little wavelets, like
a real lake; large birds flew swiftly over the Bois, as over a
real wood, and with shrill cries perched, one after another,
on the great oaks which, beneath their Druidical crown, and
with Dodonian majesty, seemed to proclaim the inhuman
emptiness of this deconsecrated forest.   (I, 512–13)

Literary self-consciousness is first supplied and then artfully
withdrawn. Proust's myrtles, unlike Stevens's, are the flowers
of perpetual wintertime. They are borrowed from the sixth
book of the *Aeneid*:

> nec procul hinc partem fusi monstrantur in omnem
> lugentes campi; sic illos nomine dicunt.
> hic, quos durus amor crudeli tabe peredit,
> secreti celant calles et murtea circum
> silva tegit; curae non ipsa in morte relincunt.
>   (VI, 440–14)

> Not far away, spreading on every side,
> The Fields of Mourning came in view, so called
> Since here are those whom pitiless love consumed
> With cruel wasting, hidden on paths apart
> By myrtle woodland growing overhead.
> In death itself, pain will not let them be.

As are the wandering shades:

> centum errant annos volitantque haec litora circum
>   (VI, 329)

> They flutter and roam this side a hundred years.

122

These lines pay homage to Book XI of the *Odyssey* and, alluded to by Proust in the last cadential paragraph of his first volume, provide the basis for a larger pattern of repetition in the novel as a whole. The wandering figures of the dead are to reappear, magnified and terrifying, in *Le Temps retrouvé*, and the narrator, as we have seen, is in that later cadence to reach backwards from Virgil to the original Homeric vision of hell. As we move further forwards in the time of the novel, gathering the litter of modernity about us as we go, we move further back in the time of Classical literature. It matters to Proust that his modern epic should travel towards the origins of the European literary tradition. But the very text that is so pointedly inlaid with literary reference is about to present us with a richly imagined retreat from art and its traditions. The Bois de Boulogne becomes, in Stevens's sense, a 'dump'. The work of the landscape gardeners who created this artificial urban pleasance is now lost from view. The fake lake and the would-be wood return to nature. The mind of the artist is removed from the scene, and an inhuman wind begins to blow.

This gesture of denial is often repeated. Even within the narrator's recreative descriptions of Vinteuil's compositions or Elstir's canvases the pull towards the artless and the art-free is powerfully felt. Art matters, Proust suggests, because it takes us out of art and allows us, for a moment at least, to shed its complex mediations. In Proust, as in Stevens, the optimism of a literary language that seems bent on supplying ever more meaning yields from time to time before a much simpler emotional need. Beyond the busyness of sentences, the foolery of puns and the festive hubbub of texts that have other texts fluttering and roaming inside them, the writer craves contact with something that is quiet and plain and still and true. From within the boom-boom of literature the writer begins his perverse return journey to silence.

There is strangeness, then, at the heart of Proust's theory and practice of art in *A la recherche du temps perdu*. While seeming to sanctify the art-object by ascribing redemptive powers to it, and while supporting its claims with a panoply of arguments and parables, Proust looks forward to an era in which the noise of art will finally have been stilled. He imagines a mode of artistic being in which there will be nothing left to imagine. He falls in and out of love with his own grand design. A tension of this kind runs also through Proust's account of art as a social phenomenon. Art was born useful and delightful but is everywhere simply exchanged. Legrandin, Charlus, the Guermantes and the Cambremers transform sublime works into empty eloquence or opinionated chatter, yet art despoiled by these unflagging art-talkers is lively subject matter for a new art. A modern Homer will listen avidly to all that conversational tumult on the ringing plains of the Faubourg Saint-Germain.

Yet the strangest and most haunting occupants of the inter-ference-zone between art as supreme value and art as nullity are Proust's artisans. On the one hand, they are gathered into the ecstatic flux of his fictional text, each contributing a dash of colour or a burst of propulsive energy to its ceaseless dithy-rambic motion. Shrimp-collectors, music editors, cellists, harp-ists, dressmakers and aviators all add their labour and their professional skill to the Proustian pageant. They are honoured guests in the narrator's exhaustive programme of speculative thinking. They help him towards that pure play of difference and similarity which might, in the end, be the creative artist's best reward for his own labours. Yet, on the other hand, they stand outside art, stained like the dyer's hand by what they work in. Cellists scratch at their instruments, editors fiddle with their variant readings, pilots loop the loop and the oxen of Laon drag their massive stones uphill, and in doing so they all recall the narrator to a real world with real stuff in it. Against a background of compulsive mental exertion, the motor activity of muscles acquires a new dignity. Art is a trap from which craftsmen and tradespeople have already escaped. They have achieved a necessary earthbound release from the otherworldly redemptions of art. These two views of art are each set out at heavenly length in the novel. Between them, Proust's reader feels the purifying, and the impurifying, change.

IV

Politics

SHE: Have you heard it's in the stars
Next July we collide with Mars?
HE: Well, did you evah! What a swell party this is.

COLE PORTER, *'Well, Did you Evah?'*

It would be unwise to think of *A la recherche du temps perdu* as a documentary record of the Third Republic, or as the fictional recreation of a characteristically French political process. Thiers, Gambetta, Clemenceau and Jaurès flit through the pages of the novel as wraiths thrown up by salon conversation or by the narrator's reverie. They have no policies worth specifying; they are not the authors of events or the instigators of legislation; and their grip upon the crisis- and scandal-laden texture of current affairs is no tighter than that of Louis XIV, Napoleon or Talleyrand, whose ghosts are also astir in Proust's book. Political parties and factions are named but not described. Upheavals within the Church, the army or the judiciary are notable only for the shock waves and the ripples of curiosity they send through dinners and receptions. And the First World War, which provides the backcloth to the closing stages of the narrative, is as inscrutable as the Fronde or the Congress of Vienna. On learning that Swann has been invited to lunch at the Elysée, Mme Verdurin begins to regard Jules Grévy, the president of the Republic, as a particularly menacing

126

bore (I, 213; I, 260). Politics, one might wish to say, fascinates Proust only in extreme dilution. It matters to him when it adds a new spice to social relationships or to his narrator's self-analysis, but is otherwise lacking in character and complexity.

Yet if we return to Proust's writing armed with a somewhat extended notion of what politics is we can see the book as imbued with political awareness and concern. Class relations, for example, are anatomised at length by the narrator himself and by Charlus, Norpois, Saint-Loup and the duc de Guermantes. Working-class, bourgeois and aristocratic characters all have developed views on the mechanisms of class society, and nice distinction-making between social positions is a conversational sport available to all comers, irrespective of the positions they themselves occupy on the class spectrum. The narrator serves a long apprenticeship in the discrimination between classes, and addresses his reader as one eager learner to another.

The aristocracy is particularly favoured by the narrator as an object of socio-political enquiry, for it has the merit of complexity. The timeless and unified character that the aristocracy possesses for the hasty observer soon breaks down, on closer inspection, into a fluid array of sub-species, each with its own animated history. The reader is reminded at great length, during the Doncières episode in *Le Côté de Guermantes*, that the Napoleonic aristocracy is not at all the same thing as the *ancien régime* aristocracy, whose titles had in many cases simply been 'confirmed' by the Emperor. Le prince de Borodino and Robert, marquis de Saint-Loup-en-Bray, are brought together by military service, but a wide gulf continues to separate the nobilities to which they belong and to create coolness between these comrades-in-arms (II, 427; III, 143). The Courvoisiers and the Guermantes belong to the same social caste, are different branches indeed of the same family, but different from each other in countless points of behaviour, sensibility and intelligence. In *La Prisonnière*, the aristocratic Charlus, who has now shrunk into an adviser on matters of status and rank to the bourgeois Mme Verdurin, schools her at length in the shadings that persist even within the 'old' aristocracy, and seeks with increasing exasperation to refashion one of her guest-lists accordingly:

> Je vois dès les premiers mots que nous ne parlons pas la même langue, puisque je parlais de noms de l'aristocratie et que vous me citez le plus obscur des noms des gens de robe, de petits roturiers retors, cancaniers, malfaisants, de petites dames qui se croient des protectrices des arts parce qu'elles reprennent une octave au-dessous les manières de ma belle-sœur Guermantes, à la façon du geai qui croit imiter le paon. (III, 739)

> I could see as soon as you opened your mouth that we don't speak the same language, since I was talking of aristocratic names and you come up with the most obscure names of lawyers, of crooked little commoners, evil-minded tittle-tattles, and of little ladies who imagine themselves patronesses of the arts because they echo an octave lower the manners of my Guermantes sister-in-law, like a jay trying to imitate a peacock. (V, 263-4)

Charlus's lofty scorn and sarcasm speak of a class system that is already in terminal disarray. The system ought to be intelligible, even to Mme Verdurin. It ought above all to have a neatly stratified pyramidal structure, but a variety of factors – including intermarriage, the buying of titles and the invention of genealogies – has caused the strata to buckle and to leak one into the next. To make matters still more difficult, the novel contains no neutral commentators. All characters speak with the bias of their own desires for social dominance or advancement and are hugely unreliable as sociological observers. Charlus rewrites his insider's account of aristocratic manners to suit his own caprice, and recomposes his letters of credence in accordance with his latest campaign of sexual conquest. Ambitious hostesses compete for the favours of the nobility, who in their turn have an unillusioned sense of their own market value. The preservation of class boundaries calls for strenuous policing, yet the task is already a futile one. The legitimacy of the Guermantes now exists only in the narrator's youthful dreams of a glorious feudal past. In the present, the family offers a sorry spectacle. Their battles and tournaments are now played out indoors, on the salon floor, in the Faubourg Saint-Germain. The 'perforating gaze' and the 'scrutinising greeting' that they bring to the newcomer in their midst are the last residue of their former valour, a final bloodless feat of arms (II, 736–7; III, 512–14).

If there is a simple initial lesson to be drawn from Proust's handling of the pseudo-politics of aristocratic society, it is perhaps that wishful fantasy is a potent political force, and one which needs to be acknowledged inside as well as outside the institutions of state. It is certainly a conviction of this kind that provides anchorage for the narrator's protracted meditations on the Dreyfus affair:

> Quand les systèmes philosophiques qui contiennent le plus de vérité sont dictés à leurs auteurs, en dernière analyse, par une raison de sentiment, comment supposer que, dans une simple affaire politique comme l'affaire Dreyfus, des raisons de ce genre ne puissent, à l'insu du raisonneur, gouverner sa raison? (II, 593)

> When we find that the systems of philosophy which contain the most truths were dictated to their authors, in the last analysis, by reasons of sentiment, how are we to suppose that in a simple affair of politics like the Dreyfus case reasons

of that sort may not, unbeknown to the reasoner, have ruled
his reason? (III, 340)

The narrator seeks to supply, as a complement to the docu-
mented public events which give the affair its visible contours,
a map of its subterranean evolution as feeling. Beneath a history
of accusations, counter-accusations, cover-ups and courts-
martial, there is a history of visceral emotion, and the two are
more than contingently connected. The nobility of the faubourg, for example, almost unanimously adopting the anti-
dreyfusard cause, bring damage upon themselves even as they
shore up their traditional allegiances. They welcome into their
circle, for the purposes of the crusade against Dreyfus, individuals who have nothing to recommend them apart from an
appropriate intensity of antisemitic and xenophobic passion.
When the case is over and Dreyfus has been freed and rehabili-
tated, these social upstarts do not obligingly melt back into the
obscurity from which they had emerged. They have taken up
a new social position during the state of emergency and are
not now to be dislodged. An aristocratic war against one group
of outsiders has ended with another group quietly claiming
victory. An embattled caste, in its crazed attempt to refortify
itself, has opened itself up to invasion; it has willed yet another
irreversible movement in its own long, slow destruction.

For Proust, then, the social and political topography of the
Dreyfus case cannot be coherently mapped or modelled without
making continuous reference to the habits of feeling that typify
the main groups involved in the case. But in addition to these
dynamic portraits of collective emotion, he provides a gallery
of individual studies, and these too are reconnected to the
world of public affairs. Charlus, for example, rehearses an
entire chronicle of antisemitic commonplaces in *Le Côté de
Guermantes*, and subjects Bloch to a sadistic *ad hominem*
attack. Yet the scenarios of torture and cruelty that are the

copper coinage of the antisemitic imagination and casually re-emerge in Charlus's talk, soon give way to a profound personal fascination: Charlus is charmed by Bloch, excited by him, driven by him into a state of sexual and political disarray. Such are the unruly fantasies and obsessions from which entrenched political doctrines grow, the narrator proposes, and the Dreyfus events are remarkable only for the variety and urgency of the libidinal energies which they mobilise. Only the Great War is to provide an equivalent series of semi-public adventures for the sexual appetite. Saint-Loup, surrounded by his troops, relishing his life in a closed order of fighting males, is described as living out sexual desires that are 'ennuagés d'idéologie' (IV, 325; 'enclouded by ideology' (VI, 68)), clinging to an out-moded chivalric ideal. But the relationship between sex and ideology in this novel is forever one of reciprocal 'enclouding'. So much so that the politics of sexual intimacy to be observed inside the relationships between Swann and Odette, the nar-rator and Albertine, or Charlus and Morel, have the same underlying structure as the politics of the salon or that of the ministries whose margins we glimpse from time to time. Power-play in each of these arenas may be described in a single language of gesture: feint, subterfuge, conspiracy, tactical lying, the deferral of gratification by mere eloquence and indirection are the very grammar of politics and bring the bedchamber and the Chamber of Deputies into piquant proximity.

There is one appealingly straightforward way of coming to terms both with the density of political reference in Proust's novel and with the wilful thinness with which it characterises statecraft, parliamentary democracy and public administration. The novel is a panoramic account of an individual's subjectivity, and catches up within itself, as the instrument of that indi-vidual's self-understanding, a dizzying profusion of alternative selves. The narrator spawns the relentless procession of 'not-me's over and against which his 'me' comes tenuously into being. It would well suit the purposes of such a book for the public domain in its turn to be submitted to the rule of subjectivity, and for society to be understood not as a durable set of suprapersonal institutions and arrangements but as the sum of the interpersonal exchanges taking place within a given community. The competing claims of republicanism and monarchism, or of the old and new aristocracies, for example, would in this view result from the solidification, and the reconfirmation generation upon generation, of what were originally personal dispositions and the spasmodic upheavals of individual desire. Understanding any social institution would not then involve looking for the system of which it was part, but would demand that detailed attention be paid to the characteristic rhythms and intensities of individual experience from which the institution itself was fashioned and into which it constantly threatens to dissolve again. Proust's narrator seems himself to be lending his support to such a view when he says in *Le Temps retrouvé*: 'je sentais cette influence capitale de l'acte interne jusque dans les relations internationales' (IV, 492; 'I felt the influence of the internal act to be dominant even in the sphere of international relations' (VI, 277)).

If we look at Proust's novel through this sort of lens many of its seeming oddities do indeed begin to make sense. The displacement of the political process as an object of enquiry by a powerful flow of personal impressions and affective states is no longer simply a long-range consequence of the Romantic emphasis on the feeling individual. It is the mainspring of a new critical and satirical vision. This novelist who places himself inside a subjectivity and on the margins of the political world is able to represent politics as a cruel dreamlike charade. But he does this not simply to press the claims of the individual and his much-vaunted 'inner life', and not simply to reduce the study of politics to a branch of social psychology. Out of the narrator's estrangement from the political sphere comes a sabre-toothed style of political critique. Having no other public role than that of a lesser courtier in a superannuated court, he develops a lucid rage against politics at large. He needs victims, and finds them everywhere.

Proust's account of an ailing aristocracy miraculously re-energised by the Dreyfus affair resembles Musil's hilarious history of the 'Collateral Campaign' in *The Man Without Qualities* (1939–42). For Musil as for Proust, countless pages of savage comedy are to be derived from a single grandiose disproportion: that between the cant and ceremonial to which political agents are devoted and the simplistic ideas which sustain them. The Collateral Campaign is an eleventh-hour attempt to rescue some last shred of coherence, some valedictory sense of past glory, from the wreckage of the Austro-Hungarian empire. This campaign is doomed to failure, yet pursued with cunning, deliberation, and an exquisite sense of protocol. The imperial substance has already rotted away, but how self-importantly its shadows continue to dance. The key 'idea', early in Musil's novel, is simply that a Prussian should take over the spiritual leadership of the great Austrian campaign, but this is mockingly introduced in the language of a new Copernican revolution:

> what distinguishes an overwhelmingly great idea from an ordinary, perhaps even incomprehensibly ordinary and mistaken one, is the fact that it is in a kind of molten state, as a result of which the ego enters into infinite expanses and the expanses of the universe enter into the ego, whereby it ceases to be possible to recognise what belongs to oneself and what to the infinite. Hence overwhelmingly great ideas consist of a body, which, like the human body, is compact but perishable, and of an eternal soul, which is what lends

them their significance, but which is not compact – on the contrary, at every attempt to get hold of it in cold words it evaporates into nothingness.

Proust's narrator dreams as a child that a fabulous feudal system has survived by an improbable grace of history into the modern era, and then, as a young adult, wakes up to an aristocracy that has long been a phantasmagoria and is now on the point of extinction. Dreyfus provides the *mondains* with the last semblance of a common cause, and brings their rituals and ceremonies back into apparent alignment with the affairs of society at large. The question 'is he or she one of us?', asked of an unknown visitor to the salon, dramatises an otherwise insignificant social occasion. Loyalty, duty, patriotism and decency can no longer be taken for granted: they are everywhere to be tested, and protected when threatened. An entire social edifice can be made to tilt and lurch by a single unguarded word. In the dying moments of their history, the aristocracy has discovered a last delusional sense of historical mission.

Proust's political comedy is nowhere closer to Musil's 'Kakania' – that hyper-ironical recreation of fin-de-siècle Austria – than in his fantasticated portrait of Théodose II, who is the king of a nameless Eastern country. If we were invited to treat *A la recherche du temps perdu* as a *roman-à-clef*, we could say that Théodose is Tsar Nicholas II and leave matters there. His numeral gives a reader a clue, and the diplomatic events evoked in the novel map so closely on to the contemporary chronicle of Franco-Russian relations that the identification seems unanswerably neat and convincing. But to look at the matter simply in these terms would be to leave Proust's astonishing powers of derision out of account. For although Théodose's visits to Paris are a talking point during a number of separate episodes in the novel, the reader's main source of information about him is the former ambassador Norpois, whose diplomatic and oratorical skills enjoy their finest hour in the effulgence of the king's first visit. Reporting, at the beginning of *A l'ombre des jeunes filles en fleurs*, on the toast proposed by the visitor at the Elysée, Norpois is entranced by a single well-chosen word:

> C'est tout simplement un coup de maître; un peu hardi je le veux bien, mais d'une audace qu'en somme l'événement a pleinement justifiée. Les traditions diplomatiques ont certainement du bon, mais dans l'espèce elles avaient fini par faire vivre son pays et le nôtre dans une atmosphère de renfermé qui n'était plus respirable. Eh bien! une des manières de renouveler l'air, évidemment une de celles qu'on ne peut pas recommander mais que le roi Théodose pouvait se permettre, c'est de casser les vitres. Et il l'a fait avec une belle humeur qui a ravi tout le monde, et aussi une justesse dans les termes où on a reconnu tout de suite la race de princes lettrés à laquelle il appartient par sa mère. Il est certain que quand il a parlé des «affinités» qui unissent son pays à la France, l'expression, pour peu usitée qu'elle puisse être dans le vocabulaire des chancelleries, était singulièrement heureuse. Vous voyez que la littérature ne nuit pas, même dans la diplomatie, même sur un trône, ajouta-t-il en s'adressant à moi. La chose était constatée depuis longtemps, je le veux bien, et les rapports entre les deux puissances étaient devenus excellents. Encore faut-il qu'elle fût dite. Le mot était attendu, il a été choisi à merveille, vous avez vu comme il a porté. Pour ma part j'y applaudis des deux mains. (I, 451-2)

'It was simply masterly; a trifle daring, I quite admit, but it was an audacity which, after all, was fully justified by the event. Traditional diplomacy is all very well in its way, but in practice it has made his country and ours live in a hermetically sealed atmosphere in which it was no longer possible to breathe. Very well! There is one method of letting in fresh air, obviously not a method that one could officially recommend, but one which King Theodosius could allow himself to adopt – and that is to break the windows. Which he accordingly did, with a spontaneous good humour that delighted everybody, and also with an aptness in his choice of words in which one could at once detect the race of scholarly princes from whom he is descended through his mother. There can be no question that when he spoke of the "affinities" that bind his country to France, the expression, unusual though it be in the vocabulary of the chancelleries, was a singularly happy one. You see that literary ability is no drawback, even in diplomacy, even upon a throne,' he added, turning to me. 'The community of interests had long been apparent, I quite admit, and relations between the two powers were excellent. Still, it needed saying. The word was awaited; it was chosen with marvellous aptitude; you have seen the effect it had. For my part, I thoroughly applaud it.'   (II, 35 – 6)

Théodose is conjured into being by Norpois's prolix commentary: the king is the author of an empty phrase, and this draws forth from the former ambassador an answering cascade of further vacuities. Proust's dark satirical genius takes wing here. Théodose is kingship become hot air. This is no longer the strong verbalisation – that of oaths, edicts and treaties – by means of which a king might perform his functions and reassert his legitimacy, but the enfeebled afterlife of power finding expression in toasts, rumours and reportage. Théodose's kingdom without name is the *nulle part* from which no diplomatic envoy ever returns. What better way of celebrating this low-water mark of the monarchical principle than with Norpois's 'two-handed' applause?

In episodes like this, and there are many of them, Proust's political imagination plunges with abandon towards the abyss. The delirium of Norpois and the nullity of Théodose spread as a contagion through the social order. The many-voiced world of opinion goes unanimously mad, and universal darkness, for a while, buries all. Yet Proust had constructed a narrator who can do many things and espouse many viewpoints. In one of his guises he thrills to danger and seeks an apocalyptic end to the posturings of the political animal, but in another he reinstates judgement and proceeds with caution. Dreyfus in particular slows him down, and prompts him to a step-by-step reconstruction of individual political choice.

While the narrator is clearly more reserved in his *dreyfusard* sympathies than Proust himself was, it is apparent from the first detailed accounts of the affair, which occur during the Doncières episode in *Le Côté de Guermantes*, that the Dreyfus case is to be a privileged site for political and moral discussion, a place where the hidden underworld of political commitment may be studied in laboratory conditions. Saint-Loup parts company with his aristocratic peers on the question of Dreyfus's innocence or guilt, and finds in the Doncières barracks a single like-minded officer: 'Saint-Loup m'avait parlé d'un autre de ses camarades qui était là aussi, avec qui il s'entendait particulièrement bien, car ils étaient dans ce milieu les deux seuls partisans de la révision du procès Dreyfus' (II, 404; 'Saint-Loup had spoken to me of another of his comrades who was present also, one with whom he was on particularly good terms since in this environment they were the only two to champion the reopening of the Dreyfus case' (III, 114)). The narrator describes himself as readily sharing in this atmosphere of fraternal warmth during his stay, and by numerous small complicit touches later in the novel identifies himself with the *dreyfusard* cause. 'M. de Cambremer avait conclu que j'étais dreyfusard', the narrator says in *Sodome et Gomorrhe* (III, 355; 'M. de Cambremer had concluded that I was a Dreyfusard' (IV, 422)), supplying no evidence to the contrary. The rhetoric of the pro- and anti-

Dreyfus camps may be similar in certain respects, as may their campaign tactics and their appeals to this or that honourable tradition, but thereafter there is no equilibrium between them: on the one side is justice, and on the other infamy. In *Sodome et Gomorrhe* Swann tells the narrator that the prince de Guermantes has changed his mind on the question of Dreyfus's supposed crime. He had discovered new facts about the case and could then no longer sustain his former view. Swann's admiration for the uprightness of the prince is echoed and amplified by the narrator in his own voice. The truth must be told, and justice done (III, 108–10; IV, 127–30).

The narrator casts a merciless eye upon the myths and superstitions of the *anti-dreyfusards*. He holds their follies up to ridicule, and, in the ironic play of his own monologue, exposes their rigidities. A perplexing question arises, however, as in all accomplished demythologising performances of this kind. Where does the critic speak from? Where can he discover a vantage point, a system of values or a set of criteria that will not themselves fall victim to his critique? The *anti-dreyfusards* settle for error while truth is at hand, but the narrator cannot simply ground his attack upon them in the superiority of truth-telling to mendacity, for lying has already been shown to have its charms and even its virtues. Yet, without anchorage of this sort, how can the observer of an animated political scene avoid being swept along in the flux of other people's views? In *A l'ombre des jeunes filles en fleurs* the narrator states the problem in an aggravated form, using a familiar visual image:

> pareille aux kaléidoscopes qui tournent de temps en temps, la société place successivement de façon différente des éléments qu'on avait crus immuables et compose une autre figure. Je n'avais pas encore fait ma première communion, que des dames bien pensantes avaient la stupéfaction de rencontrer en visite une Juive élégante. Ces dispositions

nouvelles du kaléidoscope sont produites par ce qu'un philosophe appellerait un changement de critère. L'affaire Dreyfus en amena un nouveau, à une époque un peu posté-rieure à celle où je commençais à aller chez Mme Swann, et le kaléidoscope renversa une fois de plus ses petits losanges colorés. Tout ce qui était juif passa en bas, fût-ce la dame élégante, et des nationalistes obscurs montèrent prendre sa place.   (I, 507 – 8)

like a kaleidoscope which is every now and then given a turn, society arranges successively in different orders elements which one would have supposed immutable, and composes a new pattern. Before I had made my first Com-munion, right-minded ladies had had the stupefying experi-ence of meeting an elegant Jewess while paying a social call. These new arrangements of the kaleidoscope are produced by what a philosopher would call a 'change of criterion'. The Dreyfus case brought about another, at a period rather later than that in which I began to go to Mme Swann's, and the kaleidoscope once more reversed its coloured lozenges. Everything Jewish, even the elegant lady herself, went down, and various obscure nationalists rose to take its place.
                                                   (II, 103)

Society seems to be an impersonal mechanism for the pro-duction of political change, and to have irony built into it. No sooner has one familiar form of antisemitism begun to dissolve, removing from Jews certain of their accustomed disabilities, than another form begins to gather strength. Within a genera-tion, a prominent set of social attitudes has changed and changed again, and responsibility for these shifts cannot be clearly assigned to individual agents or even to groups propelled by a common purpose. The notion that irony is immanent in social change, and need not therefore be officiously super-added by the outside observer, continues to be employed by the narrator in his report on the later stages of the Dreyfus affair, and on its aftermath. At the start of Le Temps retrouvé, yesterday's traitors and scoundrels have become today's solid citizens. A profusion of late-blooming *dreyfusards* has transformed the entire political landscape: 'Toute la Chambre étant à un certain moment devenue révisionniste, c'était forcément parmi d'anciens révisionnistes, comme parmi d'anciens socialistes, qu'on avait été obligé de recruter le parti de l'ordre social, de la tolérance religieuse, de la préparation militaire' (IV, 305; 'The whole Chamber having at a certain moment become revisionist, it was inevitably from among former revisionists – and also from among former socialists – that the party of social order, of religious tolerance, of military preparedness, had been obliged to enlist its recruits' (VI, 44)). The political kaleidoscope has turned again, and with no responsible agent anywhere in sight.

The distinguishing mark of this narrator as a chronicler of his times is that, while being caught up in local events from day to day, he is able to take a long historical view of things. He expects recurrences, *volte-faces* and reversals of fortune. He launches his commentaries not from an extraterrestrial viewpoint but from the position of one who has inhabited the turmoil of society for a long time and grown accustomed to its tricks of perspective. However, his knowledge of the world, his expectation that new events will conform to old patterns, or that new patterns will be assembled from old building-blocks, produces disenchantment but not depression. Discovering that irony is in history anyway has a tonic rather than a debilitating effect on the narrator's own ironic style. Far from waiting passively for the next echo of things already said, or the next fulfilment of a destiny long ago foretold, he is able to model his own perceptions and his own narrative on the sameness-in-difference, the surprising predictability, of social life. By the mid-point of the novel, he has seen everything before, yet is eager to continue looking. An intellectual passion propels him.

He measures tensions and stresses within systems. He points
to the gaps and flaws that the proponents of those systems
would generally wish to conceal. He values the moment when
values begin to seem insecure, or when strong-minded criteria
begin to go slack. Proust as a political commentator is an
ironist's ironist. For him there is no bedrock, no stable map
or measuring-rod, and no viewpoint from which all other viewpoints can be made to make sense. There is instead a continuous dialectical trajectory in his thinking, and a disinterested
scrupulousness in his handling of divergent political passions.
Yet he knows also that certain of those passions, the darkest
and deadliest of them, must be repudiated. In speaking of the
guiltless Dreyfus and the multitude of his accusers, Proust's
narrator offers us his own version of Zola's 'J'accuse'.

Here, surely, is the programme of the European Enlighten-
ment given a zestful, fleet-footed and thoroughly modern form.
And here is a writer who can scarcely fail to gratify the Western
liberal consensus, for he not only calls infamy by its name,
exposes delusions and rejects reactionary views, but he speaks
with such intellectual gaiety and with such *style*. How could
principled high spirits of this kind ever be politically suspect?

Yet nothing in Proust's novel is as simple as this question
makes it sound. I have spoken already of the taste for risk and
extremity that Proust ascribes to his narrator. This expresses
itself in an occasional reduction to absurdity of political meaning and in the creation of catastrophic social scenes. But the
narrator takes everyday risks too. He has an everyday power
of provocation about him, and a promiscuous will to imitate
the views of other people. These qualities bring him at times
into brutish and illiberal company. The antisemitism, for
example, that is so firmly dismantled in certain episodes of the
novel, is gleefully reinvented in others. In the following passage
from *A l'ombre des jeunes filles en fleurs*, the narrator describes

the absence of communication between Jews and non-Jews
during the holiday season at Balbec:

> Or cette colonie juive était plus pittoresque qu'agréable. Il
> en était de Balbec comme de certains pays, la Russie ou la
> Roumanie, où les cours de géographie nous enseignent que
> la population israélite n'y jouit point de la même faveur et
> n'y est pas parvenue au même degré d'assimilation qu'à
> Paris par exemple. Toujours ensemble, sans mélange
> d'aucun autre élément, quand les cousines et les oncles de
> Bloch, ou leurs coreligionnaires mâles ou femelles se rend-
> aient au Casino, les unes pour le «bal», les autres bifurquant
> vers le baccara, ils formaient un cortège homogène en soi
> et entièrement dissemblable des gens qui les regardaient
> passer et les retrouvaient là tous les ans sans jamais échanger
> un salut avec eux, que ce fût la société des Cambremer, le
> clan du premier président, ou des grands et petits bourgeois,
> ou même de simples grainetiers de Paris, dont les filles,
> belles, fières, moqueuses et françaises comme les statues de
> Reims, n'auraient pas voulu se mêler à cette horde de fillasses
> mal élevées, poussant le souci des modes de «bains de mer»
> jusqu'à toujours avoir l'air de revenir de pêcher la crevette
> ou d'être en train de danser le tango. Quant aux hommes,
> malgré l'éclat des smokings et des souliers vernis, l'exagé-
> ration de leur type faisait penser à ces recherches dites
> «intelligentes» des peintres qui ayant à illustrer les Évangiles
> ou les *Mille et Une Nuits*, pensent au pays où la scène se
> passe et donnent à saint Pierre ou à Ali-Baba précisément
> la figure qu'avait le plus gros «ponte» de Balbec.   (II, 98)

Now this Jewish colony was more picturesque than pleasing.
Balbec was in this respect like such countries as Russia or
Romania, where the geography books teach us that the
Jewish population does not enjoy the same esteem and has
not reached the same stage of assimilation as, for instance,
in Paris. Always together, with no admixture of any other
element, when the cousins and uncles of Bloch or their

co-religionists male or female repaired to the Casino, the ladies to dance, the gentlemen branching off towards the baccarat-tables, they formed a solid troop, homogeneous within itself, and utterly dissimilar to the people who watched them go by and found them there again every year without ever exchanging a word or a greeting, whether these were the Cambremer set, or the senior judge's little group, professional or 'business' people, or even simple corn-chandlers from Paris, whose daughters, handsome, proud, mocking and French as the statues at Rheims, would not care to mix with that horde of ill-bred sluts who carried their zeal for 'seaside fashions' so far as to be always apparently on their way home from shrimping or out to dance the tango. As for the men, despite the brilliance of their dinner-jackets and patent-leather shoes, the exaggeration of their type made one think of the so-called 'bright ideas' of those painters who, having to illustrate the Gospels or the Arabian Nights, consider the country in which the scenes are laid, and give to St Peter or to Ali-Baba the identical features of the heaviest 'punter' at the Balbec tables. (II, 367–8)

This passage could be politely described as a phenomenology of antisemitic feeling, and a descriptive catalogue of the images and 'ideas' on which such feeling rests. The Jews who visit Balbec annually are colonisers rather than members of a simple *colonie de vacances*; they are assimilated, yet self-proclaimingly different; they are foreigners in demeanour if not in fact, and bring a disturbing breath of Eastern European or Oriental air to the otherwise bracing Normandy coast; they are a homogeneous and exclusive group; their womenfolk are a 'horde', and their menfolk draw attention to themselves by the uncanny glare of their apparel; they are an affront to Christianity, whether by refusing to conform to the statuary of a great cathedral or by sacrilegiously re-judaising the gospels; their social behaviour brings upon itself, by its exaggeration and immodesty, the unanimous disapproval of French society; they are themselves to blame for whatever afflictions they continue to endure.

The narrative voice in this paragraph is of course much more nuanced than this bald enumeration of antisemitic motifs would suggest: the opinions of the Cambremers are always to be distrusted, and in so far as that family is associated with the charge of Jewish 'exclusivism', the charge must itself be an object of suspicion; the Parisian grain-merchants too, with their statuesque daughters, are unreliable arbiters in matters of taste and social conduct. Yet there is still something alarming about the cornucopian generosity with which this list unfolds and the seeming warmth with which the narrator embraces each vindictive vignette. Xenophobia has expanded to fill the entire social field. Its characteristic assumptions explain everything in sight, and provide the space of casino or ballroom or beach with a cogent geometry. In its monothematic accumulation of detail, if not in its undercurrents and inflections, the rhetoric of this passage is close to the pamphleteering style of Edouard Drumont in *La France Juive* (1886) or of Céline in *Bagatelles pour un massacre* (1937). Later in the novel, in *Le Côté de Guermantes*, a thoroughgoing critique of 'orientalist' antisemitism dissolves into a rhapsodic recreation of orientalism in all its paranoid over-insistence (II, 487–9; III, 214–16).

It would be unsatisfactory to say of such writing simply that it represents one voice in a polyphony of voices in the book as a whole, and that its venom is amply neutralised by the narrator's sympathetic accounts elsewhere of Bloch and his family, and of the beleaguered Jewish community at large. The extremity of this writing deserves to be heard, and its searing aggression felt, before the problem of its presence in Proust's book is 'solved'.

During another episode in *Le Côté de Guermantes* a remarkable dialogue is established between Charlus, whose cruelty is deplored by the narrator, and the narrator himself, who seems to rediscover his own cruelty by imitation of his conversational partner. Charlus has just claimed that Dreyfus cannot be called a traitor because, being a Jew, he cannot be thought of as French, or as having responsibilities towards France; and Charlus has sketched for the narrator a fantasy scene in which Bloch would appear as David to the Goliath of his own father:

> Cela composerait une farce assez plaisante. Il pourrait même, pendant qu'il y est, frapper à coups redoublés sur sa charogne, ou, comme dirait ma vieille bonne, sur sa carogne de mère. Voilà qui serait fort bien fait et ne serait pas pour nous déplaire, hein! petit ami, puisque nous aimons les spectacles exotiques et que frapper cette créature extra-européenne, ce serait donner une correction méritée à un vieux chameau.　(II, 584–5)

> 'That would make quite an amusing farce. He might even, while he was about it, give his hag (or, as my old nurse would say, his "haggart") of a mother a good thrashing. That would be an excellent show, and would not be unpleasing to us, eh, my young friend, since we like exotic spectacles, and to thrash that non-European creature would be giving a well-earned punishment to an old cow.'　(III, 331)

The narrator recoils from Charlus at this point and from his 'terrible, almost insane' ravings, but the report he then interpolates on a conversation between Bloch senior and Nissim Bernard ends upon this cadence:

> S'attristant du malheur des Juifs, se souvenant de ses amitiés chrétiennes, devenant maniéré et précieux au fur et à mesure que les années venaient, pour des raisons que l'on verra plus tard, il [Bernard] avait maintenant l'air d'une larve préraphaélite où des poils se seraient malproprement implantés, comme des cheveux noyés dans une opale.
>
> 　　　　　　　　　　　　　　　　　　　　　(II, 586)

> Saddened by the misfortunes of the Jews, remembering his old Christian friendships, grown mannered and precious

> with increasing years for reasons which the reader will learn
> in due course, he [Bernard] had now the air of a pre-
> Raphaelite grub on to which hair had been incongruously
> grafted, like hairs in the heart of an opal.   (III, 332)

Some of the grotesquerie here is designed to give a foretaste
of Nissim Bernard's sexuality, which is to be unveiled later in
the novel: homosexuality is an incongruity and a pollution
inside the jewel-like consistency of the procreative heterosexual
group. But the image, which on the surface resembles such
fin-de-siècle inventions as Odilon Redon's eye-flower or decapi-
tated cactus-man, has another disturbing dimension too. *Larve*
retains its classical Latin sense of 'mask' or 'ghost', but has a
more modern meaning in the field of natural history. The Jew
as larva, surreptitiously invading and devouring the body of
Christian society, already had a long European history by this
point, and had been given new currency by the biologising
tendency of much antisemitic writing in the later part of the
nineteenth century. Wagner, to name only the most celebrated
pamphleteer within this tradition, had spoken in such terms in
his essay 'Judaism and Music' (1850). Proust's image, sweet-
ened somewhat by its nod towards pre-Raphaelite painting,
then switches 'almost insanely' towards a further vision of corruption: Nissim Bernard, from having been a larva becomes an
opal. Hair that had previously sprouted from a surface is now
trapped inside a volume. It stands out as clearly and indissolu-
bly against the surrounding radiance of the precious stone as
the procession of Bloch family members had stood out against
the pure concentrations of Frenchness gathered together in the
Balbec casino. Fantasies of this kind have the peculiarity that
they remove fears of uncleanness and contamination from the
unruly inner world of feeling and project them into a stable,
measurable outside space: 'foreigners', strangers, dirt and invas-
ive organisms are material presences in an otherwise clear and

unspoilt material medium. Social hygiene, like bodily hygiene, then becomes a simple art of repositioning matter. Ethnic cleansing beckons.

The language of calumny in modern France is for the most part inert and formulaic, and what novelty it has comes more often from the discovery of a new target individual or group than from the display of unusual verbal invention. Proust is a true innovator, in this as in so much else: he has discovered, for long moments, a vilifying diction that unmistakably sings and dances. Writing like this does not belong to, say, an adolescent developmental phase in the narrator's personal history, and its presence in *A la recherche du temps perdu* cannot be explained as a feature of the growth and maturation that the novel traces in the long term. The states of heightened awareness and self-awareness that the narrator eventually reaches in *Le Temps retrouvé* are presented as the finest flowering of an always restless and experimental mind, and as a worthy destination for a long tale of mental strife. But on his way towards this happy outcome the narrator does not simply slough off earlier and less perfect mental states in favour of the later and more perfect states that they prefigure. He does not gradually purge himself of his delinquencies. He darts about, improvises, regresses, anticipates, and becomes in one incarnation what he most opposes in another. This Dreyfus sympathiser suddenly seeks consensus with members of the opposing camp. This enlightened and debonair ironic voice suddenly seeks to know hatred from within. Indeed the book has been put together in such a way as to allow the narrator to be delinquent whenever he chooses, and after as well as before his late moments of illumination.

If there is an irony governing Proust's entire account of the Dreyfus case it is irony of a recklessly careering, self-overtaking kind – rather like that of Erasmus's *Praise of Folly* (1509) or

Swift's *A Tale of a Tub* (1704). One value system is used to expose another to ridicule, but the relation is a reversible one: the instrument of ridicule may become its object as the satirical text presses manically ahead. One of the hallmarks of the Proustian political vision is to be found in this extreme instability, in this resistance to all principles of social order and continuity. And this instability is jealously protected by Proust's text, even if this means giving house room from time to time to reprehensible views.

Outside the grand experimental laboratory that the Dreyfus case represents for the narrator, it is in his account of the working class that his relish for contradiction is most clearly on display. The narrator's attitudes towards the working class are sketched in considerable detail, and trenchantly enough to counterbalance his still more detailed portraits of the bourgeoisie and the aristocracy. On the one hand, workers, and especially family servants, are of interest to the narrator for what they tell of the past. They are embodiments of folk wisdom. They are a living link with feudalism, and their language, for all its malapropisms and faults of grammar, is a philological treasure-house, a rich layer of sedimented medieval forms. Through Françoise, or the street-traders whose cries echo in the opening pages of *La Prisonnière*, an otherwise lost antiquity continues to speak. On the other hand, however, certain workers have the glamour of modernity about them: electricians, mechanics, telephonists and employees in the rapidly expanding aviation industry are participants in a huge technological revolution, and, however small their individual roles, they are seen collectively by the narrator as standard-bearers for enterprise and invention. The *mondains*, who would hesitate before visiting a bourgeois home for fear of meeting a republican there, would also as a matter of course wish to preserve oil-lamps and horse-drawn omnibuses in the face of modern machines (I, 507; II, 103). But the workers are alive to the poetry of the new.

If certain representatives of the working class are valued for the past they preserve and others for the bright future they seem to announce, we surely have an instructive contradiction, and the basis for a searching critical view of class society. The enlightened bourgeoisie, whose values the narrator often takes pains to reproduce, already knows, in Proust's account of it, that working-class identities are constructed and modified to suit the requirements of capitalist employers. The plasticity of this class during an era of social upheaval and rapid industrialisation would seem to confirm the narrator's 'kaleidoscopic' view of social events and processes: the exact causes of change in the social order may be difficult to ascertain, but its effects are visible everywhere and, over the span of a generation, can radically alter the texture of daily living. Previously silent members of the community are starting to make a stir. Yet the narrator who comments in these terms on the passage of socio-historical time, and is often excited by the exploits of technocratic modernity, also looks back with unashamed nostalgia to an *ancien régime* of artisanal production methods and stable class relations. Perhaps silence was preferable after all to the new clamour.

The tension point between these two views is to be found in *Sodome et Gomorrhe*. Although the relationship between the narrator and Albertine is by now a very modern affair, receiving stimulus from the motor car and benediction from the 'aéroplane', the narrator is still positively chivalric in his protracted discussions of class:

> Car pour la chose, je n'avais jamais fait de distinction entre les classes [. . .] je n'avais jamais fait de différence entre les ouvriers, les bourgeois et les grands seigneurs, et j'aurais pris indifféremment les uns et les autres pour amis, avec

une certaine préférence pour les ouvriers, et après cela pour les grands seigneurs, non par goût, mais sachant qu'on peut exiger d'eux plus de politesse envers les ouvriers qu'on ne l'obtient de la part des bourgeois, soit que les grands seigneurs ne dédaignent pas les ouvriers comme font les bourgeois, ou bien parce qu'ils sont volontiers polis envers n'importe qui, comme les jolies femmes heureuses de donner un sourire qu'elles savent accueilli avec tant de joie.   (III, 414–15)

For in point of fact I had never made any distinction between the classes [. . .] I had never made any distinction between working people, the middle classes and the nobility, and I should have been equally ready to make any of them my friends. With a certain preference for working people, and after them for the nobility, not because I liked them better but because I knew that one could expect greater courtesy from them towards working people than one finds among the middle classes, either because the nobility are less disdainful or else because they are naturally polite to anybody, as beautiful women are glad to bestow a smile which they know will be joyfully welcomed.   (IV, 492)

As anti-bourgeois polemic goes, these remarks are far from inflammatory. Indeed the familiar sins of the bourgeoisie – complacency, small-mindedness, self-interest, mercantilism, prudishness and the like – are omitted altogether, and the narrator stops short of complete absolution for members of this class because they occasionally behave badly towards their social inferiors. Exemplary politeness towards workers can, however, be expected from the aristocracy, as the narrator has already had occasion to note in his many sympathetic portrayals of Saint-Loup. The narrator thus projects himself, in two directions at once, away from his own class position: he identifies with the *grands seigneurs* as the givers, and with the workers as the receivers, of benevolence. Equality can be rediscovered between seeming non-equals, but only on condition that the bothersome bourgeois is removed from the scene.

This long discussion of the permeable and impermeable barriers between classes then takes a comparative turn. Where the narrator himself is a self-proclaimed strict egalitarian, his mother, though perfectly well disposed towards servants, mechanics, and other working people, insists on observing certain physical and verbal boundaries. She would be reluctant to shake a working person's hand, and distressed to hear him address one of her own class equals in the second rather than the third person. What makes the entire passage so unusual as proto-sociology, however, is not the air of anxious gentility that hangs over it, but on the contrary its whiff of impending scandal. There is perhaps something promiscuous and narcissistic in the aristocratic cult of good manners, the narrator suggests, and an over-willingness to woo: the *grands seigneurs* are like pretty women whose smiles go everywhere. And again the mother's fear of a handshake between classes is perhaps a screen for the deeper fear of a transgressive sexual intimacy:

> Quand elle voyait un chauffeur d'automobile dîner avec moi dans la salle à manger, elle n'était pas absolument contente et me disait: «Il me semble que tu pourrais avoir mieux comme ami qu'un mécanicien», comme elle aurait dit, s'il se fût agi de mariage: «Tu pourrais trouver mieux comme parti.» (III, 415)

> When she saw the driver of a motor-car dining with me in the restaurant, she was not altogether pleased, and said to me: 'It seems to me you might have a more suitable friend than a mechanic,' as she might have said, had it been a question of my marriage: 'You might have found somebody better than that.' (IV, 493)

If mechanics are to be allowed into the dining room, what can prevent them from making further improper advances? They will be marriage partners next, or worse.

These local injections of sexual fantasy into the narrator's account of class relationships are not at all unusual in the novel. Indeed we glimpse briefly in this passage one of the organising ideas of the book: beyond equality of the kind that radical politicians might campaign for – an equality which concerns, say, voting rights and citizenship – there lies an egalitarianism of desire in which the enfranchised and the disenfranchised alike share. A prince may look at a bell-boy, and an electrician at a countess. The only problem with equality thought of in these terms is that it gives class politics a profoundly conservative tone. Class distinctions have to be retained rather than abolished in this world of indefinitely desiring individuals, for such differences are a powerful source of erotic stimulus. Rigidly stratified societies multiply the opportunities for pleasure that are available to sexual adventurers, and can enrich the fantasies of even the most austere stay-at-home.

This picture of social class as one erogenous element in an encompassing libidinal economy culminates in *Le Temps retrouvé*, during the extended scene in Jupien's brothel. This brings together in a grandiose comic set-piece a number of bold reversals. War with Germany brings colour and animation to the capital: exotic military uniforms from the outposts of Empire make Paris into a new Venice or Constantinople, and kilted Scots send a tremor of excitement through the *demi-monde*. The nightly black-out offers freedom rather than restriction: in the shadows sexual contacts can be made without conversational preliminaries. Enemy bombing raids bring not terror but imposing drama to every street: daily life is lived out under the volcano, and, in true Pompeian fashion, any embrace between lovers could prove to be their last. But by far the boldest reversal involves the status of the brothel itself. Anticipating Genet's *Le Balcon* (*The Balcony*, 1956) or Buñuel's *Belle de jour* (1966), but already outstripping them in satirical exuberance, Proust turns Jupien's establishment into a model of class-bound society, and at moments into a social utopia. Professional and class identities must be preserved in order to be recreated in the sexual pantomime, but a sublime vision of classlessness still hovers over the scene: everyone is entitled to his desire, and entitled to exploit others in seeking outlet for it. The only blemish in what could otherwise have been a perfect circuit of sexual and monetary transactions is the hypocrisy that afflicts certain social groups. Where members of the higher social classes have an acquired nonchalance and candour in matters of sex, working people, who may also seek sado-masochistic adventures of the kind in which Jupien specialises, are constrained by the opinion of their fellows:

> Pour un employé d'industrie, pour un domestique, aller là c'était comme pour une femme qu'on croyait honnête, aller dans une maison de passe. Certains qui avouaient y être allés se défendaient d'y être plus jamais retournés et Jupien lui-même, mentant pour protéger leur réputation ou éviter des concurrences, affirmait: «Oh! non, il ne vient pas chez moi, il ne voudrait pas *y* venir.» Pour des hommes du monde c'est moins grave, d'autant plus que les autres gens du monde qui n'*y* vont pas, ne savent pas ce que c'est et ne s'occupent pas de votre vie. Tandis que dans une maison d'aviation, si certains ajusteurs *y* sont allés, leurs camarades les espionnant, pour rien au monde ne voudraient *y* aller de peur que cela fût appris.   (IV, 415)

For a man with a job, whether in industry or in domestic service, to go to Jupien's was much the same as for a woman supposed respectable to go to a house of assignation; some, while ready to admit that they had gone there, denied having gone more than once, and Jupien himself, lying to protect their reputations or to discourage competition, would declare: 'Oh, no, he doesn't come to my establishment, he wouldn't go *there*.' For men with a social position it was not so serious, particularly as other men with a social position who do not go *there* know nothing about the place and do not concern themselves with your life. But in an aeroplane factory, for instance, if one or two fitters have gone *there*, their comrades, who have spied on them, would not dream of following their example for fear of being found out. (VI, 180)

At this point the narrator, who appears throughout this scene as an excitable and not easily shockable observer, discovers the first glimmerings of a true political cause: aviation workers whose sexual wishes are thwarted in this way deserve to be emancipated. Their case is especially strong because, unlike the indolent, non-serving aristocrats who figure prominently among Jupien's customers, these plane-makers are active contributors to the common good and to the war effort. Where utopian thinkers would ordinarily attend first to the public rights and obligations that a successful civil society might prescribe for its members, and give sexual arrangements a subsidiary role in their planning, Proust's narrator places the demands of a dissident and unquenchable sexual drive at the centre of his scheme. Once overweening desire has been appropriately provided for, then lesser questions of economic and social policy can be decided in its wake. Honest toilers on the production line will then be able to pursue their pleasure without shame or ostracism.

Le Temps retrouvé brings class relationships, which have been unstable throughout the novel, to the brink of incoherence. The bourgeois Mme Verdurin re-emerges, twice widowed and twice remarried, as the princesse de Guermantes, and the narrator declaims an almost operatic lament for the lost worlds of poetry and enchantment that such usurpations leave behind them. Perhaps an ideal and indestructible princess, the purest distillation of class feeling, will rise up and haunt the procession of impostors that Mme Verdurin has unleashed:

et toujours, sans interruption, viendrait comme un flot de nouvelles princesses de Guermantes, ou plutôt, millénaire, remplacée d'âge en âge dans son emploi par une femme différente, une seule princesse de Guermantes, ignorante de la mort, indifférente à tout ce qui change et blesse nos cœurs, le nom refermant sur celles qui sombrent de temps à autre sa toujours pareille placidité immémoriale.

(IV, 533–4)

and yet for ever and ever, without interruption, there would come, sweeping on, a flood of new Princesses de Guermantes – or rather, centuries old, replaced from age to age by a series of different women, of different actresses playing the same part and then each in her turn sinking from sight beneath the unvarying and immemorial placidity of the name, one single Princesse de Guermantes, ignorant of death and indifferent to all that changes and wounds our mortal hearts.   (VI, 330)

But it is in the brothel episode that Proust's re-imagining of a class system in catastrophic decline reaches its most extreme and most ambiguous form. On the one hand, the flames of hell are to be seen lighting up the night sky, and premonitions of disaster are everywhere. Indeed, the *Titanic* has already gone down and Vesuvius has already erupted, although the bacchanal carries on in seeming unawareness under Jupien's benign supervision. The brothel, like Dante's inferno, is 'composite', cellular, divided up into separate scenes of punishment and degradation. Art history has become a collection of lascivious images, and philology has been reduced to the study of low-life sexual jargon. And most alarmingly of all, class characteristics have been turned into mere erotic accoutrements, and are valued, like whips, chains and spy-holes, only in so far as they produce or prolong arousal. On the other hand, the brothel is a place of refuge for desire. Many of Jupien's customers are on leave from the trenches, and all of them are the potential victims of bombing and bombardment. Where the crowned heads of Europe, and its politicians and generals, have produced carnage on a previously unimaginable scale, Jupien, who is 'intelligent comme un homme de lettres' (IV, 394; 'with an intelligence worthy of a man of letters' (VI, 154)), devotes himself to altogether more civilised pursuits: he stages a restrained and playful form of belligerence, the outcome of which is not death or mutilation but pleasure and financial reward.

The voice of Charlus is to be heard coming from inside one of the rooms as the narrator listens at the door: '«Je vous en supplie, grâce, grâce, pitié, détachez-moi, ne me frappez pas si fort, disait une voix. Je vous baise les pieds, je m'humilie, je ne recommencerai pas. Ayez pitié»' (IV, 394; ' "I beseech you, mercy, have pity, untie me, don't beat me so hard," said a voice. "I kiss your feet, I abase myself, I promise not to offend again. Have pity on me" ' (VI, 154)). This is the exultant sound of what we might call, paraphrasing a celebrated expression of Eluard's, 'le dur désir de désirer'. A prince, who can trace his ancestry beyond the Capetian kings, now seeks his pleasure at the hands of a brutish serf, and, to enhance that pleasure, expects an array of antiquated torture instruments to be found for him. The transactions between torturer and masochist, and the playful reversal of master and slave relationships that these involve, are thus conducted in a self-consciously historical fashion. The aristocrat comes to terms with modernity, and with the dubious population of murderers and slaughtermen who, in his fantasies at least, crowd the back streets of the metropolis, by constructing for himself a medieval stage-set in which he can enjoy a paying victimhood. Class relationships have been exhaustively eroticised and commodified, and are now up for sale in a modern market economy, but the call of desire that is to be heard throughout this scene still has its dignity in the narrator's eyes and still manages to break free, at the last, from the grasp of commerce: 'Or les aberrations sont comme des amours où la tare maladive a tout recouvert, tout gagné. Même dans la plus folle, l'amour se reconnaît encore' (IV, 418; 'And perversions in the narrower sense of the word are like loves in which the germ of disease has spread victoriously to every part. Even in the maddest of them love may still be recognised' (VI, 184)). In the brothel, in wartime, love holds out against death. In the darkness, in the private rooms of this composite hell, in the farcical reinventions of an unequal society that Jupien stage-manages, love and fraternity have found their last stronghold.

This account of the working class is indeed contradictory, and part of a wider view in which politics itself is the science of contradiction in the social sphere. Working-class people, when they are not servants or artisans, are panders, spies and go-betweens. When they are not serving other people's sexual needs in these indirect ways, they are compliant small fry whose favours can be bought and sold at first hand. The fact that the narrator will share his table with a mechanic, and express solidarity with prostitutes during one extended episode, cannot do much to offset one's sense that, all in all, this self-proclaimed egalitarian would rather spend his time in other company. In the book as a whole, the abjection of the aristocracy weighs much heavier than that of the labouring poor. And although in part this emphasis flows from the superior absurdity of superior people, and from the freer rein this gives to Proust's satirical imagination, there are other reasons for it too. The narrator is presented as a bourgeois who has an affinity, and in due course a complicity, with the aristocrats whose company he seeks. Certain major elements in his own creative project seem to be reliant upon the inveterate inequalities that the class system embodies.

From an early stage in the novel it is clear that old and new aristocrats, even when risible in other respects, are to be valued for their sense of style, and that the excellences and excesses of their speech are particularly fascinating. Their dress, manners and deportment are all worthy of study, but their flamboyant verbal performances charm the narrator much more. Even the marquis de Norpois, who is introduced at the beginning of *A l'ombre des jeunes filles en fleurs* and is a figure of caricature during this and all subsequent appearances, brings a touch of genius to his unstemmable tirades. By the sheer force of his rhetoric he is able to transform clichés, proverbs, and fashionable phrases from the newspapers into a rich and strange delirium. In *Le Côté de Guermantes*, for example, he addressed Bloch torrentially on the need for caution among those who call for the Dreyfus case to be reopened:

> «si, avant même que fût séchée l'encre du décret qui instituerait la procédure de révision, obéissant à je ne sais quel insidieux mot d'ordre vous ne désarmiez pas, mais vous confiniez dans une opposition stérile qui semble pour certains l'*ultima ratio* de la politique, si vous vous retiriez sous votre tente et brûliez vos vaisseaux, ce serait à votre grand dam. Êtes-vous prisonnier des fauteurs de désordre? Leur avez-vous donné des gages?» Bloch était embarrassé pour répondre. M. de Norpois ne lui en laissa pas le temps. «Si la négative est vraie, comme je veux le croire, et si vous avez un peu de ce qui me semble malheureusement manquer à certains de vos chefs et de vos amis, quelque esprit politique, le jour même où la Chambre criminelle sera saisie, si vous ne vous laissez pas embrigader par les pêcheurs en eau trouble, vous aurez ville gagnée. Je ne réponds pas que tout l'état-major puisse tirer son épingle du jeu, mais c'est déjà bien beau si une partie tout au moins peut sauver la face sans mettre le feu aux poudres [. . .]»   (II, 542–3)

'should you, before even the ink has dried on the decree ordering the retrial, obeying I know not what insidious word of command, fail, I say, to disarm, and band yourselves in a sterile opposition which seems to some minds the *ultima ratio* of policy, should you retire to your tents and burn your boats, you would be doing so to your own detriment. Are you the prisoner of those who foment disorder? Have you given them pledges?' Bloch was at a loss for an answer. M. de Norpois gave him no time. 'If the negative be true, as I sincerely hope and trust, and if you have a little of what seems to me to be lamentably lacking in certain of your leaders and your friends, namely political sense, then, on the day when the Criminal Court assembles, if you do not allow yourselves to be dragooned by the fishers in troubled waters, you will have won the day. I do not guarantee that the whole of the General Staff is going to get away unscathed, but it will be so much to the good if some of them at least can save their faces without putting a match to the powder-barrel [. . .]' (III, 280–81)

And so it goes on. In a sense, Norpois in spate has all the faults and none of the artistry that one might expect from professionalised political discourse. His language is by turns archaic and self-consciously modern, learned and exaggeratedly colloquial, circumlocutory and condescendingly plain-spoken. Whatever its register, it assiduously collects banalities and strings them together: the shortest route from one ready-made expression to another lies by way of a third such expression. Norpois's talk is all bluster, an accumulation of verbal waste-matter, an antidote to thinking.

Yet this is mastery of a kind. Norpois enjoys copiousness, puts pressure on his syntax to accommodate qualifications and grace-notes, and clearly believes that length is the soul of wit. His speech comes alive in its commonplaceness and reaches grotesquely towards an *arioso* continuity of line. Just as Proust in his literary pastiches brings off the rare feat of sounding like Balzac, Flaubert or the Goncourts while continuing to sound

159

like himself, so here he endows Norpois with certain of his
own stylistic habits. Norpois in his harangues, like Legrandin
in his over-embroidered accounts of silence and moonlight,
speaks pidgin Proust. His language is ornate but not complex,
expansive but intellectually undernourished. In displaying the
absurdities of the Norpois verbal style Proust not only draws
attention to the risks his own 'grand manner' willingly runs
but causes a current of fellow feeling to flow between his
narrator and the aberrant linguistic performers whose portraits
emerge from his pen. Norpois knows something important
about language: that it abhors a vacuum and can muster huge
forces with which to invade and occupy social space. His
table-talk has gone irretrievably to the bad, but in certain major
respects it remains exemplary. In his attention-seeking, his
fondness for length and his inventive transformation of ready-
made expressions, Norpois is rather like a novelist.

Norpois's class position and his profession license him to
speak voluminously, and to tyrannise his social inferiors with
opinions and reminiscences. But two other aristocratic figures,
while enjoying the same privilege, exert a much more powerful
influence on the narrator in the development of his literary
vocation: Saint-Loup and Charlus. Both are prolific talkers on
politics and international affairs, but their talk is more seductive
than Norpois's for having a pronounced historical axis. Saint-
Loup, during the Doncières episode, takes the narrator on a
bold retrospective tour of European battles and traces a direct
line of descent from the *Iliad* to the skirmishes of the modern
day:

> On ne fait pas un atelier de peinture avec n'importe quelle
> chambre, on ne fait pas un champ de bataille avec n'importe
> quel endroit. Il y a des lieux prédestinés. Mais encore une
> fois, ce n'est pas de cela que je parlais, mais du type de
> bataille qu'on imite, d'une espèce de décalque stratégique,

de pastiche tactique, si tu veux: la bataille d'Ulm, de Lodi, de Leipzig, de Cannes. Je ne sais s'il y aura encore des guerres ni entre quels peuples; mais s'il y en a, sois sûr qu'il y aura (et sciemment de la part du chef) un Cannes, un Austerlitz, un Rossbach, un Waterloo, sans parler des autres. Quelques-uns ne se gênent pas pour le dire. Le maréchal von Schlieffen et le général de Falkenhausen ont d'avance préparé contre la France une bataille de Cannes, genre Hannibal avec fixation de l'adversaire sur tout le front et avance par les deux ailes, surtout par la droite en Belgique, tandis que Bernhardi préfère l'ordre oblique de Frédéric le Grand, Leuthen plutôt que Cannes. (II, 410-11)

You don't make an artist's studio out of any old room; so you don't make a battlefield out of any old piece of ground. There are predestined sites. But, once again, that's not what I was talking about so much as the type of battle a general takes as his model, a sort of strategic carbon copy, a tactical pastiche, if you like. Battles like Ulm, Lodi, Leipzig, Cannae. I don't know whether there'll ever be another war, or what nations will fight in it, but, if a war does come, you may be sure that it will include (and deliberately, on the commander's part) a Cannae, an Austerlitz, a Rossbach, a Waterloo, to mention a few. Some people make no bones about it. Marshal von Schlieffen and General von Falkenhausen have planned in advance a Battle of Cannae against France, in the Hannibal style, pinning their enemy down along his whole front, and advancing on both flanks, especially on the right through Belgium, while Bernhardi prefers the oblique advance of Frederick the Great, Leuthen rather than Cannae. (III, 122)

Saint-Loup's easy mastery of the historical archive and his ability to trace over long periods the migration of classic tactical or strategic devices speak directly to the narrator's own artistic ambitions: he too already has extensive tracts of historical time to manage and inherits formal models from his predecessors ancient and modern. What is so impressive about Saint-Loup's historiography is that he seems to be the author rather than the mere chronicler of events. His family lost its place on the historical stage long ago, but he speaks as if they held it still. He is the originator of speech-events only, but in his witty, rhythmic, overflowing tirades he sustains the glorious illusion of political power.

Charlus dwells with comparable ease in the historical dimension, and bases his claims to consideration both on his aristocratic titles and on the swagger with which he enumerates them. This is his response in *Sodome et Gomorrhe* to one who had presumed to draw attention to the modest-sounding rank of *baron*:

> «Permettez, répondit M. de Charlus avec un air de hauteur, à M. Verdurin étonné, je suis aussi duc de Brabant, damoiseau de Montargis, prince d'Oléron, de Carency, de Viareggio et des Dunes. D'ailleurs cela ne fait absolument rien. Ne vous tourmentez pas.» (III, 333)

> 'Pardon me,' M. de Charlus haughtily replied to the astonished Verdurin, 'I am also Duke of Brabant, Squire of Montargis, Prince of Oléron, of Carency, of Viareggio and of the Dunes. However, it's not of the slightest importance. Please don't distress yourself.' (IV, 395)

There is an element of high farce in Charlus's self-fashioning, of course. His ancestry may reach far back into history and spread well beyond the confines of France, but Carency brings *carence*, or deficiency, into the picture, and *damoiseau* not only makes him improbably youthful but, by contagion from the far commoner *damoiselle*, feminises him. For all his proud self-promotion, this male damsel is perhaps more remarkable for what he lacks than for what he has. A similar sense of ironic reservation pervades the narrator's description of Doncières: Saint-Loup's spontaneous exercises in military history reflect the youthful bravado of an officer cadet who has not yet made the transition from training camp to battlefield.

Aristocrats such as these can be made fun of for their arrogance, but at the same time admired for their boldness in exploiting history for their own ends. There is a resourceful and rapacious quality about their narrative performances, and from this the narrator eagerly learns. Earlier in the novel, Charlus had offered to take the narrator's worldly education in hand, and, as part of this process, to initiate him into the secret history of European political institutions. The Emperor of Austria had recently praised Charlus for the depth of his knowledge and expressed regret that the last Bourbon pretender to the French throne had not had access to Charlus's advice: if he had had this good fortune, he would now be king. What the would-be king could so easily have enjoyed is now spread tantalisingly before the upwardly mobile narrator:

> J'ai souvent pensé, monsieur, qu'il y avait en moi, du fait non de mes faibles dons, mais de circonstances que vous apprendrez peut-être un jour, un trésor d'expérience, une sorte de dossier secret et inestimable, que je n'ai pas cru devoir utiliser personnellement, mais qui serait sans prix pour un jeune homme à qui je livrerais en quelques mois ce que j'ai mis plus de trente ans à acquérir et que je suis peut-être seul à posséder. (II, 583)

> I have often thought, Monsieur, that there was in me, thanks not to my own humble gifts but to circumstances which you may one day have occasion to learn, a wealth of experience, a sort of secret dossier of inestimable value, of which I have not felt myself at liberty to make use for my own personal ends, which would be a priceless acquisition to a young man to whom I would hand over in a few months what it has taken me more than thirty years to acquire, and which I am perhaps alone in possessing. (III, 329)

Such claims are preposterous, and the narrator has on numerous earlier occasions mocked Charlus for making them; there is always self-interest behind Charlus's professions of altruism, and a low motive beneath his high eloquence. Yet his vision of himself as a walking archive, a historical record in human form, is powerful enough to overcome certain of the narrator's scruples. There is a lesson to be had from Charlus, although not the one that he himself is eager to teach. For the narrator as novelist-in-waiting, Charlus points the way towards a necessary sense of the past. And the extreme plasticity that Charlus's views acquire as soon as they are pressed into the service of his erotic campaigns provides the spectacle not of promiscuity but of an ever-alert and ever-resourceful speculative intelligence. Charlus remakes the world to suit the passions of the moment, and in doing so acquires enviable lightness and dexterity. Again, any prospective novelist should take note.

Charlus and Saint-Loup share these qualities with Talleyrand (1754–1838), the exemplary political survivor, and in *Le Temps retrouvé* Charlus indeed compares himself with this illustrious aristocratic predecessor (IV, 339; VI, 87). But where Talleyrand travelled lightly from one high office to another, adapting himself to the requirements of his successive political masters, Charlus and Saint-Loup have no masters and no power. They are a political irrelevance, yet move from one airy verbal fabrication to another with undiminished self-confidence and wit. Where Talleyrand had helped redraw the map of Europe at the Congress of Vienna, these latecomers merely talk, and their talk gains a special sinister brilliance as Europe descends into darkness. Talleyrand's disengaged political adroitness has become sublime frivolity. Proust's narrator insists upon the term, places a positive valuation upon it, and thinks of the mental quality it names as an inheritable characteristic. Saint-Loup's style is 'in the blood', and the inventiveness of Charlus also has a seeming genetic basis: 'il échafaudait volontiers en matière mondaine des théories où se retrouvaient la fertilité de son intelligence et la hauteur de son orgueil, avec la frivolité héréditaire de ses préoccupations' (III, 736; 'he was always ready, in social matters, to elaborate theories in which his fertile intelligence and lordly pride were combined with the hereditary frivolity of his preoccupations' (V, 260)). What aristocrats inherit, in the mental as well as in the material sphere, the bourgeois has to work for. Charlus and Saint-Loup have recourse to history and situate themselves in genealogical time, yet they glory in the gratuitousness of their inventions. The narrator, on the other hand, has no history and only the briefest of genealogies. He looks to the work of art, and to the exertions that it will require of him, to make good these deficiencies and to usher him into an enviably frivolous world.

The play of affinity and distance between the narrator and these aristocratic masters reaches its culmination in *Le Temps retrouvé*. Saint-Loup, on leave from the front and still fired by patriotic fervour, weaves playful verbal arabesques from the horrors of war. Even as he faces his own death, his nonchalance and intellectual disengagement are defiantly intact. Charlus and Saint-Loup, uncle and nephew, fellow customers in Jupien's establishment, grow more alike, in spite of the fact that Charlus's war is distinguished only by his suspected Germanophilia and by the consummate greed with which he continues to pursue his pleasures under the eye of the invader. But it is Charlus who has the greater originality, and who comes closer to being the supreme artist that the crazed and death-haunted tenor of the times seems to demand. The narrator defends Charlus in these terms against a fashionable society for whom his conversational style is now outmoded:

En fait ils étaient ingrats, car M. de Charlus était en quelque sorte leur poète, celui qui avait su dégager de la mondanité ambiante une sorte de poésie où il entrait de l'histoire, de la beauté, du pittoresque, du comique, de la frivole élégance. Mais les gens du monde, incapables de comprendre cette poésie, n'en voyaient aucune dans leur vie, la cherchaient ailleurs, et mettaient à mille piques au-dessus de M. de Charlus des hommes qui lui étaient infiniment inférieurs, mais qui prétendaient mépriser le monde et en revanche professaient des théories de sociologie et d'économie politique [. . .] Bref, les gens du monde s'étaient désengoués de M. de Charlus, non pas pour avoir trop pénétré, mais sans avoir pénétré jamais sa rare valeur intellectuelle. (IV, 345–6)

In this they were ungrateful, for M. de Charlus was to some extent their poet, the man who had been able to extract from the world of fashion a sort of essential poetry, which had in it elements of history, of beauty, of the picturesque, of the comic, of frivolous elegance. But people in society, incapable of understanding this poetry, did not see that it existed in their own lives; they sought for it rather elsewhere, and placed on an infinitely higher peak than M. de Charlus men who were much stupider than him but who professed to despise 'society' and liked instead to hold forth about sociology and political economy [. . .] In short, people in society had become disillusioned about M. de Charlus, not from having penetrated too far, but without having penetrated at all, his rare intellectual merit. (VI, 93–4)

How many more creative virtues can a would-be poet acquire and still not be a poet? To Charlus's historical sense and his frivolity, the narrator now adds comic and descriptive talents, a love of beauty, intellectual prowess and a happy freedom from professorial pedantry. The narrator is bringing Charlus uncomfortably close to the sort of poet he might himself become, and this means, within the logic of the narrator's self-creation, that Charlus must be discarded. Like Swann, Elstir, Bergotte and Vinteuil, he must be seen to be excellent and seen to fail. Only flawed role-models can serve this bringing to birth of a new artist.

The repudiation of Charlus is completed during the brothel scene, and at a moment when the baron, coming closer still to the narrator himself, has almost become a novelist. The narrator has been listening to Jupien's compassionate account of Charlus's sexual needs, and in reaction to this arrives at a moment of cruelty as shocking as Prince Hal's rejection of Falstaff at the end of *Henry IV*:

> Et en écoutant Jupien je me disais: «Quel malheur que M. de Charlus ne soit pas romancier ou poète! Non pas pour décrire ce qu'il verrait, mais le point où se trouve un Charlus par rapport au désir fait naître autour de lui les scandales, le force à prendre la vie sérieusement, à mettre des émotions dans le plaisir, l'empêche de s'arrêter, de s'immobiliser dans une vue ironique et extérieure des choses, rouvre sans cesse en lui un courant douloureux. Presque chaque fois qu'il adresse une déclaration, il essuie une avanie, s'il ne risque pas même la prison.» Ce n'est pas que l'éducation des enfants, c'est celle des poètes qui se fait à coups de gifles. Si M. de Charlus avait été romancier, la maison que lui avait aménagée Jupien, en réduisant dans de telles proportions les risques, du moins (car une descente de police était toujours à craindre) les risques à l'égard d'un individu des dispositions duquel, dans la rue, le baron n'eût pas été assuré, eût été pour lui un malheur. Mais M. de Charlus n'était en art qu'un dilettante, qui ne songeait pas à écrire et n'était pas doué pour cela. (IV, 410)

> And listening to Jupien, I said to myself: 'How unfortunate it is that M. de Charlus is not a novelist or a poet! Not merely so that he could describe what he sees, but because the position in which a Charlus finds himself with respect

167

to desire causes scandals to spring up around him, and compels him to take life seriously, to load pleasure with a weight of emotion. He cannot get stuck in an ironical and superficial view of things because a current of pain is perpetually reawakened within him. Almost every time he makes a declaration of love he is violently snubbed, if he does not run the risk of being sent to prison.' A slap in the face or a box on the ear helps to educate not only children but poets. If M. de Charlus had been a novelist, the house which Jupien had set up for him, by reducing so greatly the risks – at least (for a raid by the police was always a possibility) the risk emanating from an individual casually encountered in the street, of whose inclinations the Baron could not have felt certain – would have been a misfortune for him. But in the sphere of art M. de Charlus was no more than a dilettante, who never dreamt of writing and had no gift for it.

(VI, 173–4)

Everything is now in place for Charlus to become an artist. To the qualities that have already been listed the narrator now adds recklessness, an appetite for suffering, a willingness to be humiliated. Only a hair's breadth separates Charlus from the calling and the condition of the novelist, but the barrier is uncrossable. Charlus cannot write. The blow is delivered with offhanded insolence, and in the absence of its victim, but it strikes home as terribly as 'I know thee not, old man'. Charlus, like Falstaff, has outlasted his usefulness.

If the political dimension of *A la recherche du temps perdu* were to be articulated solely in terms of class conflict, we could say that it represents yet another Pyrrhic triumph for the professional bourgeoisie. The aristocracy is seen off by the narrator in his search for his own artistic vision and voice. Sometimes this process is brutal and peremptory, as when Mme de Surgis presents to Charlus her two sons, Victurnien and Arnulphe, who combine the twin perfections of beauty and stupidity (III, 96–8; IV, 112–15). And sometimes, as we have just seen in the case of Charlus himself, it is slow and filled with lingering admiration. The working class is often treated more charitably, but is always at several removes from effective political action. Whereas aristocrats, in this social universe, have only the memory of power, and workers only the remotest foretaste of it, the narrator himself has the real thing. A reliable sign of his new-found potency is that he can offer himself both as a representative of the bourgeoisie in his daily habits and expectations and as miraculously class-neutral and unaligned in his artistic endeavours. His tireless capacity for introspection and self-analysis is fed by unshakeable self-belief. He can lose himself in reverie, and find himself again in sententious utterance which projects his personal experience towards mankind at large. He can lose himself in mimicry as he travels back and forth between the speech habits of different social groups, and find himself again in his own singular and obdurate vocal style. He triumphs where his fellow bourgeois Bergotte, Swann, Vinteuil and Elstir do not, for he has more staying power and single-mindedness than they have.

The price to be paid for this confident assumption of the artistic vocation is that of being a helpless bystander before real political events. The artistic ego can consume and transform everything in its path; it can look upon class wars and world war and not be shaken; it can assemble a ship of fools and yet rise clear of folly; it can even become an archive, a compacted mass of historical data given memorable artistic form. But although power converges upon Proust's artist from all these directions and heaps all these honours upon him, he still cannot either assume power in his own person or imaginatively reinvent the spheres in which it is exercised by others. The bourgeois artist cannot see the ground on which he himself is standing, or come to grips with the forces which make it possible for him to exercise freely his own inventiveness. He works

hard to dissociate himself from a tribe of obsolete and gratuit-
ous-seeming aristocrats, but a new gratuitousness, more terrifying than theirs, is his reward.

Yet this cannot be the whole story of Proustian politics. For
although Proust's narrator skilfully negotiates his own release
from the class identities by which others are bound, and blithely
removes political parties and policies from the scene, he does
not create for himself in the process a motionless observational
platform. On the contrary, the particular virtue of this narrator,
put together by Proust from so many competing loyalties,
enthusiasms and antipathies within himself, is that he remains
mobile and many-voiced throughout a very long novel. The
political realm is alive with pretension, vanity and self-deceit.
Intellectually, it produces paradoxes and absurdities in
unstoppable profusion. The narrator is at home there, tempera-
mentally, and wants his politics to be as complicated and incon-
sequential as possible.

The narrator's will to complication can produce dizzying
short-term effects inside the narrative. Indeed there are passages
where the personality of the narrator seems to come apart into
an infinitely mischievous play of ironies. Where can he possibly
ground his own observations and judgements when *all* classes
and political groups, past and present, launch into a *danse
macabre* before his eyes? A critical moment of this kind occurs
in *Sodome et Gomorrhe*, when the narrator joins Saniette, Cottard, Brichot and other members of the Verdurin clan for a
pilgrimage by train to La Raspelière. This property near Balbec,
owned by the Cambremers but rented seasonally to the Verdurins, itself lacks secure social anchorage, and the narrator's
journey to it is a stormy passage through troubled class feelings.
Cottard is alarmed that princesse Sherbatoff might have to
share a compartment with a farmer, Saniette fears a new peasants' revolt when he sees a railway platform crowded with

members of the rural community, and Brichot tells the narrator
of the pleasures that await him at their journey's end:

> «Si ce sont vos débuts chez Mme Verdurin, monsieur, me
> dit Brichot, qui tenait à montrer ses talents à un 'nouveau',
> vous verrez qu'il n'y a pas de milieu où l'on sente mieux
> la 'douceur de vivre', comme disait un des inventeurs du
> dilettantisme, du je m'enfichisme, de beaucoup de mots en
> 'isme' à la mode chez nos snobinettes, je veux dire M. le
> prince de Talleyrand.» Car, quand il parlait de ces grands
> seigneurs du passé, il trouvait spirituel et «couleur de
> l'époque» de faire précéder leur titre de monsieur et disait
> monsieur le duc de la Rochefoucauld, monsieur le cardinal
> de Retz, qu'il appelait aussi de temps en temps: «Ce *struggle
> for lifer* de Gondi, ce 'boulangiste' de Marcillac.»
>
> (III, 268–9)

> 'If this is your first appearance at Mme Verdurin's, Mon-
> sieur,' Brichot said to me, anxious to show off his talents
> before a newcomer, 'you will find that there is no place
> where one feels more the *douceur de vivre*, to quote one of
> the inventors of dilettantism, of pococurantism, of all sorts
> of "isms" that are in fashion among our little snoblings – I
> refer to M. le Prince de Talleyrand.' For, when he spoke
> of these great noblemen of the past, he felt that it was
> witty and added 'period colour' to prefix their titles with
> 'Monsieur', and said 'M. le Duc de La Rochefoucauld', 'M.
> le Cardinal de Retz', referring to these from time to time also
> as 'That *struggle for lifer* Gondi', 'that *Boulangist* Marcillac'.
>
> (IV, 316)

Brichot is the embodiment here of the social malady that Nietz-
sche had called *ressentiment*. Speaking from within a citadel
of bourgeois complacency, he trains the full force of his eru-
dition on those who enjoy a social and intellectual status
superior to his own. His envy and animosity find expression
in a heavy-handed teasing of the distinguished dead. In a single

171

gesture, Cardinal de Retz (1613–79) and La Rochefoucauld (1613–80) are reminded of what they were before they found fame, and transported abruptly into the modern world, the one becoming a crude social Darwinist and the other a supporter of General Boulanger, whose brief period of reactionary insurgency belongs to the late 1880s. What gives Brichot's pedantic fantasy its special air of dementia, however, is that he should proclaim Mme Verdurin's ascendancy while cutting Talleyrand down to size. *La douceur de vivre*, the celebrated phrase that Talleyrand had used, apocryphally, of the last years of the *ancien régime*, is now reapplied to the Verdurins' seaside residence, while Talleyrand himself becomes a vulgarian of the present day: *je m'enfichisme* or 'couldn't-care-lessery' was a coinage of the early 1890s, and even more up-to-date in Proust's France than, say, 'jingoism' in Britain at the same period.

The narrator's own position in all this criss-crossing of social perspectives is, to say the least, fragile and uncomfortable. He takes sides against Brichot, yet shares a great deal with him. The narrator, like Swann before him, has his own reasons for seeking temporary admission to the clan of which Brichot is an honoured member. Brichot's attack upon the aristocracy echoes the narrator's own resentful demythologising of the Guermantes. Brichot in his time-travels through the history of France is a paltry and envious version of the all-knowing free spirit that the narrator aspires to become. His attention flickers between the peasants on the platform and the buffoonish bourgeois on the train, between the Verdurins and their aristocratic landlords, between low-grade, high-grade and purely imaginary princesses, and nowhere finds its point of rest. Class values are so much in crisis that an astute observer can do no more than conduct comparative measurements at chosen points in the social landscape, hoping to discover pockets of dignity, true feeling or intellectual probity hidden away in odd corners of the scene. Surviving in this world, and in due course perhaps breaking through into Talleyrand's *douceur de vivre*, is a matter of diplomacy and negotiation, of not insisting too much or trying too hard. The nascent artist must recognise that he too is a 'struggle for lifer', and that his essential gift is an indefinite power of adaptation.

What is true of episodes like the journey to La Raspelière is to some extent true of the novel as a whole. Proust aestheticises politics, following the example of Saint-Loup, Charlus and other characters of his own invention. One is reminded at moments of Disraeli, for whom politics was uniformly dramatic and rhetorical whether played out at the hustings and in Parliament or recreated in *Coningsby* (1844) and *Sybil* (1845). Proust's political creatures are much given to rhetorical flights and to verbal displays bordering on madness. Salon discussion of contemporary politics is artfully whipped into a froth of fatuous opinions and slogans. The narrator has to a spectacular degree the adaptability and dexterity that in his youth he admired in Norpois and Stendhal's Mosca (II, 405; III, 115), and, in addition, is master of an inexhaustible singing line that carries his narration through the din of divergent political voices.

Yet there is also something much more violent and dissonant in Proust's portrayal of the political life. All human situations are matters for negotiation, the narrator seems often to suggest, and inventiveness and adaptation should be watchwords for the artist quite as much as for the politician or the diplomat. But beyond this delicious play of possibility, real, non-negotiable conflicts and contradictions continue to exist, and these too find their way into the texture of Proust's novel. Here is a work which is in considerable part a pro-Dreyfusard satire, and comparable in this to Anatole France's *L'Île des pingouins*

(1908), yet one which incorporates into itself currents of visceral antisemitic feeling; a work which defends and celebrates the working class, yet offers a democratically improved form of prostitution as a cure for social ills; and a work which, while endlessly proclaiming the nullity of the aristocracy, locates and ingeniously exploits ever more sources of poetry in this discredited social class. This vision of politics has neither ease nor *douceur* in it, but offers at best a bracing pessimism. When even this breaks down, Proust's book leaves us with politics as an art of the impossible, and with ample reason for despair.

V

Morality

Let Earth unbalanc'd from her orbit fly,
Planets and Suns run lawless thro' the sky,
Let ruling Angels from their spheres be hurl'd,
Being on being wreck'd, and world on world
ALEXANDER POPE, *An Essay on Man*

Early in *Du côté de chez Swann*, Proust's narrator describes the
Giotto panels depicting the Virtues and the Vices that are to
be found in the Arena chapel in Padua, and draws attention
to a quality of these allegorical emblems that it is tempting to
associate with Proust's own procedures as a novelist. There is
no charity about the figure labelled *Caritas*, the narrator says,
and there is no envy about the figure labelled *Invidia*. The
one, energetic and coarse, passes her inflamed heart upwards
to her creator rather as a cellar-worker might pass a corkscrew
up through a grating to someone who had asked for it on the
ground floor. The other is so completely locked in a struggle,
muscle against muscle, with the serpent protruding from her
mouth that she has no time or energy left for the thinking of
envious thoughts. The moral characteristic ostensibly being
symbolised has in fact been reincarnated or reinvented, the
narrator says, as a fragment of the real world – 'comme effectivement subi ou matériellement manié' (I, 81; 'as a reality,
actually felt or materially handled' (I, 96)). When he visits
Padua for the first time, in *Albertine disparue*, the Virtues and

175

the Vices, and other figures in the chapel, continue to give this impression of an 'action effective, littéralement réelle' (IV, 227; 'actual movement, literally real activity' (V, 744)).

There is an encouragingly straightforward precept for the would-be novelist somewhere here: by verbal magic, let your moral agents become materially manipulable stuff, let them become flesh or speech-sound or both. And a lesson, for the reader of Proust's book, about the kinds of portraiture that he or she can expect to find in it. Just as the moral character of Uriah Heep in *David Copperfield* (1849–50) may be thought to be immanent in the dampness of his palms and the 'snaky twistings of his throat and body', and that of Henry James's Isabel Archer in the exquisite feints and obliquities of her drawing-room conversation, so the moral character of Albertine, Charlus, Saint-Loup, the Verdurins and the whole glorious fresco of Proust's inventions is perhaps simply to be found in the chronicle of their words and deeds and mannerisms.

But this is only a fragment of the larger picture. For Proust's narrator, while being at times a disinterested spectator at the scene of moral action, and at others an empty space in which his fellow characters acquire, deploy and transform their individualities, is also a moral activist in his own right. He has views, innumerably many views. He is a *moraliste* in the manner of La Rochefoucauld and La Bruyère; an unsystematic moral philosopher at moments in the manner of Victor Cousin (1792–1867); a *moralisateur* at moments in the manner of Molière's Tartuffe or Alceste. He is not only a moral theorist but one who monitors the language of theory and brings to the words in which moral judgements are expressed a tireless philological curiosity.

What is strange, however, is that the narrator, having these concerns and so elaborately characterised as a maker of judgements and a fabricator of theories, is seldom detained by Proust's critics for further questioning on moral matters. The narrator is an introspective psychologist of unusual virtuosity; an art critic, a cultural, scientific and political commentator, and a historian of manners. In all these guises, he produces theoretical statements, catches his characters in a theoretical net, and propels his narrative forward almost as if the telling of a story were an exercise in devising a set of appropriate experimental tests for a number of cherished psychological or metaphysical hypotheses. In all these guises, Proust's narrator's theories have been thought of as the obvious starting point for anyone who seeks to understand what manner of artefact *A la recherche du temps perdu* is, and what designs it has upon its reader. Yet among statements of this kind, moral statements, of which the book contains thousands, have not been put to work in rewarding ways. Perhaps they have not been thought singular enough, or varied enough, or hazardously heterogeneous enough, to be worth spending time on. Summarising a complex situation briefly, we could say that Proust and his narrator have been found very impressive indeed on questions of time, memory and desire, and really rather unimpressive on questions of vice and virtue.

Yet the moral language of Proust is sufficiently strange and provocative to repay close reading, and his book has a distinctive moral design to it that deserves to be included among the splendours of the Proustian imaginary world – together with his account of memory and desire and serving to make certain aspects of that account fully intelligible. Vice and virtue, I shall claim, are essential critical concepts that the Proust reader cannot afford to be without.

The novel is a comprehensive portrait of individual wilfulness and desire. '[T]out être suit son plaisir' (III, 23; 'every individual follows the line of his own pleasure' (IV, 24)), the narrator says in *Sodome et Gomorrhe* as he contemplates the comedy of sexual appetite in its endlessly resourceful quest for satisfaction, and the multitude of interweaving routes towards pleasure create, in the novel as a whole, the unstable environment in which all moral choices and adjudications occur. This is a world in which virtue still exists, but under conditions of extreme turbulence and stress. It ought to be possible, the narrator tells us, to retain a childlike power of intuition in these matters; certain deeds are virtuous and certain deeds are more virtuous than others: 'un enfant vraiment bien élevé qui entend des gens chez qui on l'a envoyé déjeuner dire: "Nous avouons tout, nous sommes francs", sent que cela dénote une qualité morale inférieure à la bonne action pure et simple, qui ne dit rien' (IV, 460; 'the truly well-brought-up child who, lunching in a strange house and hearing his hosts say: "We are frank, we don't hide our light under a bushel here," feels that the remark indicates a moral quality inferior to right conduct pure and simple, which says nothing' (VI, 236)). This passage from *Le Temps retrouvé* occurs during a long meditation on the responsibilities of the artist: it ought to be possible to create a work of art by an ingenious refashioning of the human materials to hand and without theoretical self-justification, just as a good deed ought to shine out in a naughty world undimmed by promotional activity from the doer on his own behalf. But in Proust the daily world that the artist and the moral agent inhabit is the unbounded province of the human will: values are created, maintained and defended without benefit of divine guidance or arbitration. Judgements are ungrounded, 'right conduct' has no external guarantor, and the observer of desire-driven and wilful social behaviour is constantly drawn back, desiringly, into the contest of wills. It would take a very wise child to tell the difference between goodness proper and the smooth affectations of goodness upon which society thrives.

Proust writes with exuberant comic energy about the inter-personal field in which virtue is now obliged to seek expression. And the occupants of that field are startlingly multiform and inconstant in their self-presentation each to each. After a rapturous description of Albertine's naked body, another Albertine comes into view:

> Il n'y avait que, quand elle était tout à fait sur le côté, un certain aspect de sa figure (si bonne et si belle de face) que je ne pouvais souffrir, crochu comme en certaines caricatures de Léonard, semblant révéler la méchanceté, l'âpreté au gain, la fourberie d'une espionne, dont la présence chez moi m'eût fait horreur et qui semblait démasquée par ces profils-là.
>
> (III, 587)

> When she was lying completely on her side, there was a certain aspect of her face (so sweet and so beautiful from in front) which I could not endure, hook-nosed as in one of Leonardo's caricatures, seeming to betray the malice, the greed for gain, the deceitfulness of a spy whose presence in my house would have filled me with horror and whom that profile seemed to unmask.
>
> (V, 83)

And Saint-Loup, for the most part a model of loyal friendship, is precipitated by a sudden disloyal word into a similar facial transformation:

> Du reste sa figure était stigmatisée, pendant qu'il me disait ces paroles vulgaires, par une affreuse sinuosité que je ne lui ai vue qu'une fois ou deux dans la vie, et qui, suivant d'abord à peu près le milieu de la figure, une fois arrivée aux lèvres les tordait, leur donnait une expression hideuse de bassesse, presque de bestialité.
>
> (II, 693)

> Whatever it was, his face was seared, while he uttered these vulgar words, by a frightful sinuosity which I saw on it once or twice only in all the time I knew him, and which, beginning by running more or less down the middle of his face,

> when it came to his lips twisted them, gave them a hideous
> expression of baseness, almost of bestiality.   (III, 461)

This is physiognomy become a dynamic rather than a static science of interpretation: facial features no longer reveal the mental and moral attributes of a continuous personality but the changing play of character that each individual harbours. The short-lived moral force of individual impulse and motive moulds and remoulds the compliant materials of skin, muscle and cartilage. And to make the quest for goodness or veracity or candour or disinterestedness still more difficult, the social world in which such qualities are available, however intermittently, for study is one in which a taste for paradox and surprise attracts more acclaim than any steady adherence to principle. It is difficult to negotiate any sense of common and enduring value in a world populated by such creatures as the duchesse de Guermantes, who prides herself on the improbability of her artistic enthusiasms and on the singularity of her moral judgements. She values Corneille only as a comic writer, finds the whole of Wagner's *Tristan und Isolde* tedious apart from a single horn-call, sees avarice where everyone else sees generosity . . . and so forth: 'Comme gâtées par la nullité de la vie mondaine, l'intelligence et la sensibilité de Mme de Guermantes étaient trop vacillantes pour que le dégoût ne succédât pas assez vite chez elle à l'engouement' (II, 762; 'As though corrupted by the nullity of life in society, the intelligence and sensibility of Mme de Guermantes were too vacillating for disgust not to follow pretty swiftly in the wake of infatuation' (III, 544)). But the vacuity of the social life in which she has her being, and the studied vacillation in which she excels, are caricatural versions of the working conditions in which the narrator's own moral career is pursued. Discovering where virtue resides and differentiating between its greater and lesser degrees are for the most part matters of conjecture and construal. A good deed is not radiantly and mutely good in a world where desire-driven social discourses appropriate everything in their path. Goodness is an unprotected fortress in occupied territory. Virtue has to be hunted down, rescued and conserved, and may at any moment dissolve again from view.

The extreme precariousness of positive moral judgements in the social world of the novel is further intensified by the lavish attention that Proust pays to those deeds that seem to call for negative judgement, and to modes of thought and conduct held by his narrator to be vicious. Proust is a sovereign critic of those 'fautes ordinaires' that Montaigne listed in his essay 'Des cannibales' ('On the Cannibals', 1580): treachery, disloyalty, cruelty, tyranny. To this list we might add hypocrisy and snobbery – as the late Judith Shklar did in *Ordinary Vices*, the splendid work of moral psychology for which she borrowed as her title Montaigne's phrase – and mendacity, to which Proust devotes many pages of sympathetic discussion. And it is of course the narrator's sympathy for what he terms vice, the colluding criticism to which he subjects it, that gives the moral dimension of *A la recherche du temps perdu* its complexity and power of provocation. Proust writes about vice rather as Kierkegaard writes about the seductiveness of Mozart's *Don Giovanni* – in prose that seeks to restore the shocking sensuous immediacy of disreputable desires, to re-inhabit the volitional world of the voluptuary. He does this not by anatomising psychological types, nor by bringing together representatives of socially aberrant desire in a gallery of villainous *caractères*. The language of moral speculation, the very diction in which the narrator's troubled adjudications are couched, is itself preened and glamorised. Abstract talk about vice becomes its own exercise in seduction, and in the process a massive transvaluation of values may occur. In the following passage from *La*

Prisonnière, for example, lying, from having been a species of torture and cruelty, suddenly becomes a source of illumination:

> Le mensonge, le mensonge parfait, sur les gens que nous connaissons, les relations que nous avons eues avec eux, notre mobile dans telle action formulé par nous d'une façon toute différente, le mensonge sur ce que nous sommes, sur ce que nous aimons, sur ce que nous éprouvons à l'égard de l'être qui nous aime et qui croit nous avoir façonnés semblables à lui parce qu'il nous embrasse toute la journée, ce mensonge-là est une des seules choses au monde qui puisse nous ouvrir des perspectives sur du nouveau, sur de l'inconnu, puisse ouvrir en nous des sens endormis pour la contemplation d'univers que nous n'aurions jamais connus.
>
> (III, 721)

> The lie, the perfect lie, about people we know, about the relations we have had with them, about our motive for some action, formulated in totally different terms, the lie as to what we are, whom we love, what we feel with regard to people who love us and believe that they have fashioned us in their own image because they keep on kissing us morning, noon and night – that lie is one of the few things in the world that can open windows for us on to what is new and unknown, that can awaken in us sleeping senses for the contemplation of universes that otherwise we should never have known.
>
> (V, 239)

This sentence, which encloses within its principal abstract proposition a tiny scene of dalliance almost in the manner of Boucher – 'il nous embrasse toute la journée' (literally 'he keeps on kissing us all day long') – sketches a new erotic opportunity and a new source of knowledge in a single highly inflected gesture: the moral imagination is reaching beyond mere rectitude and planning new sensory and intellectual delights for itself. Beyond the rewards of trust and candour and mutual approbation are suddenly to be glimpsed the dangerous teasing

182

incitements of the calculated lie. The art of the seducer has been introduced into a pastoral scene, and has brought with it its own syntax of flirtatious postponement. To be economical with the truth is to be prodigal with pleasure. Our lies thrill and delight us, and show us towards our new-found land: 'Le mensonge est essentiel à l'humanité. Il y joue peut-être un aussi grand rôle que la recherche du plaisir, et d'ailleurs est commandé par cette recherche' (IV, 189; 'Lying is essential to humanity. It plays as large a part perhaps as the quest for pleasure, and is moreover governed by that quest' (V, 698)).

This deferral of moral judgement in favour of ambiguous, transvaluative textual play is nowhere more apparent, or more ingeniously sustained, than in the narrator's protracted discussions of sexuality itself. These are, on the surface at least, straightforwardly and indeed sometimes straitlacedly moralised passages. Certain sorts of sexual act or inclination belong to virtue and certain other sorts to vice. The acts themselves do not need to be evaluated case by case because their broad moral character is already included in their initial terms of reference. Homosexuality is a vice, a perversion, an aberration, a wilful thwarting of natural process, a social menace . . . and so forth. Of this the narrator seems drably and distastefully convinced in many of his programmatic statements on sexual behaviour. And heterosexuality, while not being identified with virtue in and of itself, acquires its normative force by back-formation, as it were, from the homosexual disposition which competes with it and which appears to spread exponentially through Parisian society as the plot of the novel moves towards its resolution. Yet beneath the defensive moral programme that the narrator repeats and amplifies another sexuality – and another set of textual performances – trace their elaborately ambiguous path. Between the sexes, in the no man's land between straightforward homosexual or heterosexual preference, is the theatre of mobile desire. On this experimental stage all passions appear *en travesti*, and sensuality is heightened and manipulated by the artful indirections of speech. Here any sexuality whatsoever will begin to reveal its unofficial harmonics, and its capacity for dissidence.

In a celebrated scene from *A l'ombre des jeunes filles en fleurs*, which I have already had occasion to discuss, sexual indeterminacy as a cause at once of artistic delight and moral perplexity is held up to view over several lingering pages. This is the episode, which takes place in Elstir's studio, during which the narrator discovers a watercolour depicting 'Miss Sacripant'. This work, it will be remembered, proves to be an image of the youthful Odette dressed as a boy. How can Elstir not have been alarmed by the immorality of this image, by its near-depravity, the narrator asks, and how can he have settled in such circumstances for a merely aesthetic exploration of ambiguity? Yet no sooner have these doubts been raised than the narrator absorbs exactly this ambiguity into his own text, spins it out and complicates its emotional consequences:

> Le long des lignes du visage, le sexe avait l'air d'être sur le point d'avouer qu'il était celui d'une fille un peu garçonnière, s'évanouissait, et plus loin se retrouvait, suggérant plutôt l'idée d'un jeune efféminé vicieux et songeur, puis fuyait encore, restait insaisissable. Le caractère de tristesse rêveuse du regard, par son contraste même avec les accessoires appartenant au monde de la noce et du théâtre, n'était pas ce qui était le moins troublant.   (II, 205)

> Along the lines of the face, the latent sex seemed to be on the point of confessing itself to be that of a somewhat boyish girl, then vanished, and reappeared further on with a suggestion rather of an effeminate, vicious and pensive youth, then fled once more and remained elusive. The dreamy sadness

in the expression of the eyes, by its very contrast with the accessories belonging to the world of debauchery and the stage, was not the least disturbing element in the picture.

(II, 495)

The pleasurable hesitation that is enacted by the first sentence here would pose no particular problem – it would belong to the order of sensation that opera-goers are perfectly familiar with as they watch Mozart's Cherubino or Richard Strauss's Oktavian on stage – if it were not for the oddly naïve and oddly accentuated prior assumption that cross-dressing belongs to Vice. The narrator is constructed in such a way that he returns often from worldly wisdom to childlike puzzlement. There is something wrong here, he seems to be suggesting, for vicious people ought simply to be consumed by their vice: it is this that defines them after all. They ought to become visible only in the urgencies of wrongdoing. But good heavens, perhaps they dream too – 'vicieux et songeur', 'tristesse rêveuse' ('vicious and pensive', 'dreamy sadness') – or know nostalgia and regret. Perhaps they take holidays from their monomania and become pluralising poets for a while.

This constant passage from a strong-minded normative view of sexual conduct to an empathising and exploratory view makes Proust's narrator, for all his metaphors of pilgrimage and quest, into a hesitant spectator for long stretches of the text. His account of homosexuality in particular – sumptuous in its imagery, in tone derisive and august by turns, bringing together elements of epic, lyric and burlesque and of the scientific treatise – has an air of leisurely expansiveness: the various intensities of homosexual passion, the various moral colorations of homosexual living, are exhaustively rehearsed and measured one against the next. Differences matter. When homosexuality is for real, deeply ingrained in the human personality rather than a product of transient social convention, it can refine

185

intellectual performance and artistic perception. It can introduce a happy breach into the sensory apparatus, through which Beethoven becomes audible and Veronese visible (III, 710–11; V, 229–30). And for the observer of homosexual conduct the scientific stakes are high. Charlus in his courtship rituals is described in the language of anthropology or natural history, but in a language of generalised philosophical wonderment too. To understand fully what Charlus in his 'vice', or Albertine in hers, does or feels or craves would be to find a key to the most difficult and fertile of enigmas. For not only would this knowledge show forth the laws of the creaturely, embodied and socialised human mind, but it would usher in a larger vision of order and law-abidingness in the cosmos. Scientific and ethical discovery would be reunited at last.

Proust adheres, in the bemused attention he pays to the varieties and sub-varieties of sexual feeling, and in the insistent intermixing of his metaphors, to his own version of the principle of plenitude. Even in the presence of suffering, pain, despair and death the world cannot not be full, and it is full not because God, or the World-Ground, has ordained that it should be so but because the narrator's anxiously inventive intelligence abhors a vacuum. It creates gradations where meaner spirits might be content with dichotomies; it seeks out intermediate forms, fills interstitial spaces; it enjoys biological sports for the intellectual sport they afford, and sees in organic mutations a reflection and a reinforcement of the transforming capacity of the human mind.

A sure sign that the principle of plenitude is exercising its charm upon a literary work is the presence within it of those tantalising organisms the zoophytes, those plant-animals or animal-plants which call the familiar borders between biological classes into dispute. In the system of Leibniz, whose universe cannot become fuller than it already is, two kinds of evidence for the graduated continuity of nature are called upon. On the one hand, he refers us in the *Monadology* (1714) to the evidence of micro-organisms: 'though the earth and the air which are between the plants of the garden, or the water which is between the fish of the pond, be neither plant nor fish; yet they also contain plants and fishes, but mostly so minute as to be imperceptible to us.' On the other hand, he refers us rather more conjecturally to the zoophytes: 'not only, I say, should I not be surprised to hear that they had been discovered, but, in fact, I am convinced that there must be such creatures.' Proust is altogether Leibnizian in this respect. In *A l'ombre des jeunes filles en fleurs*, the narrator perceives an intermediate species coming towards him on the shore at Balbec: 'la bande zoophytique des jeunes filles' (II, 210; 'the zoophytic band of girls' (II, 502)). Again linear continuity is guaranteed twice over: these are girl-flowers, hovering between classes, and each member of the group is seamlessly connected to the others. In due course, a comparable structure is to be found in the narrator's own passions; he desires all these interconnected girls at once, zoophytically: 'le désir d'aimer [. . .] erre voluptueusement dans une zone de charmes interchangeables' (II, 269; 'the desire to love [. . .] wanders voluptuously through a zone of interchangeable charms' (II, 573)). Throughout the novel this voluptuous *errance* is maintained. The narrator takes pleasure in hybrids, androgynes and polymorphs; in images that connect seemingly remote varieties of experience; in oxymorons and parentheses that allow seepage between otherwise disparate words or propositions. Death itself, in the final tableau of the novel, moves through the assembled company as a cruel artist in metamorphosis, but as an artist none the less. Proust's narrator has an insatiable interest, we might say, in the pond's population of invisible fish.

Where Proust's cult of the plenum and the continuum differs

markedly from Leibniz's, however, is in the degree of practical moral curiosity that it involves. Leibniz's universe had a gratifying moral design to it, but this did not mean that the adventures and vicissitudes of human passion needed to be inspected or evaluated in any detail. Proust, on the other hand, brings an indefatigable optimism and a fondness for detail to his survey of human conduct. For those who care to look, there is complex moral life in the interstices. And even the bad news – Evil – is good news in so far as it actualises a further set of possibles and conduces towards a sense of plenty.

We must avoid excessive simplicity, however, when it comes to the overall effect of Proustian plenitude. It could be claimed that in Proust's novel, beneath a bare dichotomous view of the conflict between virtue and vice, a thoroughgoing moral relativism is at work, and that 'the narrator', in matters of sex in particular, occupies a point of tension between a severely legislating superego and an id that is all mischief and lubricity. This would perhaps be accurate enough as a view of the slow unfolding of the novel paragraph by paragraph: the narrator does veer and vacillate; he does bring together incompatible moral viewpoints. Proust has put him together precisely as a hybrid and an amphibian. But yet the book as a whole has an overarching moral drama as well as an elaborate and cogent plot. The book is concerned, among many other things, with the discovery and the assumption by the narrator of a morality that was not available to him at the start of the tale. Proust, we may guess, already knew something of this late-coming morality at the moment of his beginning to write the novel, and introduced into the fabric of his text, we may also assume, all manner of prophetic glimpses and intimations of it. But it takes the narrator time to find things out, and he moves through many shifting views and many conflicting moral judgements on his way towards his final moments of insight and decision.

E. M. Forster was splendidly disbelieving on these questions of overall structure. Writing in 1927, he said: 'Proust's conclusion has not been published yet, and his admirers say that when it comes everything will fall into its place . . . I do not believe this . . . The book is chaotic, ill-constructed, it has and will have no external shape; and yet it hangs together because it is stitched internally.' For the moment I shall join the chorus of those who assert against Forster that the book does indeed have an external shape, and that this is strong enough to hold things together even when its internal stitching comes apart, or is abandoned in favour of spirited improvisation. I shall also claim, and more in the manner of a soloist, that this shape comes as much from the working out of a *moral* argument as from the much more celebrated Proustian accounts of time, memory and art, and depends upon a quite specific and unusual redefinition of virtue.

This redefinition is spelled out in *Le Temps retrouvé*, but the ground has been prepared earlier. Over and against the habit of virtue – as shown in the compassion and beneficence of the narrator's grandmother, for example – Proust attends to the singularity of certain virtuous acts. Nothing has prepared the narrator for them, and they do not run with the grain of any existing personality in the novel. Selfishness and greed are for a moment overshadowed by an unplanned and seemingly gratuitous access of charitable feeling. Suddenly, a work of mercy appears in among the ordinary vices of the social world. A salient event of this kind occurs in *La Prisonnière*, in the scene where M. Verdurin suggests to his wife that something might be done to help the archivist Saniette, who is now ill and destitute: 'Alors j'avais pensé, je ne veux rien faire qui te déplaise, mais nous aurions peut-être pu lui faire une petite rente pour qu'il ne s'aperçoive pas trop de sa ruine, qu'il puisse se soigner chez lui' (III, 828; 'And so it occurred to me – I don't wish to do anything that doesn't meet with your approval, but we might perhaps be able to scrape up a small income for him so that he shan't be too conscious of his ruin, so that he can keep a roof over his head' (V, 370)). The Verdurin couple are famous for quite other qualities – notably for the firmness with which they expel offending members from their little clan – and could not in the ordinary course of things be expected to hear, let alone heed, the cry of the needy. Faced with the Verdurins' act the narrator is obliged to revise his views, and his moral vocabulary: something like 'partial goodness' must exist, he concludes (V, 373; 'bonté partielle' (III, 830)). In *Le Côté de Guermantes*, he had drawn attention to 'the connexions [. . .] between goodness and wickedness in the same heart' (III, 331; 'les rapports [. . .] entre la bonté et la méchanceté dans un même cœur' (II, 585)) as a neglected object of study. He is now doing the fieldwork himself.

The most striking spontaneous upsurge of beneficence occurs much later in the novel, however, and involves a goodness that is no longer partial. This is to be found in the episode of the Larivières, the husband and wife who appear in the work only once, only for a page, and on the strength only of their virtue. The Larivières are the wealthy cousins of Françoise. Upon hearing that their nephew has been killed at the front, they come out of retirement to support the young widow. He had been a café-owner, as had the Larivières. To the menial tasks and long hours of running a café they now return: 'Et depuis près de trois ans, elles rinçaient ainsi des verres et servaient des consommations depuis le matin jusqu'à 9 heures et demie du soir, sans un jour de repos' (IV, 424; 'And for nearly three years now they had been washing glasses and serving drinks from early morning until half past nine at night, without a day's rest' (VI, 191)).

These events are presented as moral epiphanies. They offer

the narrator a powerful alternative view of social man and woman: selflessness replaces a customary greed; an energetic, practical *caritas* replaces the mere preaching of good works. But what is still more remarkable about these moments is the dramatic discontinuity that each of them introduces into the discourse of the novel. In both cases, the new insight echoes down into the menial business of contriving, plotting and stitching together a work of prose fiction. In the first case, that of Saniette, the incident is connected by the narrator to his larger sociolinguistic investigation of the Verdurin clan. Saniette is introduced early in the novel as suffering from a speech impediment, and, by his pedantic use of archaisms in conversation, he wilfully impedes his own passage through society. Only an imbecile would talk like that, M. Verdurin had already remarked of him (III, 732–3; V, 256–7). And now, faced with the potentially troublesome consequences of his own good deed – if word of it gets about others will come asking – M. Verdurin retreats for a moment into a linguistic oddity of his own. He wants to avoid grateful speeches and touching scenes, and, in characterising these, he and his wife use a word that the narrator has not heard before and does not understand. The word is the private possession of the family or the clan: 'Ce genre d'expressions est généralement un reliquat contemporain d'un état antérieur de la famille' (III, 829; 'An expression of this sort is generally a survival from an earlier condition of the family' (V, 371)). The narrator promptly abandons his anecdote and embarks upon an exorbitant discussion of the origins and cultural role of what are now called sociolects. From Saniette's doubly imperfect speech, to the Verdurins' private language, to the violence performed by the narrator upon his own tale a connecting thread all at once passes. As the narrator's attention is massively switched from the moral to the linguistic sphere, from the mystery of an unexpected good deed to the mystery of an unintelligible word, the paradoxical task of the novelist comes back into view – that of travelling by way of linguistic particulars, which may include aberrations, conceits and nonce-words, towards a new vision of communicative solidarity between individuals, a new sense of common humanity. Referring to the grandmother's illness, the manager of the Balbec hotel uses the word *symecope* rather than *syncope* ('stroke'), and this ignorant invention encapsulates for the narrator the intensity of his own grief: the wound inflicted upon language speaks for his own loss, and for the grandmother's wounded brain (III, 175; IV, 205–6).

The Larivière episode contains a still more emphatic movement of linguistic self-consciousness on Proust's part. Faced with the Larivières' astonishing act of mercy, the ordinary proprieties and tacit agreements that govern the dealings between a novelist, his characters and his readers are suspended:

> Dans ce livre où il n'y a pas un seul fait qui ne soit fictif, où il n'y a pas un seul personnage «à clefs», où tout a été inventé par moi selon les besoins de ma démonstration, je dois dire à la louange de mon pays que seuls les parents millionnaires de Françoise ayant quitté leur retraite pour aider leur nièce sans appui, que seuls ceux-là sont des gens réels, qui existent. Et persuadé que leur modestie ne s'en offensera pas, pour la raison qu'ils ne liront jamais ce livre, c'est avec un enfantin plaisir et une profonde émotion que, ne pouvant citer les noms de tant d'autres qui durent agir de même et par qui la France a survécu, je transcris ici leur nom véritable: ils s'appellent, d'un nom si français d'ailleurs, Larivière. (IV, 424)

In this book in which there is not a single incident which is not fictitious, not a single character who is a real person in disguise, in which everything has been invented by me in accordance with the requirements of my theme, I owe it to the credit of my country to say that only the millionaire cousins of Françoise who came out of retirement to help their niece when she was left without support, only they are real people who exist. And persuaded as I am that I shall not offend their modesty, for the reason that they will never read this book, it is both with childish pleasure and with a profound emotion that, being unable to record the names of so many others who undoubtedly acted in the same way, to all of whom France owes her survival, I transcribe here the real name of this family: they are called – and what name could be more French? – Larivière.   (VI, 191)

In order to pay his homage to a sublime selflessness, Proust seemingly steps outside the confines of his own fictional text. He interrupts and overrides the voice of his carefully constructed narrator, and announces, within a work of fiction, that these particular creatures are not his, that the moral efficacy they represent is part of an empirically observable state of affairs out there in the world, and that their virtuous act somehow disempowers the novelist in the very exercise of his craft. Even those who would hasten to point out that such protestations themselves belong straightforwardly enough to the rhetoric of fiction, that a visible work of ironic self-construction is still going on here even as irony is disclaimed, can scarcely fail to be impressed by this abrupt movement between narrative registers. Again a moral singularity has found its analogue in a singular moment of upheaval in the expressive medium.

Proust is of course always a keen-eared monitor of spoken and written language. But in cases like these the philological concerns of his book acquire a new urgency. It is no longer simply a question of noting and recreating the varieties of local verbal colour that speaking creatures display: the speech of characters, their sociolects, idiolects and mannerisms, and the speech of the novelist himself, are transformed into an experimental zone, a mobile topological space, in which the inventions of the moral imagination can be mapped and modelled.

Vice, virtue and their cognates are not exclusively moral notions, needless to say, in either French or English, and Proust exploits the ambiguity of these terms throughout his work. A virtue is a power, a property, or simple operational success as well as a species of moral excellence; just as a vice is a flaw or a defect or simple operational failure as well as a species of depravity. The theoretical prose poem on homosexuality with which *Sodome et Gomorrhe* begins hesitates luxuriously between these two meanings of vice: 'car tout être suit son plaisir; et si cet être n'est pas trop vicieux, il le cherche dans un sexe opposé au sien. Or pour l'inverti le vice commence, non pas quand il noue des relations (car trop de raisons peuvent les commander), mais quand il prend son plaisir avec des femmes' (III, 23; 'for every individual follows the line of his own pleasure, and if he is not too depraved, seeks it in a sex complementary to his own. And for the invert vice begins, not when he enters into relations (for there are all sorts of reasons that may enjoin these), but when he takes his pleasure with women' (IV, 24–5)). On the one hand vicious conduct is conduct offensive to the self-appointed guardians of heterosexuality; the narrator espouses their language and insists that homosexual acts are by definition depraved. On the other hand, vicious conduct is conduct by which the human agent removes himself or herself from the 'natural' exercise of his or her desires: in this view of things a homosexual man displays virtue in seeking male sexual partners and vice in consorting sexually with women. All in an excited confusion of voices and sexual attitudes, the narrator now adopts and now discards this morally neutral position; he hovers between description and prescription, between natural history of a loosely Darwinian kind and an overwrought campaign on behalf of a threatened heterosexual norm. The linguistic medium itself moves in and out of focus as a carrier of moral meanings: speech may be vicious merely

194

in so far as some element of pronunciation or usage falls short of a generally accepted standard, but it may be vicious in the sense that it has a corrupting or morally debilitating effect on those who use it. Bad speech may lead to bad deeds, or to a lazy tolerance of such deeds. The entire distended Albertine episode of the novel is situated in a region that by turns is and is not one of moral conflict: her sexuality and her speech are vicious now in a moral and now in a merely descriptive sense. Everything about her demands to be scrutinised and tested; her seeming candour may at any moment be revealed as shameless duplicity, just as the pleasing symmetry of her full face may give way to the almost grotesqueness of her profile. Her casual remarks may switch at any moment from being benign curiosities – the sort of thing that the late Eric Partridge might have enjoyed collecting – to being points of access to a dark history of perverse desire: 'j'aime bien mieux que vous me laissiez une fois libre pour que j'aille me faire casser . . .' (III, 840; 'I'd a great deal rather you left me free for once in a way to go and get myself b . . .' (V, 385)), says Albertine, sending the narrator off in search of a missing noun. When he finds 'le pot' – the 'two atrocious words' needed to complete Albertine's sentence – he discovers that he has sunk to the lowest depths of the sexual imagination. Even the prostitutes who offer anal intercourse, he says, would not use this hideous expression to clients seeking such a service (III, 843; V, 388). Vicious language has brought him before an ineffable vision of vice.

All this slippage between categories, all this ecstatic swooning across the spectrum of moral intensities and all these delectable suspensions of judgement are encouraged by certain features only of the Proust style. Others resist them. The novel contains much crisply sententious writing on the pattern of 'on n'aime plus personne dès qu'on aime' (I, 392; 'when one is in love one has no love left for anyone' (I, 480)) and this writing, although of course caught up in the forward-flung motions of a strenuously desire-driven text, constantly reminds us of the plain propositional syntax that a hard-won and unassailable general truth about the human passions might in due course call into play. Proust's apophthegms are rehearsals or trial runs for the sort of truth-telling that his narrator's enquiries might in due course necessitate. A voice within the flux of the text is constantly drawing our attention to the *terra firma* that lies ahead, just over the horizon. And escaping from the flux is itself metaphorically prefigured and syntactically pre-enacted in the text. Virtue must have secure anchorage somewhere, the text manages to suggest even as it executes its insolent intellectual *glissandi*.

If we confine ourselves for the moment to the internal workings of the text, this escape towards breadth and fixity takes two main forms. First of all, the down-at-heel mortals whom the novelist describes with affectionate complicity are in an important sense right when they present themselves to each other as heroes and heroines, or indeed as gods and goddesses. Urged on by their colluding chronicler, they reach out, beyond the minor perturbations of salon society, towards the status of transhistorical emblem. They become Homeric, Virgilian or Dantesque. Here again is the narrator recreating his puzzlement at the courtship of Charlus and Jupien: '. . . le vice de chacun l'accompagne à la façon de ce génie qui était invisible pour les hommes tant qu'ils ignoraient sa présence. La bonté, la fourberie, le nom, les relations mondaines, ne se laissent pas découvrir, et on les porte cachés. Ulysse lui-même ne reconnaissait pas d'abord Athéné' (III, 15; 'each man's vice [. . .] accompanies him after the manner of the tutelary spirit who was invisible to men so long as they were unaware of his presence. Kindness, treachery, name, social relations, they do not let themselves be laid bare, we carry them hidden. Ulysses himself did not recognise Athena at first' (IV, 15)). This is an extraordinary exercise in euhemeristic interpretation of the kind that Jean Seznec studied in his monumental *La Survivance des dieux antiques* (1940). At first glance the mechanism seems straightforward enough: the discovery of Charlus's homosexuality, and the new meaning that this imprints retrospectively upon his behaviour, is first of all presented in Proust's famous sententious manner, and is then, in an abrupt access of sarcasm, transposed into mythical terms. The moral language strains towards a convincing generality, and myth provides this wish with an absurd premature fulfilment. The narrator plays Odysseus to the goddess Athena as played by the baron de Charlus. A voyeur watching others at their sexual sport has become the hero of heroes, newly returned to Ithaca after his long voyage.

But looked at in the wider perspective of the narrator's quest for secure knowledge of the human passions, the passage is much more intricate than this. Against the current of deflationary euhemerism, as one might call it – these gods and heroes are mere mortals after all – runs a lively current of sympathetic fantasy: these mortals are indeed divine. Charlus's snobbery often takes the form of euphoric self-promotion. He is a descendant of kings, closely related to the current crowned heads of Europe and on terms of some intimacy with countless notable personages who, for the time being, cannot be directly absorbed into his wondrously ramifying family tree. His Christian names and aristocratic titles themselves form an epic catalogue. All this is mercilessly mocked by the narrator, but a not dissimilar process of mythical amplification is to be found in Proust's own fashioning of his fictional characters: Charlus is small-minded, lame-spirited, yet beyond his false grandeur he is genuinely grand; Mme Verdurin is fatuous in her social performances, philistine in her tastes, but by the sheer extremity of these she becomes a genuinely sacred *monstre sacré*;

Albertine is duplicity itself, but a spacious arena for the speculative intellect and a personification of the scientific quest.

The narrator as moral scientist, precisely because his ambition is to articulate general truths, needs to populate his world not simply with particularised human agents but with archetypal images of human agency and with the elementary structures of the moral life. He himself does not shrink from self-identification with gods and heroes. He is at one moment Odysseus, as we have just seen, and at others gathers about him a slightly more mundane band of fellow-explorers. The 'partial goodness' of M. Verdurin was there all the time, the narrator says, before the Saniette episode revealed it to him – just as America was there before Columbus, he adds, or the North Pole before the exploration led by Robert Edwin Peary (III, 830; V, 373). Peary's exploit dates from 1909, and it is fascinating to see this contemporary traveller co-opted from the front page of the newspapers into the narrator's personal mythology. New heroes can be created instantly, provided that they conform to a time-honoured pattern.

I mentioned two escape routes from the textual flux on which Proust's comparative study of moralities is based. The second route involves not the creation of a pantheon but the articulation of abstract laws. Laws, great laws, general laws, great general laws: the refrain is an insistent one throughout the novel, and reaches its culmination in the closing pages. And the proximity of moral science to observational physical science is stressed repeatedly. Whether upwards into the heavens – 'toute cette immensité réglée par des lois' (IV, 475; 'the whole law-governed immensity' (VI, 255)) – or downwards into the hidden mental worlds of fools or imbeciles, the Proustian scientist travels with the same sort of practical-minded trust in his own inferential procedures: they are all he has with which to grasp the overarching structure of things, and it is only when that structure begins to appear among the phenomena that his task acquires its intellectual and moral worth. Proust writes with admiration about the slow, patient procedures of the scientist and places that slowness in perpetual dialogue with the happy accidents and intuitive leaps which also fuel creative intellectual and artistic work. When 'les lois générales de l'amour' (IV, 399; 'the general laws of love' (VI, 160)) or 'les grandes lois morales' (IV, 460; 'the great moral laws' (VI, 236)) have finally been elicited, the aphoristic abstract language used throughout the book – the language, lightly modernised, of La Rochefoucauld (1613–80), Vauvenargues (1715–47) and Chamfort (1740–94) – may be expected, as I have already said, to shed its merely experimental air and become the appropriate vehicle for the hard-won certainties. But this moment of adequation between a moral language and a set of tested and accredited moral ideas not only does not occur in *Le Temps retrouvé*, it is conscientiously deferred. Even as the language of the *moralistes* presses ahead to an apotheosis of sorts in Proust's final intermittent hymn to generality and law-abidingness, another kind of meaning is stealing up on the book and, with gigantic strokes, another kind of moral outcome is being sketched.

Beyond purely textual escape routes from the flux of Proust's text lies a quite different moral perspective, and this has something to do with the improbable beneficence of the Verdurins towards Saniette and with the supererogation of the Larivières. These events have prepared Proust's reader for the unusual redefinition of virtue to be found in *Le Temps retrouvé*, and the time has surely come for me to say what I understand this latecoming virtue to be.

It is related to, but far from co-extensive with, a certain variety of altruism. '[T]ous les altruismes féconds de la nature', the narrator says in the closing pages of the novel, 'se développent selon un mode égoïste' (IV, 613; 'all the fruitful altruisms of nature develop in an egotistical manner' (VI, 436)). The necessary egotistical carrying fluid within which this concern for others runs can only be, it is often assumed, the greedily appropriative artistic imagination. Martha Nussbaum in her splendid essay collection *Love's Knowledge* summarises this problematic view as held by Proust's narrator in the following terms: 'it is only in relation to the literary text, and never in life, that we can have a relation characterized by genuine altruism, and by genuine acknowledgement of the otherness of the other'. This is indeed one of the narrator's views; the textual evidence is copious. But the moral, or indeed simply the aesthetic, import of any complex fictional text cannot be expected to reside in any one view, however ringingly it is proclaimed, or in any one character, however encompassing his monologue may become. Proust's book, in its culminating vision of the moral life, crosses the threshold that the narrator establishes for himself in his account of art and dares to recreate a sense of community and communicativeness between the novelist and those who read him, and between those who write and read and the innumerable company of those who do neither. The emotion that comes into play here is pity, and the virtue accompanying it is an unconditional and improbably versatile charity. Pity of an active and inclusive kind, and a charity that is extended indifferently to the living, the dead and the unborn. There is something excessive about pity, the narrator had already said, speaking of his grandmother's last sufferings, something that exaggerates pain. But by way of its exaggerations, pity takes us towards an intolerable truth about the presence of suffering in the world (III, 172; IV, 201–2). The narrator's pity now, towards the end of the novel, moves irreversibly into the register of excess.

We may of course be inclined to ask straight away where

this emotion comes from, and what it is that authorises, in a thoroughly godless literary work, the almost sacramental tone that the narrator chooses to adopt. Compassion is of course in the air as news reaches Paris of the slaughter at the front, but he stands apart from the common feeling: 'j'avais une pitié infinie même d'êtres moins chers, même d'indifférents, et de tant de destinées dont ma pensée en essayant de les comprendre avait, en somme, utilisé la souffrance, ou même seulement les ridicules' (IV, 481; 'there were others less dear to me, or for whom I had cared nothing at all, for whom I felt an infinite pity, all those whose sufferings, or merely whose follies, my thought, in its effort to understand their destinies, had used for its own selfish purpose' (VI, 262–3)). Not only his dear ones, now dead – the grandmother and Albertine have just been mentioned – but 'les ridicules', 'les bêtes', 'les méchants' and 'les ingrats' (ridiculous, foolish, malicious and ungrateful people) are to be included in the merciful work of literary composition (IV, 480; VI, 261–2). The commonplace phrase 'à tout péché miséricorde' ('for every sin there is forgiveness') has been used satirically on a number of occasions earlier – it is one of those ready-made expressions from which Norpois weaves the weighty fabric of his soliloquies (I, 465; II, 52) – but a supreme day of reckoning has now arrived on which the shortcomings and the wrongdoings of all social creatures are indeed to be neutralised in an all-embracing act of forgiveness. It will perhaps seem pedantic, faced with the grandeur of this gesture, to point out that Proust has a source here, and one that he refers us to directly in his text. But that source, a still abundantly flowing one in the French culture of Proust's maturity, tells us something important about the scale and the tone of this episode. I am referring to the Victor Hugo of *Les Contemplations* (1856).

Mme de Guermantes, during one of her last appearances in

the novel, quotes one of Hugo's poems to his dead daughter Léopoldine (IV, 583; VI, 397), and the narrator shortly after quotes a celebrated line from another of those poems, 'A Villequier':

> Il faut que l'herbe pousse et que les enfants meurent
>
> (IV, 615)
>
> Grass must grow and children must die   (VI, 438)

But to the grandest of those poems, upon which Hugo's collection ends, no reference is made. The relationship between the novel and 'A celle qui est restée en France' ('To the woman who remained in France') is much more intimate than that. It is not the text of the poem that the narrator now incorporates, but its reach, the unqualified misericord that it intones over all creatures:

> Que sur toute existence et toute créature,
> Vivant du souffle humain ou du souffle animal,
> Debout au seuil du bien, croulante au bord du mal,
> Tendre ou farouche, immonde ou splendide, humble ou
>   grande,
> La vaste paix des cieux de toutes parts descende!
>
> Upon each existence and each creature, living by human breath or the breath of beasts, upright on the threshold of the good or crumbling on the edge of evil, gentle or fierce, hideous or splendid, lowly or exalted, may the vast peace of the heavens from all directions descend!

Hugo dated his poem 'le jour des morts', or All Souls' Day, 1855. It was written during his exile in Guernsey, and she who had remained in France, Léopoldine who was in her French grave, spoke and interceded on behalf of all the dying and the dead, on behalf of the faithful departed and of the faithless, fond and foolish departed too. This great poem of forgiveness and remembrance is of a kind that it is perhaps now difficult to imagine being imagined, let alone repeated. But Proust has the audacity, the folly even, to repeat its vast gesture of inclusion. Reading a book, his narrator says, is like wandering around in a cemetery unable to make out the obliterated names on the tombstones. In some sense the novelist must conspire with this forgetfulness in order to produce his fictions; he must oblige a mass of individual details, and indeed the coherence of individual personalities, to disappear in order to allow a truer and more generous remembering to begin:

> s'il est un moyen pour nous d'apprendre à comprendre ces mots oubliés, ce moyen ne devons-nous pas l'employer, fallût-il pour cela les transcrire d'abord en un langage universel mais qui du moins sera permanent, qui ferait de ceux qui ne sont plus, en leur essence la plus vraie, une acquisition perpétuelle pour toutes les âmes? (IV, 482)

> if there exists a method by which we can learn to understand these forgotten words once more, is it not our duty to make use of it, even if this means transcribing them first into a language which is universal but which for that very reason will at least be permanent, a language which may make out of those who are no more, in their truest essence, a lasting acquisition for the souls of all mankind? (VI, 264)

This repeats and amplifies the already very ample Hugolian commemorative act; between the community of the novelist's characters and those other shadowy communities comprising the real-life prototypes from which those characters will be derived and, beyond them, all the souls of the dead and the unborn, a new kind of connection is to become possible thanks to the work of art. When that connection has been actualised, mere works of art begin to disappear from view.

'Von Herzen – möge es wieder zu Herzen gehen!': Proust echoes the hope that Beethoven had expressed for his Missa

Solemnis. But the work of art no longer travels simply from the heart to the heart; the *oublieuse mémoire* that propels the novelist at his task creates a channel of communication between the human past, the whole of it, and the human future, the whole of that too. It is the novelist's responsibility not simply to be altruistic, but to catch up an inexhaustible array of others into the networks of his text. This is not merely a matter of requiring the individual self to acknowledge the difference of the other, the separate existence and character of each of that self's interlocutors in turn. During artistic creation, the self has the higher duty to become indefinitely porous to what lies outside it; to press no individual claim other than that of its own power of sympathy; to welcome all comers, the whole raggle-taggle procession of them, into its now hugely extended interior world. The narrator reports on his panic at the idea that a single once-real person might be excluded from his book: 'Cette jeune fille aux prunelles profondément enfoncées, à la voix traînante, est-elle ici? Et si elle y repose en effet, dans quelle partie, on ne sait plus, et comment trouver sous les fleurs?' (IV, 482; 'That girl with the very deep-set eyes and the drawling voice, is she here? and if she is, in what part of the ground does she lie? we no longer know, and how are we to find her beneath the flowers?' (VI, 264)). Beneath a floral surface, which combines graveyard flowers, flowers of rhetoric and the flowery charms of the young woman herself, a person is still to be found, and needs to be preserved. 'Comment ne le sentez-vous pas? Ah! insensé, qui crois que je ne suis pas toi!' ('How can you not feel it? Oh foolish one, who thinks that I am not you!'), Hugo had asked his reader in the preface to *Les Contemplations*. And Proust's narrator has at last, after many accidents, arrived at a comparable point of egotistical sublimity. Early in the novel, Uncle Adolphe had said of the narrator as a schoolchild 'Qui sait, ce sera peut-être un petit Victor Hugo' (I, 78; 'Who knows? he may turn out a little Victor Hugo' (I, 92)). By the end of the novel the prophecy has come true, apart from the matter of size: Proust as Hugo is not little.

This, then, is the moral outcome of the narrator's anxious journey through salon society and through the plurality of sexual worlds. He has discovered love for humankind. How satisfactory is this late illumination? Edmund Wilson, in his brilliant essay on Proust in *Axel's Castle* (1933), drew attention not only to the moral dimension of the novel but to one of its possible limitations, when he wrote: 'It seems strange that so many critics should have found Proust's novel "unmoral"; the truth is that he was preoccupied with morality to the extent of tending to deal in melodrama.' Could it be that the narrator's late discovery of love, forgiveness and redemption, triggered by the almost magical parallel discovery of his own artistic vocation, belongs to the melodramatic tendency of Proust's imagination, and that the outcome I have been describing has been insufficiently worked for in this highly worked-upon book? Is this simply a morality *ex machina*, a last-minute attempt to settle by strong-arm methods the leisurely contest of moralities that the main body of the book has staged? In my view the answer to these questions is 'no'. My reasons for thinking that there *is* a convincing match between the culmination of Proust's moral drama and the moral speculation that has gone on earlier in the work will already be plain.

When it comes to the conduct of others, Proust's narrator is shown to have a broadly coherent pattern to his preferences and admirations. On the one hand, he admires virtuous deeds that do not and cannot prate about their own origins, motives and effects. He admires singularities in the moral sphere, just as he attaches great importance to sudden and unrepeatable effects of sunlight in the natural world. In this respect, Giotto's figure of *Caritas*, passing her heart upwards as if it were a corkscrew and the Larivières uncorking bottles and washing glasses in their dead nephew's bar, are emblematic not just of the mysterious and uncovenanted goodness that is sometimes to be found among otherwise rapacious human beings but of a necessary discontinuity in the moral life. Giotto's great poem of redemption in the Arena chapel is organised in such a way that, even within the flow of divine mercifulness, *Caritas* and *Invidia* are still counterposed, separated by an unbridgeable gulf and irreducible one to the other. Proust insists on distance and discontinuity in the same way.

On the other hand, his narrator is an enthusiast for zoophytes, transitional forms, admixtures and continuous series. In the moral sphere he enjoys watching the surreptitious emergence of virtue in improbable places – among the work-force of a brothel specialising in sado-masochism, for example – and positioning the 'partial goodness' of the Verdurins among the neighbouring qualities of hypocrisy and self-interest that they continue to reveal. The quasi-Leibnizian cult of continuity and plenitude to which the narrator seems to adhere for long stretches of his narration involves him in producing an iridescent interlace of ordinary vices and ordinary virtues and in thinking of a newly discovered intermediate form as a trophy to be displayed with pride by the moral explorer. This explorer does not want to stop at the Americas with Columbus or at the North Pole with Peary, but is driven onwards by an unquenchable curiosity. New intermediate worlds await his gaze.

These two views are seriously at odds, and not simply because one belongs to the world of action and the other to the world of self-conscious speculative play, or because one belongs to the instant and the other to long-drawn-out temporal process. They are at odds because they compete for the same ground, each striving to exclude the other from it, and are combinable only in unusual and far-fetched circumstances. But it is exactly these circumstances that *Le Temps retrouvé* provides: in this section of the novel a series of singular events, discontinuous moments, visionary glimpses, allows the narrator to look with a new clarity of vision at the ship of fools whose company he has sought, but to behold their foibles, lies and cruelties with a forgiving rather than an accusing eye. By way of a singular, again almost magical, process of self-transformation, the narrator accedes to the All, to the continuum. Previously he had been there by slow routes – as a curious traveller, a deliberative tourist, a migratory *moraliste*. He is now there by virtue of a sudden ecstatic insight and a new self-granted moral legitimacy based upon it. Like the Larivières, he has reached a moment of selflessness and supererogation; his art-project, like the Larivières' life-project, is to let others be. In the narrator's case to let others numerously, variously and overflowingly be; and to do this by way of work which by turns asserts the special dispensations governing art and withdraws them in favour of the greater social All in which art has only a contributing role, if role at all.

This sounds perhaps still too much like a wish-fulfilment fantasy. Too blithely forgiving as a moral outcome to a work that has dwelt at such length upon the savagery of social man and woman. What has to be remembered, and what gives the *matinée chez la princesse de Guermantes* section of the novel its special atmosphere, its special far-fetchedness that rings uncannily true, is that the narrator's misericord is pronounced not from a happy position of resignation or artistic resolve but from one of extremity, and from a sense of common mortality that has cruelly survived the rediscovery of his own creative power. As we create, we are dying, the narrator says, and the promised book which is to be a perpetual acquisition for all souls, 'toutes les âmes', will itself in due course be consumed into oblivion. The narrator had spoken in *A l'ombre des jeunes filles en fleurs* of a house of plain exterior 'dont l'intérieur est rempli de trésors, de pinces-monseigneur et de cadavres' (II, 102; 'which inside is full of hidden treasures, crowbars or corpses' (II, 372)). Characterising Swann's reaction to Odette's confessions of past misconduct in 'Un Amour de Swann', he had spoken of a perpetuity of pain: 'Son âme les charriait, les rejetait, les berçait, comme des cadavres. Et elle en était empoisonnée (I, 364; 'His soul carried them along, cast them aside, then cradled them again in its bosom, like corpses in a river. And they poisoned it' (I, 445)). By the end of the book, pain, humiliation and cruelty have been so completely internalised by the narrator that there is in a real sense nothing left in the social world, no foible or vice, for him to forgive. We are no longer in Axel's Castle, if we ever were, but in Bluebeard's – with treasures, crowbars and corpses as the unavoidable background to our last moral exertions. It is in this shadow-world of pure loss that the narrator's strange benediction, and strange last sense of human community, make their most poignant sense.

VI

Sex

Les pertes nocturnes d'un poète ne devraient être que des voies lactées, et la mienne n'est qu'une vilaine tache
MALLARMÉ TO HENRI CAZALIS, 30 October 1864

The night emissions of a poet should be nothing but milky ways, and mine is nothing but a nasty patch

Desire has its indirections, as everyone knows. If I ask for a round-trip airline ticket to Nassau, I may also be expressing a wish not to be abandoned in a Dortmund railway siding. If I insist upon a quiet evening at home, this may be my roundabout way of goading my partner into proposing what I really want: a wild evening on the town. But desire can be very direct too. If I say 'I want a glass of water', I may well mean something precise and straightforward about the current state of my appetites. Water, and water only, is what I want. Coffee will not do, and neither will champagne, or gripe water, or soda water, or aqua vitae, or the milk of human kindness. In all such cases, whether sly or plain-spoken, my wishes would be poorly characterised by anyone who said of me 'he desires' or 'he requires' or 'wishfulness has descended upon him'. Beneath the present promptings of my organism, a continuous pleasure-seeking tide may run, and I may, becoming conscious of this, begin to feel that every one of my wishes in some sense resembles every other, but it is still important to me that the objects of my desire remain separable and particular. It would diminish the dignity of my wish for water to present it as the symptom of a universal thirst. I do not want my Bahamas travel project, with its tincture of Dortmund-avoidance, to dissolve into a vapid and undiscriminating wanderlust.

When Proust writes about sex, and he often does, he plays dangerous games in the border territories between the very particular and the very general. Sexual desire in *A la recherche du temps perdu* is highly localised, but it is also the abyss into which all other forms of desire threaten to sink. During the nocturnal reverie upon which the novel opens, the narrator encounters in a rapid associative sequence many of the desirable objects and activities upon which his attention is later to dwell: travel, reading, social advancement, personal and historical remembrance, the countryside and the artistic life. He opens a benign Pandora's box, and out spills a throng of separate pleasures. But this passage, which is grandly optimistic in so many ways, also contains its own retelling of the Fall:

Quelquefois, comme Ève naquit d'une côte d'Adam, une femme naissait pendant mon sommeil d'une fausse position de ma cuisse. Formée du plaisir que j'étais sur le point de goûter, je m'imaginais que c'était elle qui me l'offrait. Mon corps qui sentait dans le sien ma propre chaleur voulait s'y rejoindre, je m'éveillais. Le reste des humains m'apparaissait comme bien lointain auprès de cette femme que j'avais quittée il y avait quelques moments à peine; ma joue était chaude encore de son baiser, mon corps courbaturé par le poids de sa taille. Si, comme il arrivait quelquefois, elle avait les traits d'une femme que j'avais connue dans la vie, j'allais me donner tout entier à ce but: la retrouver, comme ceux qui partent en voyage pour voir de leurs yeux une cité

désirée et s'imaginent qu'on peut goûter dans une réalité le
charme du songe.   (I, 4–5)

Sometimes, too, as Eve was created from a rib of Adam, a
woman would be born during my sleep from some misplac-
ing of my thigh. Conceived from the pleasure I was on the
point of enjoying, she it was, I imagined, who offered me
that pleasure. My body, conscious that its own warmth was
permeating hers, would strive to become one with her, and
I would awake. The rest of humanity seemed very remote
in comparison with this woman whose company I had left
but a moment ago; my cheek was still warm from her kiss,
my body ached beneath the weight of hers. If, as would
sometimes happen, she had the features of some woman I
had known in waking hours, I would abandon myself
altogether to this end: to find her again, like people who
set out on a journey to see with their eyes some city of their
desire, and imagine that one can taste in reality what has
charmed one's fancy.   (I, 3)

Sexual energy, which was on the point of producing a nocturnal
emission, produces instead a long-drawn-out chain reaction. A
fully formed fantasy woman emerges from the excitation of the
narrator's nervous system, and this insubstantial Eve thereupon
not only becomes weighty but leaves real traces on his body.
The woman is a mental cause which triggers thermal and ortho-
paedic effects. These in their turn create an altered mental
state, in which a lifetime love-quest is sketched. From the
threshold of an orgasm that did not occur, there extends an
interminable desiring itinerary, which draws into itself, as of
right, the lesser journeys of the traveller or the tourist. The
huge exploratory programme of the novel as announced in
these opening pages seems to exist under the sign of an ever-
vigilant and opportunistic Eros. Other than sexual interests are
of course allowed, but one of the things that makes Proust's
account of sex so compelling is precisely that sexual appetite
is subject to displacement and endlessly transferable into other

areas of human thought and behaviour. Eros is within touching distance of everything else that the book contains. It is the base camp to which all upwardly striving spiritual and artistic adventurers regularly return, and the *quod erat demonstrandum* of all intellectual exertion.

One way of preventing the novel from seeming unseemly and monstrous in the attention it pays to sexual matters is to think of the plot itself as a regulatory device. It cannot be 'about' sex all through, or unduly lubricious in its account of, shall we say, music, religion or yachting, because it tells the story of an individual whose sexuality only gradually declares itself and only latterly goes out of control. From a childhood and adolescence in which he had had a range of concerns and pastimes, he advances, in the episodes recounted in *Sodome et Gomorrhe* and *La Prisonnière*, to an adulthood marked by obsessional jealousy and perpetual unhappy arousal. Like Swann before him, he discovers a world in which desire has no outer boundary. Sequestered with Albertine, he inhabits a saturated sexual space in which the cries of street-traders and the diurnal motions of the sun speak of one thing only. The situation had not always been thus in the narrative of his life, and is not to be thus during the multiple denouements of *Le Temps retrouvé*, but the novel contains central scenes where Eros reigns alone and uncontested. With occasional moments of respite these scenes depict the narrator at the lowest point of his fortunes as a desire-driven agent, and lead him, at the end of a long ordeal, to the path of salvation.

There is powerful evidence for this developmental view of sex in Proust's work. The exuberant erotic set pieces with which *La Prisonnière* is interspersed, and which do not have their exact equivalent elsewhere, certainly suggest that a crisis point has been reached in the narrator's self-awareness. In this extravaganza on the pleasures of ice cream, for example, are to be found ingenuities of mouth and tongue undreamed of by mainstream pornographers, and an impending extreme disorder in the relationship between lovers:

«Mon Dieu, à l'hôtel Ritz je crains bien que vous ne trouviez des colonnes Vendôme de glace, de glace au chocolat, ou à la framboise, et alors il en faut plusieurs pour que cela ait l'air de colonnes votives ou de pylônes élevés dans une allée à la gloire de la Fraîcheur. Il font aussi des obélisques de framboise qui se dresseront de place en place dans le désert brûlant de ma soif et dont je ferai fondre le granit rose au fond de ma gorge qu'ils désaltéreront mieux que des oasis (et ici le rire profond éclata, soit de satisfaction de si bien parler, soit par moquerie d'elle-même de s'exprimer par images si suivies, soit, hélas! par volupté physique de sentir en elle quelque chose de si bon, de si frais, qui lui causait l'équivalent d'une jouissance). Ces pics de glace du Ritz ont quelquefois l'air du mont Rose [. . .] De même, au pied de ma demi-glace jaunâtre au citron, je vois très bien des postillons, des voyageurs, des chaises de poste sur lesquels ma langue se charge de faire rouler de glaciales avalanches qui les engloutiront (la volupté cruelle avec laquelle elle dit cela excita ma jalousie); de même, ajouta-t-elle, que je me charge avec mes lèvres de détruire, pilier par pilier, ces églises vénitiennes d'un porphyre qui est de la fraise et de faire tomber sur les fidèles ce que j'aurai épargné. Oui, tous ces monuments passeront de leur place de pierre dans ma poitrine où leur fraîcheur fondante palpite déjà.»

(III, 636–7)

'Oh dear, at the Ritz I'm afraid you'll find Vendôme Columns of ice, chocolate ice or raspberry, and then you'll need a lot of them so that they may look like votive pillars or pylons erected along an avenue to the glory of Coolness. They make raspberry obelisks too, which will rise up here and there in the burning desert of my thirst, and I shall make their pink granite crumble and melt deep down in my throat which they will refresh better than any oasis' (and here the deep laugh broke out, whether from satisfaction at talking so well, or in self-mockery for using such carefully contrived images, or, alas, from physical pleasure at feeling inside herself something so good, so cool, which was tantamount to a sexual pleasure). 'Those mountains of ice at the Ritz sometimes suggest Monte Rosa [. . .] In the same way, at the foot of my yellowish lemon ice, I can see quite clearly postillions, travellers, post-chaises over which my tongue sets to work to roll down freezing avalanches that will swallow them up' (the cruel delight with which she said this excited my jealousy); 'just as,' she went on, 'I set my lips to work to destroy, pillar by pillar, those Venetian churches of a porphyry that is made with strawberries, and send what's left over crashing down upon the worshippers. Yes, all those monuments will pass from their stony state into my inside which thrills already with their melting coolness.'

(V, 140–41)

The narrator is touched to find that Albertine's conversation has become so image-laden and 'writerly', and looks on in helpless wonderment as his literary apprentice acquires her own powers of verbal sorcery. In Albertine's imagery, the penis travels beyond mere temporary erection to re-emerge as an edifice, a public monument. And its charisma is such that in its tumescent state it throws bridges between the worlds of industry, art and nature. What had been a pylon just before is transformed into an obelisk and a pink-headed Alpine mass. But although the passage dwells upon the delights of 'eating' in its specialised erotic sense, the penis and its icy surrogates have become too delectable for comfort: all this sweet-toothed licking, sucking and friction against the palate causes each proud emblem of potency to melt away into nothing at all.

The dark comedy of these jocular pages is to be found in the dialogue between Albertine, who has become a man-eater in the manner of her near-contemporaries Salome and Lulu, and the helpless narrator, whose silent interventions speak of pleasures he cannot share. Here is a contest between two huge appetites, neither of which is prepared to suspend its own demands in order to gratify the other. This is sexual desire in its militant and absolutist mood – conceding nothing, reciprocating nothing, and taking prisoners only in order to destroy them slowly. Albertine's consuming passion is the distorting mirror in which the narrator sees his own will to contain and control her. Her fabulous landscape, colonnaded with ice-creams, recreates in a parodic vein the narrator's wish to have and to hold his partner as the instrument of his own pleasure, and to swallow her voluptuously.

Yet it would be quite misleading to say that Proust makes his reader wait through long periods of tantalising deferral before finally ushering him or her towards such scenes of rapturous excitement. A moderately guileful pornographer might do this, but Proust does not. Sex in a precariously sublimated form is present in his book from the start, and long moments of *jouissance*, recklessly exceeding the requirements of the plot, are staged and savoured throughout. For Proust's narrator, sexual delight is a gloriously adventitious thing, and the best way of procuring it seems often to involve not trying too hard or being in search of something else. Besides, one does not have to have sex in order to have sexual experiences. Walking in the countryside, playing in the Champs-Elysées, listening to music or taking a liquescent morsel of cake into one's mouth, can stir the pleasure reflexes of the human creature in altogether unpredictable ways, and produce rapture.

Swann's first encounter with Vinteuil's 'little phrase', early in 'Un Amour de Swann', is one such episode in an extended series that all seem to be based upon a single template:

Peut-être est-ce parce qu'il ne savait pas la musique qu'il avait pu éprouver une impression aussi confuse, une de ces impressions qui sont peut-être pourtant les seules purement musicales, inétendues, entièrement originales, irréductibles à tout autre ordre d'impressions. Une impression de ce genre, pendant un instant, est pour ainsi dire *sine materia*. Sans doute les notes que nous entendons alors, tendent déjà, selon leur hauteur et leur quantité, à couvrir devant nos yeux des surfaces de dimensions variées, à tracer des arabesques, à nous donner des sensations de largeur, de ténuité, de stabilité, de caprice. Mais les notes sont évanouies avant que ces sensations soient assez formées en nous pour ne pas être submergées par celles qu'éveillent déjà les notes suivantes ou même simultanées. Et cette impression continuerait à envelopper de sa liquidité et de son «fondu» les motifs qui par instants en émergent, à peine discernables, pour plonger aussitôt et disparaître, connus seulement par le plaisir particulier qu'ils donnent, impossibles à décrire, à se rappeler, à nommer, ineffables – si la mémoire, comme un ouvrier qui travaille à établir des fondations durables au milieu des flots, en fabriquant pour nous des fac-similés de ces phrases fugitives, ne nous permettait de les comparer à celles qui leur succèdent et de les différencier.   (I, 206)

Perhaps it was owing to his ignorance of music that he had received so confused an impression, one of those that are none the less the only purely musical impressions, limited in their extent, entirely original, and irreducible to any other kind. An impression of this order, vanishing in an instant, is, so to speak, *sine materia*. Doubtless the notes which we hear at such moments tend, according to their pitch and volume, to spread out before our eyes over surfaces of varying dimensions, to trace arabesques, to give us the sensation of breadth or tenuity, stability or caprice. But the notes themselves have vanished before these sensations have developed sufficiently to escape submersion under those which the succeeding or even simultaneous notes have already begun to awake in us. And this impression would continue to envelop in its liquidity, its ceaseless overlapping, the motifs which from time to time emerge, barely discernible, to plunge again and disappear and drown, recognised only by the particular kind of pleasure which they instil, impossible to describe, to recollect, to name, ineffable – did not our memory, like a labourer who toils at the laying down of firm foundations beneath the tumult of the waves, by fashioning for us facsimiles of those fugitive phrases, enable us to compare and to contrast them with those that follow. (I, 250–51)

There is something very general indeed in this paragraph, which repeatedly calls attention to the moment of pleasure as inveterately particular. Desire belongs to everyone, and finds its opportunities everywhere. When it is not blocked or diverted, it moves in trance-like progression from its first stirrings towards its 'ineffable' outcome, and beyond into an afterlife of quietened but still intense sensation. Musical structure has become a modelling device for the structure of desire itself. Proust's procession of crossover words – *arabesque*, *largeur*, *ténuité*, *stabilité*, *caprice* and many others – allow us to move back and forth between the acoustic and the properly sexual frames of reference that organise his text. Desire as it pursues and achieves satisfaction, and gradually descends from that summit towards its own rebirth as desire, has a familiar contour to it, and Proust figures and refigures this in terms that emphasise the generalisable properties of private experiences. From the nameable to the unnameable, from structure to flux, from difference to sameness and seamlessness, the everyday course of human passion runs. And this pattern has, as its most expressive shorthand form, as its very formula, the passage from the solid to the liquid state. The 'liquidity, [the] ceaseless overlapping' into which precise musical motifs dissolve in the mind of the listening Swann is already present in the madeleine episode earlier in *Du côté de chez Swann* (I, 44; I, 51), and is to reappear much later, as we have just seen, as the fate of Albertine's pylons and obelisks. The narrator's first description of involuntary memory culminates upon a droplet (I, 46; I, 54), a liquid confined within an exact shape and about to dissolve into a delicious flow.

These versatile images allow Proust to linger in pleasurable indecision between sex, cognition and artistic experience. On the one hand they bring a reminder of specifically sexual secretions into the study, the laboratory or the recital room: love, like the rain and the mighty ocean itself, makes things wet. On the other hand, however often the writer, the scientist or the musician is reminded of his or her intimate fluids, he or she still occupies other worlds where articulateness is prized and untimely liquefaction frowned upon. Success in the arts of the mind is a matter of keeping things dry. It is impossible to say, in cases like these, in which bodily and intellectual rapture have been so consistently interfused, whether the sexual drive has been sublimated into something else or whether some 'higher' mental function has been reconnected to an inextinguishable underlayer of libidinal feeling. Proust's prose treads a tightrope between the two ways of thinking. Careful, differentiating analytic work may have joy as one of its by-products; the workman who struggles to lay his foundations among the waves may at any moment abandon himself and his project to the molten movement of the waters. To the proposition that the human quest for knowledge is sexual curiosity under another name Proust's narrator is willing to assent, but only on condition that the sexual body, with its aches, tensions and fluidic motions, is accorded high cognitive status. The narrator can and must have it both ways.

There is no clearer indication of this complementarity between sexual and other forms of awareness than in Proust's writing about sex itself, where description of the plain corporeal facts often shelves away into a disinterested and depersonalised mental dynamics. The mind, sexually energised, is worth studying because it tells us important things about how the real world is. 'Knowing' someone, in its biblical sense, is part of a much broader knowledge-seeking campaign. In this passage from *A l'ombre des jeunes filles en fleurs*, the narrator describes Albertine lying in bed, seemingly inviting him into their first sexual embrace:

La vue du cou nu d'Albertine, de ces joues trop roses, m'avait jeté dans une telle ivresse (c'est-à-dire avait tellement mis pour moi la réalité du monde non plus dans la nature, mais dans le torrent des sensations que j'avais peine à contenir) que cette vue avait rompu l'équilibre entre la vie immense, indestructible qui roulait dans mon être et la vie de l'univers, si chétive en comparaison. La mer, que j'apercevais à côté de la vallée dans la fenêtre, les seins bombés des premières falaises de Maineville, le ciel où la lune n'était pas encore montée au zénith, tout cela semblait plus léger à porter que des plumes pour les globes de mes prunelles qu'entre mes paupières je sentais dilatés, résistants, prêts à soulever bien d'autres fardeaux, toutes les montagnes du monde, sur leur surface délicate. Leur orbe ne se trouvait plus suffisamment rempli par la sphère même de l'horizon. Et tout ce que la nature eût pu m'apporter de vie m'eût semblé bien mince, les souffles de la mer m'eussent paru bien courts pour l'immense aspiration qui soulevait ma poitrine. Je me penchai vers Albertine pour l'embrasser. La mort eût dû me frapper en ce moment que cela m'eût paru indifférent ou plutôt impossible, car la vie n'était pas hors de moi, elle était en moi; j'aurais souri de pitié si un philosophe eût émis l'idée qu'un jour, même éloigné, j'aurais à mourir, que les forces éternelles de la nature me survivraient, les forces de cette nature sous les pieds divins de qui je

n'étais qu'un grain de poussière; qu'après moi il y aurait
encore ces falaises arrondies et bombées, cette mer, ce clair
de lune, ce ciel!   (II, 285–6)

The sight of Albertine's bare throat, of those flushed cheeks,
had so intoxicated me (that is to say had so shifted the
reality of the world for me away from nature into the torrent
of my sensations which I could scarcely contain), that it
had destroyed the equilibrium between the immense and
indestructible life which circulated in my being and the life
of the universe, so puny in comparison. The sea, which was
visible through the window as well as the valley, the swelling
breasts of the first of the Maineville cliffs, the sky in which
the moon had not yet climbed to the zenith – all this seemed
less than a feather-weight on my eyeballs, which between
their lids I could feel dilated, resistant, ready to bear far
greater burdens, all the mountains of the world, upon their
fragile surface. Their orb no longer found even the sphere
of the horizon adequate to fill it. And all the life-giving
energy that nature could have brought me would have
seemed to me all too meagre, the breathing of the sea all
too short to express the immense aspiration that was swelling
my breast. I bent over Albertine to kiss her. Death might
have struck me down in that moment and it would have
seemed to me a trivial, or rather an impossible thing, for
life was not outside me but in me; I should have smiled
pityingly had a philosopher then expressed the idea that
some day, even some distant day, I should have to die, that
the eternal forces of nature would survive me, the forces of
that nature beneath whose godlike feet I was no more than
a grain of dust; that, after me, there would still remain those
rounded, swelling cliffs, that sea, that moonlight and that
sky!   (II, 592–3)

Albertine's breasts are nowhere named here but their shape is
rediscovered in the cliffs, the moon, the wide horizon of the
sea and the ball of the narrator's inquisitively distended eye.
With her insistent pink flush rising to meet the narrator's gaze,
she is already a delectable and comestible Monte Rosa. Sexual

arousal, and the imminence of a promised pleasure, combine to produce a heady sense of omnipotence: the deepest secrets of the natural world are already within the narrator's grasp; knowledge of them beats with his pulses.

This is not, however, the story of a successful quest or of promises being kept. Albertine refuses the advances of the all-seeing narrator. He has misread her signs, or she has changed her mind at the last moment, but in either event she is not available to his touch, taste or smell, and the anticipated moment of perfect knowing vanishes from his mental field. Yet there is promise of another kind in Proust's moving geometry of globes, orbs and spheres. When the mind has found respite from its sexual hunger, and begun to look coldly upon the delusions and wishful fantasies that Eros calls into being, it will perhaps be able to make its own processes, its own obstinate powers of trickery and misconstrual, into proper objects of scientific study. Getting things wrong, being deluded, refusing to see the error of one's mental ways, will become a curriculum in its own right and as readily organisable into a coherent picture of the world as the curves and swellings that now echo each other across physical space. Let misreading have its map, and the sighing lover's unrepentant overvaluation of his love-object its geometry and its optics. And let the intellectual curiosity which seeks to travel beyond desire, and from some distant vantage point to inspect its mistakes and misdemeanours, have desire still palpably running through it.

'The sexual' seems often, then, to be the enveloping category of categories in Proust's novel, and to have a limitless range and warrant when it comes to explaining the order of things. Two further features of the work should be mentioned at this point, as seeming to confirm what might be called the 'pansexualist' hypothesis about its meanings. The first concerns a quality of Proust's writing – its erotic energy and guile – and the second a quality of the novel's 'coverage' – its inclusiveness, its tolerant marshalling of divergent sexual types into an endless fictional parade.

The seductive powers of language are often discussed by the narrator and by other characters in the work. Single words may hover in the air, ripe with suggestion, as when Albertine says of a fellow member of the 'little band': 'Oui . . . elle a l'air d'une petite mousmé' (II, 652; III, 412). *Mousmé*, meaning 'girl' or 'young woman', which had recently been imported into France by Pierre Loti in his novel *Madame Chrysanthème* (1887), is a borrowing from Japanese and brings an exotic micro-climate with it. The narrator, who would in principle disapprove of such faddishness, is prepared to change his plans for the evening in order to savour fully, as a lexicographer might, the peculiar structure of this complex word: when used by Albertine it connotes not simply the Orient but the tantalising cross-currents of homo-erotic feeling that are in play among Albertine's female friends. A woman looks at another woman, renames her, and is overheard by an excitable male. Later in the novel, Albertine is to provide strenuous philological exercise for her ever-observant partner by smuggling bizarre lexical items into their everyday talk and reanimating his jealousy in the process. But here her *mousmé* is as straightforwardly provoking as her bare neck had been earlier, and leads the couple into love-play of the least complicated sort.

If single words can sting the sexual imagination into activity, how much more artful in their manipulations of desire are entire sentences. Albertine's very pronunciation was carnal; her conversation 'vous couvrait de baisers' (II, 656; 'covered you with kisses' (III, 416)). One of the many worldly lessons that the narrator learns from Charlus is that sex can be injected randomly into social speech, by way of a masquerade that is transparent to all eyes. Towards the end of the epic *soirée* at

La Raspelière, in *Sodome et Gomorrhe*, Mme Verdurin invites Morel to stay overnight:

> — Mais il ne peut pas, répondit M. de Charlus pour le joueur attentif qui n'avait pas entendu. Il n'a que la permission de minuit. Il faut qu'il rentre se coucher, comme un enfant bien obéissant, bien sage, ajouta-t-il d'une voix complaisante, maniérée, insistante, comme s'il trouvait quelque sadique volupté à employer cette chaste comparaison et aussi à appuyer au passage sa voix sur ce qui concernait Morel, à le toucher, à défaut de la main avec des paroles qui semblaient le palper. (III, 355)

> 'No, he can't,' M. de Charlus replied on behalf of the absorbed card-player who had not heard. 'He has a pass until midnight only. He must go back to bed like a good little boy, obedient and well-behaved,' he added in a smug, affected, insistent voice, as though he found a sadistic pleasure in employing this chaste comparison and also in letting his voice dwell, in passing, upon something that concerned Morel, in touching him, if not with his hand, with words that seemed to be tactile. (IV, 422)

The shadow love-play of Charlus, his spoken fondlings and strokings of Morel and countless others, are an object-lesson in bad behaviour and earn him the narrator's stern reprobation. The intrusive voice of any one individual's desire cannot be allowed to unsettle the evenly flirtatious conversation of the group. An elementary contractual arrangement in salon society – 'fair shares for all' – requires that sexual innuendo be kept under control.

Yet there is an element in this code that the narrator in his own monologue refuses to observe. And this willingness on the narrator's part to infringe a rule that elsewhere he claims to support, and indeed seeks to reinforce by way of his ironic withdrawal from other people's lubricities, gives Proust's book one of its monumental internal disproportions. For the purposes of this fiction he has invented a voice that is 'complaisante, maniérée, insistante' ('smug, affected, insistent') to an unprecedented degree, anti-social through and through, and shamelessly obedient to the call of Eros. Good form can go hang. Much of Proust's syntax is of a teasing and caressing kind, and when his narrator speaks of sexual matters out there in society he does so in a language that returns them to a self-delighting inner world of reverie.

Earlier in the scene at La Raspelière the narrator had commented lengthily on the pantomime of disclosure and concealment that homosexual men are obliged to perform in their search for acquiescent partners:

> Mais quand ils voient un autre homme témoigner envers eux d'un goût particulier, alors, soit incompréhension que ce soit le même que le leur, soit fâcheux rappel que ce goût, embelli par eux tant que c'est eux-mêmes qui l'éprouvent, est considéré comme un vice, soit désir de se réhabiliter par un éclat dans une circonstance où cela ne leur coûte pas, soit par une crainte d'être devinés qu'ils retrouvent soudain quand le désir ne les mène plus, les yeux bandés, d'imprudence en imprudence, soit par la fureur de subir du fait de l'attitude équivoque d'un autre le dommage que par la leur, si cet autre leur plaisait, ils ne craindraient pas de lui causer, ceux que cela n'embarrasse pas de suivre un jeune homme pendant des lieues, de ne pas le quitter des yeux au théâtre même s'il est avec des amis, risquant par cela de le brouiller avec eux, on peut les entendre, pour peu qu'un autre qui ne leur plaît pas les regarde, dire: «Monsieur, pour qui me prenez-vous? (simplement parce qu'on les prend pour ce qu'ils sont) je ne vous comprends pas, inutile d'insister, vous faites erreur», aller au besoin jusqu'aux gifles, et devant quelqu'un qui connaît l'imprudent, s'indigner: «Comment, vous connaissez cette horreur? Elle a une façon de vous regarder! ... En voilà des manières!» (III, 311)

But when they see another man display a particular predilection towards them, then, whether because they fail to recognise that it is the same as their own, or because it is a painful reminder that this predilection, exalted by them as long as it is they themselves who feel it, is regarded as a vice, or from a desire to rehabilitate themselves by making a scene in circumstances in which it costs them nothing, or from a fear of being unmasked which suddenly overtakes them when desire no longer leads them blindfold from one imprudence to another, or from rage at being subjected, by the equivocal attitude of another person, to the injury which by their own attitude, if that other person attracted them, they would not hesitate to inflict on him, men who do not in the least mind following a young man for miles, never taking their eyes off him in the theatre even if he is with friends, thereby threatening to compromise him with them, may be heard to say, if a man who does not attract them merely looks at them, 'Monsieur, what do you take me for,' (simply because he takes them for what they are) 'I don't understand you, no, don't attempt to explain, you are quite mistaken,' may proceed at a pinch from words to blows, and, to a person who knows the imprudent stranger, wax indignant: 'What, you know this loathsome creature? The way he looks at one! . . . A fine way to behave!'

(IV, 367–8)

In single sentences built on this model, the propositional structure of the main utterance is almost smothered by subordinate material rushing forward to its aid. 'Mais . . . ceux que cela n'embarrasse pas . . . on peut les entendre . . . dire' ('But . . . men who do not in the least mind . . . may be heard to say') is the 'main' proposition, but devices of amplification are used so intensively in the build-up to this anodyne remark that much of its force has been pre-empted by the time its moment of completion arrives. The clauses beginning 'soit' are brazen queue-jumpers, and their copious display of alternative sexual motives and dilemmas in a sense tells the whole story before the sentence has developed anything resembling narrative thrust. The weakened proposition is then reinforced, but also outstripped, by the fragments of direct speech on which the sentence closes. From a list of abstract moral and psychological formulae we move to a playlet illustrating certain of these. We pass from abstraction to dramatic enactment by way of an almost characterless claim whose task, syntactically speaking, is to hold the whole thing together but whose contribution at the level of sense is easily lost in a clamour of other, subtler, voices. Meaning is destabilised by the syntactic pattern. It crystallises suddenly in this corner or that of a variegated open field, and may as suddenly dissolve again as new elements in the verbal texture rise to prominence. 'This is what it feels like to be a gay man pursuing sexual pleasure in a maze of untrustworthy signs', the sentence in its feverish motion seems to say. But inside this dynamic portrait of a specifically homosexual social scene, Proust's risk-filled syntax has another drama to enact. This is everyone's desire in perpetual displacement. This is how desire is.

What is so surprising about Proust's meditations on the sexual imperative in human conduct is their patient expansiveness, their willingness to take as much time as they need, and more. Eager attention and finely calibrated long sentences are available in limitless supply to create a contour-map of sexual feeling. Sometimes the pulses of his actors race, and sometimes they go sluggish. The sentences themselves may dramatise moral enquiries at one moment and tell bawdy tales the next. But the two activities and their countless hybrid forms have a common topography. The loss and the precarious restoration of meaning in sentences is Eros become visible. The hide-and-seek games that Proust's sentences play not only pay their imitative tribute to the feints, detours and side-glances that mark all sexual pursuit but offer themselves as a model for all speculation, all mental efforts to make headway, in a resistant medium, towards a desired goal.

There is a sentence-type in Proust akin to the 'long contending, victoriously intricate sentence' that Walter Pater describes in his essay on 'Style'. A simple rule governs its passage through syntactic intricacy: it must end well. The completion of the sentence-pattern must coincide with the announcement of good news, or the recapture of good sense, and will often seem to confirm that the news or the sense is indeed good, if the wayside distractions that the sentence offers have left the reader in any doubt. This example from the elegiac Bois de Boulogne episode on which *Du côté de chez Swann* closes gives us the structure in a convenient schematic form:

> Dans les endroits où les arbres gardaient encore leurs feuilles, ils semblaient subir une altération de leur matière à partir du point où ils étaient touchés par la lumière du soleil, presque horizontale le matin comme elle le redeviendrait quelques heures plus tard au moment où dans le crépuscule commençant, elle s'allume comme une lampe, projette à distance sur le feuillage un reflet artificiel et chaud, et fait flamber les suprêmes feuilles d'un arbre qui reste le candélabre incombustible et terne de son faîte incendié.   (I, 415)

> In the places where the trees still kept their leaves, they seemed to have undergone an alteration of their substance from the point at which they were touched by the sun's light, still, at this hour of the morning, almost horizontal, as it would be again, a few hours later, at the moment when in the gathering dusk it flames up like a lamp, projects afar over the leaves a warm and artificial glow, and sets ablaze the few topmost boughs of a tree that itself remains unchanged, a sombre incombustible candelabrum beneath its flaming crest.   (I, 507–8)

Through the travail of the syntax the writer's path leads him towards an ecstatic illumination at the moment of propositional closure. Radiance, already twice announced earlier in the sentence, achieves its definitive intensity at the end. Rough drafts and embellishments are cast aside, finally, just as the low sun, while touching the tops of the branches with light, consigns their stems to darkness. Sensuous, pleasure-seeking attention drives confidently towards its reward.

Yet this pattern, which is one of Proust's most conspicuous stylistic fingerprints, is available for many uses. The lesser ecstasies of the moral theorist or the social observer may be poured into the same mould. In the final pages of *Le Côté de Guermantes*, paying one of his periodic tributes to Charlus's virtuosity as a conversationalist, the narrator singles out a new quality of his talk. It offers a digest of social manners, a compacted portrait of *mondanité* in action:

> Parlant en artiste, il pouvait tout au plus dégager le charme fallacieux des gens du monde. Mais le dégager pour les artistes seulement, à l'égard desquels il eût pu jouer le rôle du renne envers les Esquimaux; ce précieux animal arrache pour eux, sur des roches désertiques, des lichens, des mousses qu'ils ne sauraient ni découvrir, ni utiliser, mais qui, une fois digérés par le renne, deviennent pour les habitants de l'extrême Nord un aliment assimilable.   (II, 856)

> Speaking as an artist, he could at the most bring out the deceptive charm of society people – but for artists only, in relation to whom he might be said to play the part played by the reindeer among the Eskimos: this precious animal plucks for them from the barren rocks lichens and mosses which they themselves could neither discover nor utilise, but which, once they have been digested by the reindeer, become for the inhabitants of the far North, an assimilable form of food.   (III, 656)

Charlus is not simply a hungry antlered ungulate wandering through the wastes of the Boulevard Saint-Germain, but a complex transformational device given animal form. The sentence homes in upon a single property common to the baron and the beast and edges it into the familiar final position. The epiphany is perfectly timed, but farcical, at least in the short term. It is only much later in the book that the full symmetry between Charlus and the ruminative reindeer is to be revealed: the devourer of social fodder is himself to be devoured by a voracious artist who, unlike Charlus, writes.

Whereas in sentences of this kind desire is directed towards a goal, and victorious in the face of delay and complication, others are of course more radically dispersed and fail to achieve, and seem often to desire to fail to achieve, a perfect final cadence. Alongside his stories of desire satiated, and moments of understanding seized and recorded, Proust tells of the disorganising demons that run through human discourse. In *La Prisonnière* and *Albertine disparue* in particular even the successful, well-made sentences have an overarching propensity for failure. Desire is endlessly reborn from its temporary resting-places. Jealousy and envy know no rest. But success and failure are both eroticised. 'Notre moindre désir bien qu'unique comme un accord, admet en lui les notes fondamentales sur lesquelles toute notre vie est construite' (IV, 206; 'Our slightest desire, though unique as a chord, nevertheless includes the fundamental notes on which the whole of our life is built' (V, 719)), the narrator announces in *Albertine disparue*, and Proust himself adheres to this watchword. The syntactic patterning of his book connects short-lived local wishes to the imposing invariant structures of human feeling, and brings a quality that one might call desirousness – desire stripped of its objects – into prominence in all manner of seemingly non-sexual scenarios. The sentences last as long as they do, sub-divide and reassemble themselves as intricately as they do, because they have this generalising task to perform. Wherever desire is to be found it is in an important sense, for Proust, the same desire, and must sound so. Beyond the unique pang or prickling of individual experience, in which precisely this pleasure and none other is being pursued, the larger music of human wishes must be audible. Eros belongs to everyone, and becoming aware of this is a fortunate Fall for the creative writer.

Even more remarkable than the erotic texture of Proust's writing, and more disturbing to the liberal sensibilities of the present day, is the plasticity of the narrator's sexual appetite. In person or under an alias, his desire goes everywhere. In part, the programme of sexual research that he sketches for himself is benign and emancipatory. Practices that are often stigmatised as deviant or perverse re-emerge in *A la recherche du temps perdu* as instructive curiosities or as sources of astonishment. That there should be such a variety of sexual preferences in the human world enchants the narrator rather as the apparently limitless range of beetle species enchanted Darwin. And when an organising taxonomic eye is trained upon these preferences the three great classes into which they fall – heterosexual, homosexual and bisexual – produce another thrilling scientific result: people in all three classes, for all their differences of 'object-choice', seem to desire in much the same way. The narrator talks often about homosexuality as a vice, and real guilt and shame can be heard echoing in his language at these points, but in between such comments he imaginatively reinvents the straightforwardness of non-straight sex. Gay men and lesbians are often obliged to be more guarded in their search for sexual outlet than their heterosexual counterparts, but for Proust, as we have seen, the underlying dynamic of desire is identical in both groups. Coming out as a homosexual is a matter of repositioning oneself inside a desire-world from which there is no exit. Envy, suspicion, rivalry, nostalgia, greed, egotism . . . these are the elements which, in varying combinations, give any sexual life whatsoever its characteristic grain and coloration. The worst that can be said of Charlus and Morel, or Mademoiselle Vinteuil and her friend, is that they behave like everyone else. When their behaviour begins to acquire a sado-masochistic edge, this simply enlarges the narrator's sense of sexual possibility. The perversions themselves are surprising and fascinating because they open his eyes still wider to a world of human desire that is all one yet unstemmably various.

The area in which Proust's account of sexual curiosity is likely to produce the most acute feelings of unease in his modern readers involves the exploitation of children. Although the later 'Albertine' episodes of the book primarily portray a sexual monomania, they have an insistent pluralising descant too. Desire is morbidly concentrated upon a single person, and has the single 'rational' objective of studying her every movement, motive and mood, but beyond the sequestered couple runs an oceanic surge of alternative sexual partners. The narrator's capacious obsession with Albertine has room within it for a scurrying population of lesser game animals. Laundry-girls, dairy-girls, delivery-girls from the local fruiterer or baker, pass by in an animated frieze, and it would be tempting, the narrator observes, to pluck one of them from the throng as 'ornithologists or ichthyologists' might in their attempt to bring order into the proliferation of species (III, 645; V, 151).

When the narrator visits Venice after Albertine's death to find forgetfulness, he finds instead a city offering innumerable incitements to memory. Venice is copious, as Paris had been, but self-consciously so, and in the manner of a historical pageant: it calls upon its great artists to celebrate its diversity, and gears its tourist trade to the artful display of its component races, trades and professions. Reminders of Albertine are everywhere, but so too are the multifarious junior members of the urban working classes: 'les allumettières, les enfileuses de perles, les travailleuses du verre ou de la dentelle, les petites ouvrières aux grands châles noirs à franges que rien n'empêchait d'aimer' (IV, 205; 'match-sellers, pearl-stringers, glass or lace makers, young seamstresses in black shawls with long fringes, whom there was nothing to prevent me from loving' (V, 719)). In fantasy, at least, the narrator embraces this titillating community of child workers as eagerly as he explores the back-streets, the alleys and the remoter canals of the city itself. He says of young Venetian girls what Ovid's narrator in the *Amores* had said of their Roman counterparts:

> Denique quas tota quisquam probet urbe puellas,
> noster in has omnis ambitiosus amor   (II, iv)

> In short, there's a vast cross-section of desirable beauties in the city – *and I want them all!*

Venice has of course for many centuries been one of the European capitals of desire, and prostitution, including child prostitution, has been a main element of its appeal to travellers and tourists. In rediscovering the *mille e tre* objects of his own desire in Venice of all propitious places, the narrator is furnishing his fantasies with a historical dimension and re-emerging from his amorous miseries as a predatory libertine in the grand manner. Unlike Don Giovanni and Casanova, however, he travels with a chaperone – his mother.

Even during the final *matinée* of the novel, a version of this fantasy persists. When Gilberte offers to arrange intimate social gatherings on the narrator's behalf, he responds with a suggestion of his own:

> je lui dis qu'elle me ferait toujours plaisir en m'invitant avec de très jeunes filles, pauvres s'il était possible, pour qu'avec de petits cadeaux je puisse leur faire plaisir, sans leur rien demander d'ailleurs que de faire renaître en moi les rêveries,

les tristesses d'autrefois, peut-être, un jour improbable, un
chaste baiser.   (IV, 566)

I said merely, in answer to her offer, that I should always
enjoy being invited to meet young girls, poor girls if possible,
to whom I could give pleasure by quite small gifts, without
expecting anything of them in return except that they should
serve to renew within me the dreams and the sadnesses of
my youth and perhaps, one improbable day, a single chaste
kiss.   (VI, 373)

Later, returning to this wish, he speaks of 'de très jeunes
jeunes filles' (IV, 605; 'young girls' (VI, 425)). What gives this
paedophilic strain in the later volumes of the novel its particular
power of provocation, however, is not so much the slow delectation with which the narrator's attention spreads across the
multitude of Parisian or Venetian girls as the concentration of
his gaze upon certain of them. In passages which discover the
enticements of Lolita long before *Lolita* (1955), the narrator
presents himself as an innocent among innocents, seeking consolation in the company of children for a lost love that had
always had its childishness:

Devant la porte d'Albertine, je trouvai une petite fille pauvre
qui me regardait avec de grands yeux et qui avait l'air si
bon que je lui demandai si elle ne voulait pas venir chez
moi, comme j'eusse fait d'un chien au regard fidèle. Elle en
eut l'air content. À la maison je la berçai quelque temps sur
mes genoux, mais bientôt sa présence, en me faisant trop
sentir l'absence d'Albertine, me fut insupportable. Et je la
priai de s'en aller, après lui avoir remis un billet de cinq
cents francs. Et pourtant, bientôt après, la pensée d'avoir
quelque autre petite fille près de moi, mais de ne jamais
être seul sans le secours d'une présence innocente fut le
seul rêve qui me permit de supporter l'idée que peut-être
Albertine resterait quelque temps sans revenir. (IV, 15–16)

233

Outside the door of Albertine's house I found a little poor girl who gazed at me with huge eyes and who looked so sweet-natured that I asked her whether she would care to come home with me, as I might have taken home a dog with faithful eyes. She seemed pleased at the suggestion. When I got home, I held her for some time on my knee, but very soon her presence, by making me feel too keenly Albertine's absence, became intolerable. And I asked her to go away, after giving her a five-hundred franc note. And yet, soon afterwards, the thought of having some other little girl in the house with me, of never being alone without the comfort of an innocent presence, was the only thing that enabled me to endure the idea that Albertine might perhaps remain away for some time.   (V, 494)

This episode, from the beginning of *Albertine disparue*, recapitulates an earlier moment in which a dairy-girl had been summoned to run an errand for the narrator, and had in due course been dismissed with five francs as her reward. Between the two episodes the sum has increased a hundredfold, and the offence has become correspondingly graver: the narrator is brought before the police and accused of corrupting a minor. He is presented as naïve and incompetent as he attempts to establish his innocence both in the eyes of his accusers, who are the parents of the girl, and of the police chief, who shares his alleged sexual tastes and advises him to be prudent in his attempts to satisfy them.

These passages have in them an awkward blend of pathos and farce, and seem almost to contain, in an early draft form, their own theory of paedophilia. The narrator, infantilised by his mother and cruelly mistreated by his sexual partner, seeks refuge in the company of what are, in his misperception of the scene, simply compliant fellow children. The adult seducer of children suffers from a nostalgic infatuation with his own lost youth and its innocent love games, or so the narrator's theory seems to run. Could it be that his perverse sexuality is a form of narcissism which uses randomly selected girls – passers-by, members of the anonymous urban crowd – as its momentary mirror? 'Ce que j'aimais c'était la jeunesse' (IV, 207; 'what I loved was youth' (V, 721)), he says at the end of a long development on this theme during the Venice episode, in which adolescent girls figure as a screen behind which the memory of desirable pre-adolescent girls is still alive. 'Elle ressemblait à ma jeunesse', the narrator says of Gilberte's young daughter in *Le Temps retrouvé* (IV, 609; 'she was like my own youth' (VI, 430)).

But the gazing narrator is often much more insistent and less 'theoretical' than this. The sight of the human body detains him. And the body of a real dairy-girl wholly captivates him, where a simulated dairy-girl working in a brothel would not:

> Une fois, j'étais entré commander un fromage chez le cré-
> mier, et au milieu des petites employées j'en avais remarqué
> une, vraie extravagance blonde, haute de taille bien que
> puérile, et qui au milieu des autres porteuses, semblait rêver,
> dans une attitude assez fière. Je ne l'avais vue que de loin,
> et en passant si vite que je n'aurais pu dire comment elle
> était, sinon qu'elle avait dû pousser trop vite et que sa
> tête portait une toison donnant l'impression bien moins des
> particularités capillaires que d'une stylisation sculptuaire des
> méandres isolés de névés parallèles.   (III, 646)

> Once, I had gone to order a cheese at the dairy, and among
> the various young female employees had noticed a startling
> towhead, tall in stature though little more than a child, who
> seemed to be day-dreaming, amid the other errand-girls, in
> a distinctly haughty attitude. I had seen her from a distance
> only, and for so brief an instant that I could not have
> described her appearance, except to say that she must have
> grown too fast and that her head supported a mane that
> gave the impression far less of capillary characteristics than
> of a sculptor's stylised rendering of the separate meanderings

of parallel snowtracks on a mountainside.   (V, 151–2)

Je levai les yeux sur les mèches flavescentes et frisées et je
sentis que leur tourbillon m'emportait, le cœur battant, dans
la lumière et les rafales d'un ouragan de beauté.   (III, 650)

I raised my eyes to those flavescent, frizzy locks and felt
myself caught in their swirl and swept away, with a throbbing
heart, amid the lightning and the blasts of a hurricane of
beauty.   (V, 157)

The full resources of *précieux* diction are brought to bear upon
this casually observed head of hair. The narrator's gaze is
arrested, and its own fixity is transferred to the object on which
it dwells. The hair is monumentalised – first as a sculpture and
then as a glacial expanse opening up among the high hills.
Later, in the second passage, it becomes atmospheric motion
in triplicate – a whirlwind, a squall, a hurricane – but retains
the stillness of a fetish. Not only is the gaze fascinated and
transfixed, but the narrator tricks his description out with
sound-echoes, learned terms and a literary cross-reference: *flavescent* ('becoming yellow'), used by Balzac in *Eugénie Grandet*
(1833), is as rare as the *flave* that it embellishes. Visual enchantment is spiced and spangled by self-conscious literary art. We
are already in the world of Nabokov's erudite sensation-hunter
Humbert Humbert, who caresses his child lover with fancy
words between motel rooms, recreates her in prose poetry
when she has fled, and to the end has an eager ear for 'the
melody of children at play'.

Proust could of course have conducted this whole experiment in transgressive sexual imagining far more prudently. He
could have taken his distance from his narrator in a more
determined fashion, and sheltered him from controversy with
a reassuring play of alibis and excuses. What he in fact does,
on this occasion and others, is move in the opposite direction

entirely. He pinpoints the cruelty of his narrator's desire. The dairy-girl owed her mobility, and her sense of human potentiality, to the narrator's willingness to imagine her in motion. When he withdraws this investment in her, she ceases to be: 'Ce vol capturé, inerte, anéanti, incapable de rien ajouter à sa pauvre évidence, n'avait plus mon imagination pour collaborer avec lui' (III, 650; 'This flyaway caught on the wing, inert, crushed, incapable of adding anything to its own paltry appearance, no longer had my imagination to collaborate with it' (V, 156)). Earlier, unwittingly playing procuress, Françoise had introduced the girl to the narrator as a Little Red Riding Hood (III, 647; V, 153). He now accepts his own allotted place in this tiny drama: within the limits imposed by his reticent conduct towards the girl, he is all wolf.

At this moment in the narrator's fantasy, his victim is not simply toyed with and discarded but obliterated. Beyond the desire to enjoy her, a desire for her destruction runs. And Proust does not consign the voice of this dark passion to quotation marks, as Goethe does with the voice of his child-murdering Erlkönig. He gives it direct to a narrator who has earlier been the vehicle for much benign philosophising, and whose bracingly sceptical views on social man and woman have made him easy to trust. Quotation marks surround everything in the book, of course, in so far as it offers a tranquil retrospective account of emotions and opinions that are ostensibly no longer in force at the time of writing. The narrator reports on follies he has already outgrown. The wisdom of his earlier years always needs updating. Besides, each of the child-haunted passages is superseded, we must remember, by a further extension of the 'Albertine' plot: the narrator rebounds from each dangerous liaison with children into the endless complications of an adult affair or its aftermath.

Yet the purpose of the strange concoction we call 'the

narrator' is to allow the varieties of human passion to speak their name, wisely and unwisely. Erotic experience is thoroughly socialised for long expanses of the narration, and the singularity of individual desire glistens in a web of interpersonal arrangements and negotiations, but Proust knows all about the sullenness and the solitary urgency of desire too, and writes them into his text. Unsociable and anti-social sex fascinates him. Incest, voyeurism, sadism, the profanation of fathers, at Montjouvain (I, 161; II, 194), and of mothers, 'which deserves a chapter to itself' (III, 300; IV, 354) – all such currents are swept into the tidal flow of his sexual curiosity. He wants his book to be full, copious, overbrimming with character and incident, and he wants the manifold voice of desire to sound in it tirelessly. While many of his European contemporaries were constructing topographies of sexual aberration on the model of Krafft-Ebing's celebrated *Psychopathia sexualis* (1886), drawing firm lines of demarcation between the normal and deviant modes of sexual behaviour, and prescribing strong doses of normal sex as if it were a social panacea, Proust considers nothing in the field of human sexuality foreign to him. Monsters are human too, his narrator plausibly urges, and the cruel extremities of desire, together with its waywardness, its dissidence and its long lackadaisical afternoons, must all be moulded into the unstoppable sexual frieze. The humanistic purpose of this project would be thwarted if children were simply removed from the scene and protected from the glare of the predator's gaze. And Proust's 'homo sum . . .' would be incomplete if it held back from desire that said 'Kill!'

'Pansexual Proust' seems an accurate enough designation, therefore, if we look simply at the texture of his writing, and at the polymorphous pleasure-seeking of his narrator. And the whole project can easily seem optimistic if it is described in this way: the depravities of the drawing-room and the murderous energies that may dwell behind the eyes of a mild-mannered literary apprentice are worth collecting and collating because they provide an encouraging sense of abundance in the social world. Eros is not an abyss after all, but a treasure-trove of discriminable sub-species. Time spent classifying them all, and gliding through the welter of them all, is time well spent. Yet although it is possible to describe *A la recherche du temps perdu* as a bacchanal in which lively figurations of desire stretch to the horizon in all directions, and to find evidence for this view on every page, optimism is still not quite the right word for its predominant mood. There is too much disenchantment in it. There are too many long-nourished miseries and farcical mishaps, and too many characters 'wrecked by success', as Freud would have said. Schemes designed to bring sexual satisfaction have an inveterate tendency to go wrong, and Proust is the epic cataloguer of moments when they do.

At the simplest level, Proust extracts a rich vein of comedy from the sheer inopportuneness with which sexual arousal and release may occur. The narrator, who had been poised on the threshold of a nocturnal emission at the very beginning of his tale, offers a quizzical cost-benefit analysis of the same bodily mechanism in *Sodome et Gomorrhe*:

> Les plaisirs qu'on a dans le sommeil, on ne les fait pas figurer dans le compte des plaisirs éprouvés au cours de l'existence. Pour ne faire allusion qu'au plus vulgairement sensuel de tous, qui de nous, au réveil, n'a ressenti quelque agacement d'avoir éprouvé en dormant, un plaisir que si l'on ne veut pas trop se fatiguer, on ne peut plus, une fois éveillé, renouveler indéfiniment ce jour-là. (III, 372)

> We do not include the pleasures we enjoy in sleep in the inventory of the pleasures we have experienced in the course of our existence. To take only the most grossly sensual of them all, which of us, on waking, has not felt a certain

irritation at having experienced in his sleep a pleasure which, if he is anxious not to tire himself, he is not, once he is awake, at liberty to repeat indefinitely during that day.

(IV, 441–2)

In the same 'grossly sensual' vein, he gives a detailed account of unwilled orgasm as it overtakes his youthful self in the company first of Gilberte and then of Albertine. This aspect of the young male's sentimental education had for the most part been discreetly omitted by earlier novelists: it so clearly belongs to a specific phase of psychosexual development that it had no doubt seemed lacking in general import. But for Proust's narrator something more significant than adolescent precocity is clearly at stake. Early in *A l'ombre des jeunes filles en fleurs* he struggles with Gilberte in the Champs-Elysées, seeking to regain possession of the long letter he had recently written to her father:

> Elle la mit dans son dos, je passai mes mains derrière son cou, en soulevant les nattes de cheveux qu'elle portait sur les épaules, soit que ce fût encore de son âge, soit que sa mère voulût la faire paraître plus longtemps enfant, afin de se rajeunir elle-même; nous luttions, arc-boutés. Je tâchais de l'attirer, elle résistait; ses pommettes enflammées par l'effort étaient rouges et rondes comme des cerises; elle riait comme si je l'eusse chatouillée; je la tenais serrée entre mes jambes comme un arbuste après lequel j'aurais voulu grimper; et, au milieu de la gymnastique que je faisais, sans qu'en fût à peine augmenté l'essoufflement que me donnaient l'exercice musculaire et l'ardeur du jeu, je répandis, comme quelques gouttes de sueur arrachées par l'effort, mon plaisir auquel je ne pus pas même m'attarder le temps d'en connaître le goût; aussitôt je pris la lettre. (I, 485)

> She thrust it behind her back; I put my arms round her neck, raising the plaits of hair which she wore over her shoulders, either because she was still of an age for it or

240

because her mother chose to make her look a child for a little longer so as to make herself seem younger; and we wrestled, locked together. I tried to pull her towards me, and she resisted; her cheeks, inflamed by the effort, were as red and round as two cherries; she laughed as though I were tickling her; I held her gripped between my legs like a young tree which I was trying to climb; and, in the middle of my gymnastics, when I was already out of breath with the muscular exercise and the heat of the game, I felt, like a few drops of sweat wrung from me by the effort, my pleasure express itself in a form which I could not even pause for a moment to analyse; immediately I snatched the letter from her. (II, 76)

This is horse-play transformed by the narration into a scene of Ovidian metamorphosis. Everything is on the verge of being something else: the young girl, cherry-ripe in her spirited resistance, becomes a shrub; semen becomes sweat, and the breathless exertions of the gymnast melt into those of the lover. All particulars are lost to a swooning motion of the remembering mind in which the precise moment of pleasure can no longer be localised. It occurs, to be sure, but on the margins of its precipitating cause. Even as young Apollo enjoys his Daphne, she escapes from his embrace. Time itself is askew: before the event can be registered as exceptional, its blossoming has passed. The event has become a memory almost before it has occurred.

The scene is repeated in plainer terms in *Le Côté de Guermantes*, when Albertine accepts the narrator's advances as unaccountably as she had rejected them at an earlier stage, in the episode of their bedtime rendezvous at Balbec:

En tout cas, quelles que fussent les modifications survenues depuis quelque temps dans sa vie (et qui eussent peut-être expliqué qu'elle eût accordé si aisément à mon désir momentané et purement physique ce qu'à Balbec elle avait

241

avec horreur refusé à mon amour) une bien plus étonnante se produisit en Albertine, ce soir-là même, aussitôt que ses caresses eurent amené chez moi la satisfaction dont elle dut bien s'apercevoir et dont j'avais même craint qu'elle ne lui causât le petit mouvement de répulsion et de pudeur offensée que Gilberte avait eu à un moment semblable, derrière le massif des lauriers, aux Champs-Élysées.   (II, 661)

In any case, whatever the modifications that had occurred recently in her life and that might perhaps have explained why it was that she now so readily accorded to my momentary and purely physical desire what at Balbec she had refused with horror to allow to my love, an even more surprising one manifested itself in Albertine that same evening as soon as her caresses had procured in me the satisfaction which she could not fail to notice and which, indeed, I had been afraid might provoke in her the same instinctive movement of revulsion and offended modesty which Gilberte had made at a similar moment behind the laurel shrubbery in the Champs-Elysées.   (III, 422)

Again, the summit of pleasure is reached by what looks like a wrong route or a false trail, and described in syntax that imitates the apartness of the partners in an encounter that is not yet an exchange: the longed-for moment of pleasure occurs twice over, first in brackets and then in a subordinate clause. Sex is a matter of bringing bodies into adjacency. One cannot have it without some such adjustment of matter in physical space, or of body-images in mental space. Sex is not something that the human body does in and for itself. But the amatory style being characterised here, and belonging not just to impatient young people but to sexual agents at large, is one in which couples and coupling do indeed point back to a primordial narcissism, an objectless inward rapture. The paragraph culminates not upon a meeting between persons, but on the memory of an earlier meeting that did not take place: Gilberte, turned to laurel in the laurel-grove, become Elysian in the Champs-Elysées, is not a person but the memory of one. Albertine, even at the moment of settling herself eagerly on to the narrator's bed, is the memory of a memory. A pretext for pleasure. An internal summons to a joy that can best be sought within.

Proust's long-range plotting in this novel is such that the extended scene of love-making towards the beginning of *La Prisonnière* draws much of its force from a studied re-use of images and ideas from these earlier episodes. These pages of seething and exultant erotic reverie are a triumph of linguistic invention and mark a culminating point in the cumulative *ars amatoria* of the West. Proust writes of love as if no other subject existed. His syntax is attuned to the intimate fluctuations of desire, and his metaphors again connect that desire to the tidal movements of the sea, the phases of the moon and the inscrutable world of vegetable growth. The text relives its own past, sometimes to the point of *da capo* repetition, but reinvents its image-stock in the process.

Although desire here speaks more expansively than ever before in Proust's novel, it does so in familiar tones and with a renewed emphasis on the non-presence of the lovers to each other. Their bodies are contiguous, interlaced indeed, but one of them is asleep:

> Parfois [le sommeil d'Albertine] me faisait goûter un plaisir moins pur. Je n'avais besoin pour cela de nul mouvement, je faisais pendre ma jambe contre la sienne, comme une rame qu'on laisse traîner et à laquelle on imprime de temps à autre une oscillation légère pareille au battement intermittent de l'aile qu'ont les oiseaux qui dorment en l'air. Je choisissais pour la regarder cette face de son visage qu'on ne voyait jamais et qui était si belle [. . .] Le bruit de sa respiration devenant plus fort pouvait donner l'illusion de l'essoufflement du plaisir et quand le mien était à son terme,

je pouvais l'embrasser sans avoir interrompu son sommeil. Il me semblait à ces moments-là que je venais de la posséder plus complètement, comme une chose inconsciente et sans résistance de la muette nature. (III, 580–81)

Sometimes [Albertine's sleep] afforded me a pleasure that was less pure. For this I had no need to make any movement, but allowed my leg to dangle against hers, like an oar which one trails in the water, imparting to it now and again a gentle oscillation like the intermittent wing-beat of a bird asleep in the air. I chose, in gazing at her, the aspect of her face which one never saw and which was so beautiful [. . .] The sound of her breathing, which had grown louder, might have given the illusion of the panting of sexual pleasure, and when mine was at its climax, I could kiss her without having interrupted her sleep. I felt at such moments that I had possessed her more completely, like an unconscious and unresisting object of dumb nature. (V, 74–5)

The narrator reaches his climax under cover of his partner's breathing, and wills her downwards to ever deeper recesses of non-awareness. She has become mute nature, for all the noise her breath makes, and her sleep is that of all things. The narrator steers himself towards pleasure with navigational movements of his leg. Stretched out beside his partner, he becomes first an oarsman and then a bird, but a bird which is asleep on the air and in no need of consciousness to perform its life-preserving feats of muscular control. This sequence of images offers us a wondrous contraption almost in the manner of Marcel Duchamp. It is an amphibious desiring machine, airborne in the end but water-borne and bed-borne just before. Yet the destiny of the narrator, once he has been mechanised in this way, is not to become ingenious and technocratic, all in a defiant retreat from the natural world, but on the contrary to give himself up to the pantheistic energies of nature, and to find release, as Albertine already has, from the demon of consciousness. His sleeping partner is the transient instrument of a grandiose narcissistic project, which is not that of seeking to become, as commoner spirits might, a self insolently enclosed upon its own singularity, but that of flowing outwards to encompass the world's curiosities. In the middle section of Proust's paragraph, which I have not quoted, Albertine in profile and Albertine in full face are compared with Siamese twins, and not with the Platonic idea of twinhood in its extreme form but with Rosita and Doodica, real twins who had become famous as circus exhibits in the early years of the century. Desire rolls through all things, moon-bathed ocean billows and Barnum freak-shows alike, and unpartnered sex is the individual's return route to this ever-flowing All.

While it would be preposterous to suggest that sexual arrangements producing delight on this scale are in any way dysfunctional, there is clearly a danger in them, and on this danger much of Proust's plot turns. Albertine, emptied of characteristics and exerting little pressure on the narrator towards the fulfilment of her own sexual wishes, becomes a spacious arena for fantasy. She is imagined in the procession of her secret lives – sending coded signals, contriving assignations, touching and being touched in unfathomable new ways – and progressively lost to the relationship of mutual satisfaction with the narrator that had for brief moments seemed to him possible. Something was going wrong even as things were going right, the narrator suggests, and this has to do not merely with the flight of this particular love-object, but with a strain of perversity and self-defeat that appears to him to inhere in the love relationship itself. If things can go wrong they will.

While this mechanism is often described in psychological terms – as if the human mind simply had among its abiding features a tendency to botch things up – Proust's most memorable accounts of love gone awry trace the problem back to the structure of the body itself. The sensory apparatus, and the erogenous zones in particular, are imperfectly equipped to perform even the simplest tasks of courtship and foreplay. The memory of a first kiss calls forth this tragi-comic fantasia on the anatomical deficiency of lovers:

> je croyais qu'il est une connaissance par les lèvres; je me disais que j'allais connaître le goût de cette rose charnelle, parce que je n'avais pas songé que l'homme, créature évidemment moins rudimentaire que l'oursin ou même la baleine, manque cependant encore d'un certain nombre d'organes essentiels, et notamment n'en possède aucun qui serve au baiser. À cet organe absent il supplée par les lèvres, et par là arrive-t-il peut-être à un résultat un peu plus satisfaisant que s'il était réduit à caresser la bien-aimée avec une défense de corne. Mais les lèvres, faites pour amener au palais la saveur de ce qui les tente, doivent so contenter, sans comprendre leur erreur et sans avouer leur déception, de vaguer à la surface et de se heurter à la clôture de la joue impénétrable et désirée. D'ailleurs à ce moment-là, au contact même de la chair, les lèvres, même dans l'hypothèse où elles deviendraient plus expertes et mieux douées, ne pourraient sans doute pas goûter davantage la saveur que la nature les empêche actuellement de saisir, car dans cette zone désolée où elles ne peuvent trouver leur nourriture, elles sont seules, le regard, puis l'odorat les ont abandonnées depuis longtemps. (II, 659–60)

I believed that there was such a thing as knowledge acquired by the lips; I told myself that I was going to know the taste of this fleshly rose, because I had not stopped to think that man, a creature obviously less rudimentary than the sea-urchin or even the whale, nevertheless lacks a certain number of essential organs, and notably possesses none that will serve for kissing. For this absent organ he substitutes his lips, and thereby arrives perhaps at a slightly more satisfying result than if he were reduced to caressing the

beloved with a horny tusk. But a pair of lips, designed to
convey to the palate the taste of whatever whets their appetite, must be content, without understanding their mistake
or admitting their disappointment, with roaming over the
surface and with coming to a halt at the barrier of the
impenetrable but irresistible cheek. Moreover at the moment
of actual contact with the flesh, the lips, even on the assumption that they might become more expert and better
endowed, would doubtless be unable to enjoy any more
fully the savour which nature prevents their ever actually
grasping, for in that desolate zone in which they are unable
to find their proper nourishment they are alone, the sense
of sight, then that of smell, having long since deserted them.

(III, 419–20)

The nuzzlings of sea-urchins and whales produce pleasures
that are commensurate with the needs of these unusual creatures, but those of human lovers are encounters with the
impossible. Albertine's pink cheeks, much praised during all
the main love episodes, are strictly unreachable by kisses. A
conventional lover's guide would speak of the ways in which
the five senses can complement or supplement each other in
a rising curve of sexual excitement, and Proust's narrator does
indeed occasionally portray his desire for Albertine in these
terms: 'mes sens tressés ensemble l'enveloppaient tout entière'
(III, 681; 'my interwoven senses enveloped her completely' (V,
194)). But here he describes at length a desolate alternative
pattern: failure in one sense-field is echoed by further failure
in each of the others. Success is first denied to the exploring
mouth and then to the eye, an organ that normally has special
privileges in the love manuals of the West. The moving image
of Albertine's cheek dissolves into an unsatisfactory series of
stills. Desire as it travels towards its object is handed from
sense to sense in an endless relay-race and in the end simply
runs past its object, leaving the beloved unsavoured and
unknown.

Nowhere in the novel is the human anatomy subject to stranger fantasmatic distortions than in the scene of sexual triumph in *La Prisonnière*. Albertine's body, disrobed by the narrator, is described as a rough-and-ready assemblage of individual parts:

> Les deux petits seins haut remontés étaient si ronds qu'ils avaient moins l'air de faire partie intégrante de son corps que d'y avoir mûri comme deux fruits; et son ventre (dissimulant la place qui chez l'homme s'enlaidit comme du crampon resté fiché dans une statue descellée) se refermait, à la jonction des cuisses, par deux valves d'une courbe aussi assoupie, aussi reposante, aussi claustrale que celle de l'horizon quand le soleil a disparu. (III, 587)

> Her two little uplifted breasts were so round that they seemed not so much to be an integral part of her body as to have ripened there like fruit; and her belly (concealing the place where a man's is disfigured as though by an iron clamp left sticking in a statue that has been taken down from its niche) was closed, at the junction of her thighs, by two valves with a curve as languid, as reposeful, as cloistral as that of the horizon after the sun has set. (V, 82)

The whole passage from which this cameo is taken is a witty amalgam of Darwinian and biblical or 'creationist' elements. On the one hand, we are back in Eden and Albertine is an incarnate successor to the Eve merely dreamt of in the opening pages of the book. She grows the forbidden fruit upon her person. The 'two valves' of her external genitalia, on the other hand, return us as surely as the earlier sea-urchin did to the world of primitive organisms. *Valve* takes us directly to the molluscs, to the bivalves in particular, and indirectly too in that the word has been used earlier (I, 44; I, 51) to describe the scallop-shaped mould from which Petites Madeleines, those now famous cakes, acquire their characteristic contour. In desiring Albertine's sex, the narrator willingly aligns himself with the most rudimentary of desire-driven organisms. What propels him and them is a single irresistible natural force, and an evolutionary process in which all creatures take part. The fact that *valve*, which comes within punning distance of *vulve*, contains a reminiscence of the madeleine, the novel's supreme edible object, opens up another biological vista: the desire to eat and the desire to mate as interconnected versions of one inextinguishable *élan vital*.

All this would betoken an ingenious rather than a perverse sexual imagination if it were not for the violent image which appears in parenthesis. Here the male member is doubly under attack. It is both a dislodged statue and a tenacious contrivance designed to hold statues in place. It should be invisible but insists on being seen. Either way, as statue or as clamp, it is jarring and ungainly. (It is in brackets that the statue falls from its bracket.) The restful curves of the equivalent female parts offer respite from the phallic obsession. The intrusive penis turns towards its sunset and gently slips from view. The vulva offers an enclosed space, a cloister, into which anxious and over-protesting male sexuality can quietly retreat.

What happens in this paragraph, then, is that human sexual anatomy is radically defamiliarised. The male and female organs shadow each other in a two-way haunting. Sexual pleasure comes not from the complementarity of bodily parts or from their capacity for reciprocal stimulation, but from their discrepancies, interferences and failures of fit. The sexual act itself dramatises the difference between the participants, and, rather than bring them to the threshold of a shared self-loss, dissolves itself into a series of stoppages and incongruities. Eros thrives on the improbable, on the almost-but-not-quite of human attraction, and on things misperceived and misunderstood. In the book as a whole moments of simple-seeming sexual delight are regularly chaperoned by admonitory accounts of bodily contacts going wrong. It is almost as if intense pleasure can be had only when a threatening, de-sexing angel is at hand.

A further surprising feature of Proust's opulent phenomenology of sexual experience is that it can cope memorably, inside its slow rhythms and involved textures, with the suddenness of desire. Desire teases, spins things out, but it swoops and pounces too. Everyone will have his or her treasured examples of the textual effect by which deliberation yields to the concentrated energy-spasm of an image. Bunyan, in his autobiographical *Grace Abounding* (1666), speaking of himself as a man caught in spiritual transport, writes: 'my mind was now so turned, that it lay like a horse leech at the vein, still crying out, *Give, give*.' James Carker, pursuing Edith Dombey in the closing stages of Dickens's *Dombey and Son* (1848), seems for a moment to have her within his grasp, despite her proud resistance, knife in hand: 'He would have sold his soul to root her, in her beauty, to the floor, and make her arms drop at her sides, and have her at his mercy.' In James's *The Golden Bowl* (1904) aggression is from time to time rediscovered in its pure state, unalloyed by the cruel civilities of the drawing-room: 'what was Maggie's own sense but that of having been thrown over on her back, with her neck, from the first, half broken and her helpless face staring up?' Proust is a master of this minor art: he times his violence well. Only an infinitesimal variation in the lines of a human face, his narrator says of Albertine's volatile behaviour, allows us to distinguish between the look of someone who is helping a wounded man and that of someone who is finishing him off (II, 661; III, 422). The narrator, still pondering on Albertine's repertory of facial expressions and the gradations of desire that they seem to indicate, suddenly remembers the dark intensity of her gaze as it plays upon passers-by in the street: 'son regard étroit et velouté se fixait, se collait sur la passante, si adhérent, si corrosif qu'il semblait qu'en se retirant il aurait dû emporter la peau' (III, 656; 'her intense and velvety gaze fastened itself, glued itself to the passer-by, so adhesive, so corrosive, that you felt that, in withdrawing, it must tear away the skin' (V, 163–4)). More terrifying than looks that kill are those that flay their victims alive.

In all these cases the relations between the narrator and his protagonists are complex ones. There is already complexity enough, one might have thought, in the dealings depicted between the narrated Bunyan character and his God, between Carker and Edith, Maggie and Charlotte, or the narrated self and Albertine, but the interposed narrative voice adds to this. 'Where does he stand?', we may find ourselves asking of the speaker. It is difficult, in particular, to place the extreme violence that threatens in each scene, for this seems often to flow as a contagion between narrator and 'narratee'. Violence is caught by those who behold it, or impute it to others, or tell tales in which it occurs or is imagined in the possibility of its occurrence. Viewpoints multiply. The Almighty becomes a mighty horse demanding that his leech-adherents suck his blood. Charlotte is peremptorily switched into the executioner's role by Maggie's fantasy of herself as victim through and through. The jealous narrator stands behind the figure of Albertine as she gazes upon a woman in the street, and gathers to himself, in the energy of his imagining and his imputation, a lethal power over his partner. But the special force of these images lies in their bringing divergent viewpoints back together: over and against the evasions of syntax, the interplay between characters, and the disguises that authors and readers alike wear, the excessive image simplifies and seems for a moment salutary. The reader may discover an incriminating sense of community in the face of an unspeakable deed.

In 'Un Amour de Swann', Odette, confirming Swann's suspicions and admitting that she has lied to him, strikes 'avec une netteté et une vigueur de bourreau' (I, 364; 'with all the precision and force of a headsman' (I, 446)). Swann finds his whole past altered by this new knowledge, destroyed 'stone by stone' as if by the hideous beasts that destroyed Nineveh in the prophecy of Zephaniah (I, 365; I, 447–8). The narrator, standing before a painting by Carpaccio in *Albertine disparue* and suddenly remembering the dead Albertine, finds his jealousy reborn: 'je sentis au cœur comme une légère morsure' (IV, 226; 'I felt a slight gnawing at my heart' (V, 743)). In all these cases desire gathers cruelty into itself; an aggression turns outwards upon other people and then inwards upon the self. The suddenness of the moment is dramatised by these brief intrusions of pain into the narrative texture. The jealous imagination has struck against an uncrossable threshold, an indissoluble traumatic residue.

Proust's book is a celebration, then, of the accidents and misadventures that befall the sexual appetite, and of the distinctive darkness of human desire that in the end separates it from the mating behaviour of whales, wolves or shellfish. Desire as humans know it in this work has to do not simply with slowness and indirection – *homo sapiens* has, after all, nothing to teach whales about the ceremonies of courtship or molluscs about the need to take time over love-making – but with the will to fail. It has to do both with prompt action and with the resolute refusal of action. Desire thrives upon difficulty and the threat of disappointment, and can positively shrivel when the possibility of satisfaction comes too plainly into view. Proust's description of things going wrong and getting in the way is hugely insistent and overdetermined. And the narrative of *A la recherche du temps perdu* is endlessly stalled in its forward motion towards consummation and closure by a playback device that can be activated by any passing detail. The narrator/Albertine plot replays the story of the affair between Swann and Odette and is itself in part replayed in the story of Charlus and Morel, and in the short valedictory account, at the very end of the novel, of the affair between Odette and the duc de Guermantes (IV, 592–4; VI, 408–10). The book reduplicates its plot structures, and returns with ever-renewed zest to the archetypal story of loss and disenchantment that each of those structures reinvents. Moreover this parsimonious re-use of building materials and design ideas occurs not just on the grand scale but in the local interlocking of episodes.

No sooner has the narrator, after many delays, begun his sexual relationship with Albertine, than he harks back to mere expectancy, and subjects himself to a further series of delays, by seeking to begin a relationship with Mme de Stermaria. He arranges to meet this tantalising new partner in the Bois de Boulogne, and discovers that the long wait which separates the promise of sexual favours from their delivery has a temporality of its own:

> La papauté, dit-on, compte par siècles, et peut-être même ne songe pas à compter, parce que son but est à l'infini. Le mien étant seulement à la distance de trois jours, je comptais par secondes, je me livrais à ces imaginations qui sont des commencements de caresses, de caresses qu'on enrage de ne pouvoir faire achever par la femme elle-même (ces caresses-là précisément, à l'exclusion de toutes autres).
>
> (II, 678)

> The Papacy, we are told, reckons by centuries, and indeed may perhaps not bother to reckon time at all, since its goal is in eternity. Mine being no more than three days off, I counted by seconds, I gave myself up to those imaginings which are the adumbrations of caresses, of caresses which one itches to be able to make the woman herself reciprocate

253

> and complete – precisely those caresses, to the exclusion of
> all others.   (III, 442)

The three days of waiting, in which Albertine figures in a modest supporting role, recreate the earlier drama of deferred pleasure in which she had been a protagonist. The three-day period ends, after an accumulation of circumstantial detail in which the narration seems to reach upwards from the personal to the papal time-scale, on an abrupt disappointment. Where Albertine had rung a bell to stop desire in its tracks, Mme de Stermaria writes a note: 'Je suis désolée, un contretemps m'empêche de dîner ce soir avec vous à l'île du Bois' (II, 686; 'Am so sorry – am unfortunately prevented from dining with you this evening on the island in the Bois' (III, 452)). The Bois de Boulogne is not, of course, in this novel, a trysting-place like any other. It is, on the one hand, an ornament-laden open-air brothel and, on the other, a public memorial to sexual panic: it was on this very island, in a bygone age, that Swann had been subjected to jealous torment by Odette (I, 360; I, 441). The Stermaria narrative self-consciously remembers many earlier episodes and rediscovers the elegiac poetry of lost love which the narrator had extracted from the landscape of the Bois in the closing pages of *Du côté de chez Swann*. Loss feeds upon the memory of loss. Desire must be protected from the banality of satisfaction. If it looks back into the historical past, it seeks out premonitory visions of its own unappeasable rage. But, all things considered, it is preferable for it to look not back but forwards, to the always imminent caress in which skin never touches skin.

In Proust's novel, sex itself is, in one sense, an unreally straightforward business. His characters enter liaisons easily, and, if they are male, make use of prostitutes with the same lack of ceremony as they show towards any other class of personal servants. In *A l'ombre des jeunes filles en fleurs* Bloch

boasts to the narrator that he had met Odette, now married
and seemingly respectable, on a train, and enjoyed her three
times in a row between Paris and the Point-du-Jour (II, 136–
7; II, 414). The snobbish Mme Leroi speaks for an entire
community when she announces: 'L'amour? je le fais souvent
mais je n'en parle jamais' (II, 492; 'Love? I make it often but
I never talk about it' (III, 220)). It is against this background
that Proust's chronicle of insatiable desire takes shape. People
have sex, but that is all they have. The act of physical possession
– in which, as the narrator says in a phrase that has become
famous, one possesses nothing (I, 230; I, 281) – does not even
mark a significant staging post on the endless itinerary of desire.
It tranquillises for a brief moment, but that is all it does. And
in this demotion of the sex act in favour of a cult of non-
fulfilment we touch upon another of the book's astonishing
features. Sexual agents, even as they 'make catleya', to re-use
the flower-code of Swann and Odette (I, 230; I, 281), are
moved beyond it into a new world of enforced chastity, a new
Petrarchism almost. Fantasy reasserts itself over the conjoining
of bodies, and the Proustian narrative is made over, for long
tracts of time, to pain, yearning and a fertile, image-filled hope-
lessness.

The comparison with Petrarch himself is worth making, for
both writers are indefatigable in their pursuit of what is now-
adays called 'sublimation' or 'substitutive satisfaction'. For the
author of the *Rime sparse* (1374), the impossibility of physical
union with the beloved set going a magical process of textual
invention. Laura was nowhere to be had, but once the rules
of literary art had been properly understood and internalised,
once the flowers of rhetoric had been allowed to blossom, she
could be had everywhere:

Da' be' rami scendea
(dolce ne la memoria)
una pioggia di fior sovra 'l suo grembo,
    et ella si sedea
umile in tanta gloria,
coverta già de l'amoroso nembo;
    qual fior cadea sul lembo,
qual su le treccie bionde
ch' oro forbito et perle
eran quel dì a vederle,
qual si posava in terra et qual su l'onde,
qual con un vago errore
girando parea dir: 'Qui regna Amore.'

From the lovely branches was descending (sweet in memory) a rain of flowers over her bosom,/ and she was sitting humble in such a glory, already covered with the loving cloud;/ this flower was falling on her skirt, this one on her blond braids, which were burnished gold and pearls to see that day; this one was coming to rest on the ground, this one on the water, this one, with a lovely wandering, turning about seemed to say: 'Here reigns Love.'

Where is the sublimation in lines like these? What starts as a powerful sexual urge is transposed into images of exuberant natural growth and then rediscovered, as the enveloping blossom falls from the trees on to the beloved's lap, as the selfsame urge, still sexual and at least as powerful as before. By way of his figures and tropes, the poet-narrator is able to become a supreme fecundating force, moving across the landscape and causing pleasure wherever he goes.

Proust's narrator, on the other hand, hurries through his real sexual encounters towards a promised sadness. Even before Albertine has been had, genitally, and in deed rather than in thought, another truer adventure has already begun. This is the predator's pursuit of an untrappable prey. Precautions may be taken in advance to prevent the beloved – immobilised in the lover's gaze and about to be catalogued in her bodily parts – from slipping out from her house arrest to enjoy pleasures of her own, for although possession is impossible in sex, short-term domestic captivity is not. But in the longer term, such precautions do not work. They are thwarted from within, by the narrator's will not to have, not to hold, and not to enjoy.

As so often happens in this novel, an emotional contradiction is placed centre stage. Beyond the interplay between arousal and gratification, another simpler and more desperate tension comes into view: between anxiety and *apaisement*. The very word is like a bell tolling relentlessly in *La Prisonnière*, and it means many things. Calming, quietening, soothing, allaying, assuagement, appeasement . . . These actions all involve the satiation of physical need in this volume of the work, but they are effects which have vastly outgrown their cause. Speaking of Albertine's possible lovers, the narrator says: 'Et cependant, chez moi aimer charnellement, c'était tout de même pour moi jouir d'un triomphe sur tant de concurrents. Je ne le redirai jamais assez, c'était un apaisement plus que tout' (III, 585; 'And yet to love carnally was none the less, for me, to enjoy a triumph over countless rivals. I can never repeat it often enough: it was more than anything else an appeasement' (V, 80)). Yet despite the narrator's excessive emphasis on the peace of mind that intercourse may bring, this causal relationship is often extremely unstable. Sexual assuagement also offers itself, and here is the contradiction, as a perverse port of entry to a world of necessary, unsubduable pain. Let us imagine that pain not pleasure were the true driving force in affairs of the heart, the narrator suggests, in a passage that provides the novel's central sexual tableau with its climactic insight:

257

C'est justement parce que cette douceur a été nécessaire pour enfanter la douleur – et reviendra du reste la calmer par intermittences – que les hommes peuvent être sincères avec autrui, et même avec eux-mêmes, quand ils se glorifient de la bonté d'une femme envers eux, quoique, à tout prendre, au sein de leur liaison circule constamment d'une façon secrète, inavouée aux autres, ou révélée involontairement par des questions, des enquêtes, une inquiétude douloureuse. Mais celle-ci n'aurait pas pu naître sans la douceur préalable; même ensuite, la douceur intermittente est nécessaire pour rendre la souffrance supportable et éviter les ruptures; et la dissimulation de l'enfer secret qu'est la vie commune avec cette femme, jusqu'à l'ostentation d'une intimité qu'on prétend douce, exprime un point de vue vrai, un lien général de l'effet à la cause, un des modes selon lesquels la production de la douleur est rendue possible.

(III, 588)

It is precisely because this tenderness has been necessary to give birth to pain – and will return moreover at intervals to calm it – that men can be sincere with each other, and even with themselves, when they pride themselves on a woman's lovingness, although, taking things all in all, at the heart of their intimacy there lurks continuously and secretly, unavowed to the rest of the world, or revealed unintentionally by questions and inquiries, a painful disquiet. But this could not have come to birth without the preliminary tenderness, which even afterwards is intermittently necessary to make the pain bearable and to avoid ruptures; and concealment of the secret hell that a life shared with the woman in question really is, to the point of parading an allegedly tender intimacy, expresses a genuine point of view, a universal process of cause and effect, one of the modes whereby the production of grief and pain is rendered possible.

(V, 83–4)

It takes only a tiny consonantal shift to turn *douceur* into *douleur*, and the narrator toys relentlessly with this accidental verbal association as he moves forward to his final nightmare vision of desiring humankind. Pain is what we want, and plenty of it. Between the precipitating cause, which is the desire to suffer, and the eventual effect, which is the discovery of a hell internal to the human mind, there will be moments of pleasurable respite, and even a hint from time to time that pleasure may itself be a worthy human goal, but overall the movement of these sentences is abrupt and disconsolate. The production of pain is our business on earth. All those syllables, trippingly arranged and seemingly so inventive, have as their dour underlying purpose the extraction of *douleur* from *douceur*. Beneath the playful repetitions that crowd the textual surface at this point, a powerful compulsion to repeat is at work. Beneath the logic-chopping, a powerful logic is to be found. A passing theorem, in a novel that contains many such, is also, in summary form, an immovable human destiny. In love, *douceurs* always change into *douleurs* (III, 607; V, 106): this almost has the status of a physical law. It is the artist's responsibility, we are told in *Le Temps retrouvé*, to assume this destiny, to enshrine it in his person: 'Quant au bonheur, il n'a presque qu'une seule utilité, rendre le malheur possible' (IV, 486; 'As for happiness, that is really useful to us in one way only, by making unhappiness possible' (VI, 269)).

What is remarkable about this Via Dolorosa as traced in *La Prisonnière* is that so many of the lesser pathways taken by the narrator's sexual curiosity should rejoin it. Shadows are perpetually cast over the interlacing of lovers. Albertine's 'rose-flush coming and going' is a sexual signal and an erotic provocation, but it is also, as in Hardy's 'After a Journey' from which I quote the phrase, a memory that triggers other memories. Upon this scene of dalliance figures from an unquiet past suddenly begin to intrude: Gilberte first of all, but then the narrator's mother, father, grandmother and aunt Léonie. They gather as a ghostly crowd round his bed. Far from observing these visitors as a procession of lost souls, he finds himself transformed into them, each in turn. The soul of aunt Léonie migrates into the narrator's adult person, and the relationship with Albertine allows a whole childhood past to be re-enacted:

> Voici de même que je parlais maintenant à Albertine, tantôt comme l'enfant que j'avais été à Combray parlant à ma mère, tantôt comme ma grand-mère me parlait. Quand nous avons dépassé un certain âge, l'âme de l'enfant que nous fûmes et l'âme des morts dont nous sommes sortis viennent nous jeter à poignée leurs richesses et leurs mauvais sorts, demandant à coopérer aux nouveaux sentiments que nous éprouvons et dans lesquels, effaçant leur ancienne effigie, nous les refondons en une création originale. Tel, tout mon passé depuis mes années les plus anciennes, et par delà celles-ci le passé de mes parents mêlaient à mon impur amour pour Albertine la douceur d'une tendresse à la fois filiale et maternelle. Nous devons recevoir, dès une certaine heure, tous nos parents arrivés de si loin et assemblés autour de nous.
>
> (III, 586–7)

> [H]ere I was talking now to Albertine, at one moment as the child that I had been at Combray used to talk to my mother, at another as my grandmother used to talk to me. When we have passed a certain age, the soul of the child that we were and the souls of the dead from whom we sprang come and shower upon us their riches and their spells, asking to be allowed to contribute to the new emotions which we feel and in which, erasing their former image, we recast them in an original creation. Thus my whole past from my earliest years, and, beyond these, the past of my parents and relations, blended with my impure love for Albertine the tender charm of an affection at once filial and maternal. We have to give hospitality, at a certain stage in our lives, to all our relatives who have journeyed so far and gathered round us.　　　　(V, 82)

Two things are going on at the same time here. An episode in the life of an adult, a bedchamber scene marked by excitement and dread, is suddenly visited by a blessed childhood memory. The narrator combines in himself the child he once was with the mother he once had. He is at one and the same time the giver and receiver of tenderness, and a vision of *apaisement* steals across the stage. A lost paradise is momentarily regained. A mother's care and nurturing, to which the full power of a mother's possessive passion has been added, re-emerge into later experience as the cure for all ills. If only the pattern of the narrator's relationship with Albertine could be made to conform to this model of blissful reciprocity, all would be well henceforth. Other threads in Proust's textual weave, however, are simultaneously pointing in the opposite direction. Memories of a lost childhood are a monstrous intrusion into grown-up affairs. They give a retrospective cast and an air of fatedness to the progress of love. They haunt the present, and drive its affections awry. Passions that only a moment ago seemed to have a future to them are now no more than re-enactments of this or that early family scene. An imp of the perverse is turning the quest for *apaisement* into a cult of dissatisfaction and pain. Contradiction conquers all.

The narrator's love for Albertine, like Swann's for Odette, moves from an initial period in which it had seemed impossible, through a brief moment of sexual enjoyment, into an aftermath in which the earlier sense of impossibility returns in a new and definitive form. All too soon, the kissing has to stop, and the catleya begins to wither on its stalk. But where Swann is able to make a fairly dignified exit from his tortured affair by dwindling into a husband for his elusive love-object, the narrator seeks to prolong the indignity and jealous torment of it all. Even after Albertine's death, the jealousy she inspired lives on. 'Sic ego nec sine te nec tecum vivere possum', Ovid had said in the *Amores*, compressing a complex psychological state into a single formulaic line: 'Thus I can live neither with you nor without' (III, xi). Proust amplifies this state into a slowly unfurling and all-enveloping analytic texture. Being between love and unlove is where the being of human beings comes into its own. It is more than a supreme piece of subject-matter for a fictional work: it is the condition of possibility for fiction itself, the uncertain desirousness without which there would be no tales to tell.

What I have been describing in these pages has the air of a large-scale natural rhythm. Human sexual feeling rises and subsides like the moon or the tide, and Proust provides us with a portrait of its periodicity, a double diagram of desire in action. On the one hand, Proustian desire is an energising greed. It ventures out from the inner world of narcissistic self-absorption to track down delectable objects in the external world, or to surrender itself to their flow when they are liberally available. On the other hand, it seems to want very little of the external world, to be propelled by an active will to depletion, and to cling to its own disappointments. Desire is sprightly and acquisitive at one moment, and morbidly minimalist at the next. It swings between mania and anxiety, between pleasure as a goal and pleasure as a relay-point on the road towards pain. The narrator of Proust's novel is all appetite at one moment and all shrinking and vanishing at the next. In either case he has a prose manner to match: writing that had bristled with antennae and been studded with sensors a moment ago, now seems suddenly to have lost its nerve and ambition. Where it had formerly striven for an impossible plenitude, it now starves itself down to a repetitious murmur. From the brink of sensory overload it descends to a perpetual refiguration of absence.

Broadly speaking, a rhythm of this kind fits the facts of the narrator's case rather well as he passes from the keen pleasures of boyhood and adolescence to the confusions of his early manhood. Proust describes each of these phases with assured inventiveness. Indeed it is one of the miracles of *A la recherche du temps perdu* that its author, having written so compellingly about sex in a register of youthful optimism, should be able to move into the alternative world of pain and dispossession and remain compelling. The sexual content of *La Prisonnière* and *Albertine disparue* takes the form of a protracted spiritual exercise in which the hope, meaning and delight recounted at an earlier stage in the book are relentlessly pared away. The narrator's *via negativa* is pursued with exorbitant precision and patience, as his earlier sensuous awakening had been. The volumes which precede *Le Temps retrouvé* offer us, one might say, the adjoining panels of a mighty diptych on Eros in its expectant and melancholic moods.

Yet while a snapshot of this kind will perhaps suffice as a brief characterisation of Proust's sexual plot, it does not take us far in understanding the local textures of his writing. These are thoroughgoingly erotic, as we have seen, but in a special way. Eros, far from being the abyss into which all other forces are absorbed, and far from impelling the intellectual fabric of the book towards an over-simple 'pansexualist' explanation of the world, appears page by ingenious page in Proust's book as a guarantor of complexity and discrimination. All the book's artists, scientists and intellectuals, together with the narrator himself who is a tireless defender of creative thinking wherever it occurs, are situated in the force-field of their desire. They measure, scan, reason, ruminate, seek patterns, build theories, track likenesses and regularities inside the multifarious daily surge of experience, make a show sometimes of dryness and dogmatism in their adherence to an individual system of ideas, but in doing all these things they have their passions and their vulnerability on display. Vinteuil at work upon a composition resembles Lavoisier or Ampère: all three are experimentalists 'découvrant les lois secrètes d'une force inconnue' (I, 345; 'discovering the secret laws that govern an unknown force' (I, 423)), but all three, artist and scientists alike, are propelled in their creative work by the unknowable force of their own wishes. Proust's complex verbal textures are a working model of desirous thinking. They spring from such thinking, and require it of anyone who reads them.

Proust invokes the libidinal substratum in human affairs with differentiating tact. At one extreme, the aroused body becomes a versatile but unreliable instrument of cognition: the narrator glimpses Albertine's bosom and finds that the whole surrounding landscape has acquired a new geometry of breast-shaped surfaces and volumes; he looks at her external sex organs and dreams himself backwards in evolutionary time. But at the other extreme, sex is present where our commonplace habits of thought least expect it: in sunlight as it falls on the branches of a tree or on the nondescript walls of a hotel room; in the flight of aircraft or the upwards progress of a social climber; in the movement of astral bodies or in the consecutive steps of a syllogism. The species of the natural world, the productions of human culture and the inner processes of thought, once they have been re-immersed in the desire of individuals, gain a new distinctness and singularity. Desire may in the end prove to be a grand unificatory force, binding everything to everything else in the human world, but before the end, in the interim, in the medium term that the act of writing always inhabits, desire-light, falling upon objects or mental processes, reveals differences and sharpens outlines. The eroticised texture of Proust's writing is a mobile lattice in which anything can indeed suddenly resemble anything else, but which at the same time protects and fortifies our sense of diversity. This is a textual world in which no one can have the same experience twice.

Expectation turns to melancholy between the two main phases of Proust's ample *Bildungsroman*, but these phases are alike in that both produce writing of this kind. The despair that he recreates in *La Prisonnière* and *Albertine disparue* is enlivening and rich in insights. It is magnanimous despair, one might say, remembering Marvell's 'The Definition of Love'. The narrating voice that speaks of lost love and insists on replaying the sufferings of the past moves with undiminished stealth and wit:

> Hélas, en me rappelant mes propres agitations chaque fois que j'avais remarqué une jeune fille qui me plaisait, quelquefois seulement quand j'avais entendu parler d'elle sans l'avoir vue, mon souci de me faire beau, d'être avantagé, mes sueurs froides, je n'avais pour me torturer qu'à imaginer ce même voluptueux émoi chez Albertine, comme grâce à l'appareil dont, après la visite de certain praticien lequel s'était montré sceptique devant la réalité de son mal, ma tante Léonie avait souhaité l'invention, et qui permettait de faire éprouver au médecin, pour qu'il se rendît mieux compte, toutes les souffrances de son malade.   (IV, 125–6)

> Alas, remembering my own agitation whenever I had caught sight of a girl who attracted me, sometimes when I had merely heard her spoken of without having seen her, my anxiety to look my best, to show myself to advantage, my cold sweats, I had only, in order to torture myself, to imagine the same voluptuous excitement in Albertine, as though by means of the apparatus which, after the visit of a certain practitioner who had shown some scepticism about her malady, my aunt Léonie had wished to see invented, and which would enable the doctor to undergo all the sufferings of his patient in order to understand better.   (V, 622–3)

This sentence from *Albertine disparue* seeks and eventually finds its moment of closure. It is well-made and well-behaved, but centred on a scandal. Where aunt Léonie had merely wished, from the depths of her hypochondria, for a diagnostic device that would overcome the doubts of her physician, the narrator is already in possession of such a device. His jealousy and his envy together are a morbid syndrome, but an instrument of cognition too. They distort things but they also tell us how things are.

Proust's versatile comic intelligence dwells with relish upon an outrage, a lack of proportion and right-mindedness, that is inherent in human sexuality. His text goes to work with unsubduable energy upon the fabric of desire, and mimics its characteristic rhythms. It moves from *volupté* to scientific reasoning, threading the one into the other, and from *douceur* to *douleur*. And by way of this text, Proust creates one of European literature's most engaging monsters – a protagonist who is by turns a Lothario and a spoiled child, a visionary and a pathological case, a hero of the speculative intellect and a paragon of self-defeating folly.

VII

Death

For the stars of heaven and the constellations thereof
Shall not give their light;
The sun shall be darkened in his going forth,
And the moon shall not cause her light to shine.

Isaiah, 13:10

Of the innumerable outbreaks of plague that have occurred in Europe in the current millennium, several have left their mark upon literary history. Writers as diverse as Defoe in his fictionalised *Journal of the Plague Year* (1722), Artaud in his essay 'La Littérature et la Peste' ('Literature and Plague', 1934) and Camus in his allegorical novel *La Peste* (*The Plague*, 1947) have all hastened from simple questions of sanitation and public health towards catastrophic visions of human mortality. Indeed, until the invention of mechanised mass slaughter in the twentieth century, the plague offered the writer the spectacle of death on an otherwise unimaginable scale. The streets of the plague city were piled high with corpses while an invisible contagion passed from person to person among those who were still alive. A new economics and politics of death sprang into being. Mortality could not have been more grandly staged.

If we decided, perversely, to look at the plague solely as a theme within the history of literature, two outbreaks – those which began in Florence in 1348 and in Milan in 1630 – would have a special place, for they are commemorated in two of the supreme masterpieces of Western literature. Boccaccio's *Decameron* (1352) was written in the immediate aftermath of a long episode in what came to be known as the Black Death, and in its opening pages describes the pestilential townscape in chilling detail. Two hundred years after the Milan plague, Manzoni revisited the city in the huge closing tableau of *I Promessi Sposi* (*The Betrothed*, 1827) and, in a sublime feat of historical imagination, recreated the Milanese lazaretto, its roadways overflowing with the dying and the dead, as the setting in which his young lovers were eventually to be reunited. The plague opens the one work, and closes the other; it acts as an incitement to storytelling for Boccaccio and his narrators, and, for Manzoni, as a device whereby a well-made tale may be brought to its almost tragic end. For each writer, the plague is the whole of human death in convenient paraphrase; it can fill a peroration as easily as an exordium; for the teller of tales it is the grandest of punctuation marks.

Proust punctuates in the same way, placing death, boldly figured, both at the end and at the beginning of his lengthy tale. While having little to say about epidemic disease and only slightly more to say about the technologies of destruction that the First World War had brought to prominence, he gives his novel over to grandiose death-haunted tableaux at either end. The final scene is perhaps the simpler and more memorable of the two, for it is greatly concerned with ageing, and in particular with its effects on the human face. The last reception in this novel of many receptions is held by Mme Verdurin, the new princesse de Guermantes, and for the narrator takes the form of a *bal de têtes*, a costumed ball in which only the head is disguised. A wide cross-section of the novel's characters are brought together for this one occasion, and pictured as the victims of a monstrous facial injustice. Their costume is none other than their own mortality. They could almost be plague sufferers, so swollen, disfigured and contorted are their faces. Death is everywhere on display. Everyone is enjoying a brief stay of execution to enable them to attend a last, lingering *matinée*, but the grave has already claimed them. Proust seizes upon the commonplace phrase 'un pied dans la tombe' (IV, 557; 'one foot in the grave' (VI, 362)) and restores much of its literal meaning: staying alive involves muscular resistance to a continuous downwards and deathwards pressure. The narrator, whose artistic project has by now acquired a sudden new impetus, has himself recently been brushed by a dark wing and does not know whether he will live to complete his task.

Yet although Proust's macabre vision of social man and woman herded together in death's antechamber provides the novel with a terrifying last scene and an abiding sense of closure, it is in the opening pages of the book that a deeper and more elusive terror is to be felt. The child the narrator once was hovers between sleep and waking, desiring darkness but recoiling from it too. His candle is already out, but he is woken from the sleep into which he has readily fallen by the thought that it is time to blow out his light. Silence, loss, emptiness, departure, abandonment . . . these are the ideas that are kindled by the surrounding darkness. And the narrative voice itself, playing upon these childhood memories, hovers between utterance and extinction. It cannot think straight, keeps losing its thread, and discovers intellectual obscurities in the obscurity of the night. This is consciousness feeding on the thought of its own destruction, and finding signs of its destructibility wherever it looks. The narrated child and the narrating adult are not the same person at all; growing up has driven them apart; they are at either end of a continuous procession of selves and now feel foreign to each other; and their apartness and non-identity gives the narrative, from its earliest moment on, distances to measure and analytic work to do. Yet child and adult are very much alike in their fever and uncertainty; in the sense of personal discontinuity they share; and in their common intuition that if the world is ever to become intelligible it will become so as a result of solitary mental exertion. The responsibility for making sense of things rests not with the mutually supporting members of a community, not with shared memories, customs or pieties, but with an individual self-discovered in his isolation, defying his own death and craving it at the same time.

In these opening pages, Proust's narrator reports on a magnificent and strange delusion: 'il me semblait que j'étais moi-même ce dont parlait l'ouvrage: une église, un quatuor, la rivalité de François Ier et de Charles-Quint' (I, 3; 'it seemed to me that I myself was the immediate subject of my book: a church, a quartet, the rivalry between François I and Charles V' (I, 1)). He has become the subject-matter of his bedtime reading, and for a moment or two after waking up cannot shake himself free of this belief: 'elle [. . .] pesait comme des écailles sur mes yeux' (I, 3; 'it [. . .] lay like scales upon my eyes' (I, 1)). What is doubly strange is that the self should retreat into the monuments of the European past, and into its larger-than-life personalities, in order to find its character, and that that past should be entirely dependent on the curatorial inter-ventions of a single human self for its own survival. So much historical substance rests upon these childish eyelids. Were it not for the individual's power of remembrance, selflessly exercised, the entire historical and cultural archive of Europe would be lost to an enveloping darkness. First as a reader and then as a writer, the individual expects himself to bear all that weight. And a death that is internal to consciousness, a plague that spreads invisibly as the mind thinks, shadows the writer as he sets to work, casting a dark glow upon his life-affirming celebration of the narrative arts. Proust's novel is our *Decameron*, and he begins it where Boccaccio began his – in a deathscape.

This is not the place in which to retell the complex story of how bourgeois artists came to think of themselves as occupying such positions of unaided responsibility as the new century began, but it is as well to remember that Proust was not in fact alone as he inaugurated his vast fiction in death-defying solitude. Other subjectivities were appointing themselves as the bearers of a similar burden. The narrator of Valéry's 'Le cimetière marin' ('The Graveyard by the Sea') (1922) positions himself, and his poem in the making, 'entre le vide et l'événement pur' ('between emptiness and pure event'). Yeats is 'hurt into poetry' between a long moment of historical retrospection and a coming apocalypse. And Hugo von Hofmannsthal, Proust's younger contemporary, imagines the frail voice of the lyric poet as the point where human history and the fluctuations of the cosmos converge:

Ganz vergessener Völker Müdigkeiten
Kann ich nicht abtun von meinen Lidern,
Noch weghalten von der erschrockenen Seele
Stummes Niederfallen ferner Sterne.

I cannot put off from my eyelids the weariness of totally forgotten peoples, nor can I ward off from my terrified soul the silent fall-out of distant stars.

Small wonder that the human eyelid can sometimes yield under pressures as intense as these. In the short prose text originally published as 'Ein Brief' (1902), but usually known in English as *The Lord Chandos Letter*, Hofmannsthal's Chandos describes to his friend Francis Bacon a 'terrible empathy' ('ein ungeheures Anteilnehmen') by which he feels himself connected to all other creatures, including cows and rats, and to the creative efforts of all other artists and artisans, and bids a dignified farewell to literature: no language yet exists in which his enlarged sentience could find expression. 'Je passais en une seconde par-dessus des siècles de civilisation' (I, 5–6; 'in a flash I would traverse centuries of civilisation' (I, 4)), Proust's narrator says, a little later in his opening reverie, but, unlike Chandos, he finds in this alarming sense of ubiquity a spur to eloquent speech. If the inner texture of things has been revealed to him, and if their history suddenly rushes in upon him, what can he as a writer do but write? And if they depend for their survival on his power of remembrance, he will need a prose that keeps reminding him that the odds against survival are immeasurably long. A prose in which the impending death of things, as well as their vitality and variety, speaks.

The constructions of consciousness are so insistently depicted as mutable and short-lived in this novel, and its component narratives are subjected to so much smudging, that it would be tempting to say that an all-pervading awareness of death was its native soil. It would be convenient to claim that a narrator who begins his story in the dark cannot ever get darkness out of his mind. Long complex books cry out for simple skeleton keys. Death in Proust would then resemble death in Artaud, or Rothko, or the other Francis Bacon. It would be the condition of possibility for art, and a constant insinuating presence in the art-work itself. Just as Artaud's writing has its characteristic spasm of pain, Rothko's brushwork its power to cancel meaning even as it supplies its massive banks of colour, and Bacon's version of the human face its blurring or its bulbous bruises, so Proust, we might want to say, finds death at every street corner and in every mental manoeuvre of the cornered human animal. It would simplify things if we could find Proust's imagination uniformly fired by the knowledge of its own mortality, and his writing bearing always a deathly trace upon it. In a book as various as this, it would be good to find any one feature that was always present and never likely to play tricks on us.

Yet Proust's insistent representation of death is not that feature, for it has too many tones and moods, breeds too many paradoxes, and is devoted to trickery. We can begin to get the measure of this variety by reminding ourselves of the emotional extremes towards which Proust's account takes us at different moments. Death is a daily presence in human affairs. It is a fact needing to be acknowledged, rather than a problem needing a solution. There is no promise of survival in Proust's book, other than in the provisional afterlife afforded by human memory, and in the longer-lasting but still transient power of endurance that works of art possess. But the plain incontrovertible fact of death draws forth from the narrator responses that vary from stoic resignation at one extreme to an indignant *danse macabre* at the other. The narrator, faced with the death of others, is the vehicle both for a boundless compassion and for a frenzied cruelty.

The scenes devoted to the final illness and death of the narrator's grandmother seem often to belong to a world apart, in which the ironic imperative that governs so much of Proust's writing is by sheer force of grief suspended. There are two principal episodes, widely separated but closely linked. The first, in *Le Côté de Guermantes* (II, 609–41; III, 359–97), concerns the death itself and the long period of suffering which precedes it; the second, which appears in *Sodome et Gomorrhe* under the sub-heading 'Les intermittences du cœur' ('The Intermittences of the Heart') (III, 148–78; IV, 174–209), describes the delayed action of mourning and the discovery of pain and loss on a scale that the grandmother's death had not provoked at the time of its occurrence.

273

These scenes are remarkable for their dignity and pathos. Maxims on human mortality abound, but these seldom detach themselves from the descriptive texture and often have the air of a restrained folk-wisdom: 'La malade fait sa connaissance de l'étranger qu'elle entend aller et venir dans son cerveau' (II, 612; 'We make the acquaintance of the Stranger whom we hear coming and going in our brain' (III, 363)). Even when a commonplace view is being repudiated, the language of these sentences still makes a straightforward appeal to shared experience:

> Une fois qu'elle est morte, nous aurions scrupule à être autre, nous n'admirons plus que ce qu'elle était, ce que nous étions déjà, mais mêlé à autre chose, et ce que nous allons être désormais uniquement. C'est dans ce sens-là (et non dans celui si vague, si faux où on l'entend généralement) qu'on peut dire que la mort n'est pas inutile, que le mort continue à agir sur nous. (III, 166)

> Once she is dead, we hesitate to be different, we begin to admire only what she was, what we ourselves already were, only blended with something else, and what in future we shall be exclusively. It is in this sense (and not in that other sense, so vague, so false, in which the phrase is generally understood) that we may say that death is not in vain, that the dead continue to act upon us. (IV, 195)

The power of this language lies in its rediscovery of simplicity in the midst of hard-working verbal artifice, and the figure of the narrator's grandmother is the presiding moral genius who oversees this linguistic transformation. She represents unconditional tenderness and compassion surviving in an otherwise brutish system of social arrangements, and she is appropriately plain-spoken. Indeed her reassuring taps on the wall separating her hotel room from the narrator's have an eloquence that could not be improved upon by speech (III, 160; IV, 188).

The authority that the narrator ascribes to his grandmother is such that she is summoned up in fantasy to console him for the pain her own death has caused; in an uncanny revision of the traditional *pietà* the dead maternal figure provides comfort for the still-living son (III, 154; IV, 181). And the narrator's simple speech is part of the same process of resurrection: he catches her voice into his and speaks as she would have spoken.

There can of course be rhetorical cunning behind a sudden refusal of rhetoric. *Brevitas* is no less a verbal device than amplification or circumlocution, and the narrator, as an expert observer of linguistic behaviour, puts the device to work knowledgeably in his own narrative. Immediately after suffering the stroke that is soon to kill her, the grandmother is taken to see a physician, who agrees to examine her despite a pressing social engagement: 'Votre grand-mère est perdue' ('Your grandmother is doomed') is the professional verdict he delivers while preparing himself for departure. The whole episode takes the form of a commentary on social speech. The doctor worries about his buttonhole while his patient continues her dying, and the narrator comments:

> Le professeur tempêtait toujours pendant que je regardais sur le palier ma grand-mère qui était perdue. Chaque personne est bien seule. (II, 614)

> The Professor continued to storm while I stood on the landing gazing at my grandmother who was doomed. Each of us is indeed alone. (III, 365)

From the brevity of a diagnosis cruelly delivered, we move to the bare speech of the feeling individual suddenly faced with death, and with the pity of it. This profoundly affecting tone is to be found again in the later scenes of bereavement:

> Elle était ma grand-mère et j'étais son petit-fils. Les expressions de son visage semblaient écrites dans une langue

qui n'était que pour moi; elle était tout dans ma vie, les autres
n'existaient que relativement à elle, au jugement qu'elle me
donnerait sur eux; mais non, nos rapports ont été trop
fugitifs pour n'avoir pas été accidentels. Elle ne me connaît
plus, je ne la reverrai jamais. Nous n'avions pas été créés
uniquement l'un pour l'autre, c'était une étrangère.

(III, 172)

She was my grandmother and I was her grandson. Her facial
expressions seemed written in a language intended for me
alone; she was everything in my life, other people existed
merely in relation to her, to the opinion she would express
to me about them. But no, our relations were too fleeting
to have been anything but accidental. She no longer knew
me, I should never see her again. We had not been created
solely for one another; she was a stranger to me. (IV, 202)

I am tempted to say that only great writers, or writers in
possession of limitless rhetorical energy, can ever be expected
to write as simply as this. Dante and Shakespeare have this
audacity of plain speaking, and Montaigne who, in his essay
'De l'amitié' ('On Friendship'), provided French literature with
two prototypical simple sentences which can be heard echoing
in Proust's elegy:

Si on me presse de dire pourquoy je l'aymois, je sens que
cela ne se peut exprimer, qu'en respondant: «Par ce que
c'estoit luy; par ce que c'estoit moi.»

If you press me to say why I loved him, I feel that it
cannot be expressed except by replying: 'Because it was
him: because it was me.'

Proust's sentences are remarkable not just for the economy
with which they report a powerful feeling, but for the fact that
a complex psychological process is being described in them.
The narrator's attention passes from one emotional era to
another, from familiarity to estrangement, from having a loved

276

one to losing her, but his sentences are shorn of all causal connections. Love and loss are accidents, and no intrusive machinery of cause and effect must be allowed to suggest otherwise. The grandmother was alive, and is now dead. She was close, and is now far away. For the moment, only simple sentences can rise to the occasion. Grief must not be allowed to dissolve into self-congratulating literary style.

Yet the restraint of Proust's writing in these scenes, its hard-won philosophical calm, is intercut with moments of rage and nightmare. Both in the episode of the grandmother's death and in that of the narrator's delayed mourning for her, the human organism in its death-throes is presented as undergoing an atrocity. No appropriate words of consolation are then to be found, and if a narrative is to remain true to a dying person's pain it must allow itself to be assailed and broken apart. It must find a voice for suffering from within itself, and move by exaggeration and excess towards a supremely painful truth:

> Les coups que nous destinions au mal qui s'était installé en ma grand-mère portaient toujours à faux; c'était elle, c'était son pauvre corps interposé qui les recevait, sans qu'elle se plaignît qu'avec un faible gémissement. Et les douleurs que nous lui causions n'étaient pas compensées par un bien que nous ne pouvions lui faire. Le mal féroce que nous aurions voulu exterminer, c'est à peine si nous l'avions frôlé, nous ne faisions que l'exaspérer davantage hâtant peut-être l'heure où la captive serait dévorée. (II, 618)

> The blows which we aimed at the evil which had settled inside her were always wide of the mark, and it was she, it was her poor interposed body that had to bear them, without her ever uttering more than a faint groan by way of complaint. And the pain that we caused her found no compensation in any benefit that we were able to give her. The ferocious beast we were anxious to exterminate we barely succeeded in grazing; we merely enraged it even more,

hastening perhaps the moment when the captive would be
devoured. (III, 369–70)

The narrator speaks with the authority of an informed medical
amateur about strokes, uraemia and albumin levels, and about
the dangers of administering morphine to a patient whose blood
has already been poisoned, but where Cottard, who is treating
the grandmother, is obliged by his professional code to think
solely in such terms, the narrator seeks to plunge beneath them
towards the raw immediacy of her suffering. Her pain must
become his. The memory of her tormented body takes him
upon a dream-journey into his own viscera:

> Monde du sommeil où la connaissance interne, placée sous
> la dépendance des troubles de nos organes, accélère le
> rythme du cœur ou de la respiration, parce qu'une même
> dose d'effroi, de tristesse, de remords, agit, avec une puiss-
> ance centuplée si elle est ainsi injectée dans nos veines; dès
> que pour y parcourir les artères de la cité souterraine, nous
> nous sommes embarqués sur les flots noirs de notre propre
> sang comme sur un Léthé intérieur aux sextuples replis, de
> grandes figures solennelles nous apparaissent, nous abordent
> et nous quittent, nous laissant en larmes. (III, 157)

> World of sleep – in which our inner consciousness, subordi-
> nated to the disturbances of our organs, accelerates the
> rhythm of the heart or the respiration, because the same dose
> of terror, sorrow or remorse acts with a strength magnified a
> hundredfold if thus injected into our veins: as soon as, to
> traverse the arteries of the subterranean city, we have
> embarked upon the dark current of our own blood as upon
> an inward Lethe meandering sixfold, tall solemn forms
> appear to us, approach and glide away, leaving us in tears.
> (IV, 185)

The diagnostic eye of a would-be clinician is here turned
inwards upon his own organism, and finds not oblivion but
terrifying new remembrance as he contemplates the flow of his

own blood. To have one's fears reappear in centuplicate, or even to have one's arteries radiographically revealed in sextuplicate, is to be brought close to the extreme point where numbering, or any other system of measurement and control, breaks down. There is something about the somatic life of the body which will not go into words or numbers at all. Memories of dead loved ones are a secretion within a secretion, and cause the tear-ducts in their turn to open. Pain has its secret architecture, and the narrator's professional code as a writer in the making obliges him to explore this 'subterranean city', even – or perhaps especially – if it takes him to the brink of the unutterable.

The grandmother's death is an exemplary one, and, although none of the later deaths in the novel is to be described in such detail, the narrator is often to rediscover in himself the strange syncopations of feeling that this first disastrous loss had provoked. He finds compassion with a cruel edge to it; tenderness which shades into revulsion; and an identification with the sufferer which gradually leads to an appropriation of her pain. Watch the victim closely, he seems to murmur to himself, and become a victim in your own right. The narrator's portraits of the dying Swann early in *Sodome et Gomorrhe*, and of the dying Bergotte in *La Prisonnière*, are marked by similar contrasts and incongruities. Both characters have death written on their faces long before they die, and the narrator's fondness and esteem for them are slowly transmuted into a horrified fascination. An alien force is to be seen reshaping the familiar features of these trusted seniors and mentors, and turning their lively countenances into the mineral waste-matter of which mere heavenly bodies are made. Swann's face is like a 'waning moon' (III, 89; IV, 104), and Bergotte's entire person cools down in the manner of a 'tiny planet' (III, 689; V, 204).

There is of course much that is decent and one might almost say *wholesome* about the passage of these loved and admired characters from life into death. They have 'gone before', as popular Christian moralists used to say, gone where the narrator knows he must also go. He travels with them as far as he can and then leaves them in their last solitude. In shrinking from the *je ne sais quoi* that each of them in the end becomes, he sides with the robust human individuality that each of them once possessed. In these passages, Proust gives his narrator an active capacity for grief and exercises him remorselessly in the contemplation of ruin and decay. But Proust would not be the risky writer that he is if he did not allow his narrator a generous measure of indecency and unwholesomeness too. Human mortality is an affront to good taste and invites the novelist to be tasteless in his turn. The spectacle of death in human affairs appals him, and charms him at the same time. He can resist its ravages, yet gloat over them too. He can introduce characters into his fiction for no more salubrious reason than to watch them die.

Philip Larkin spoke, in 'The Old Fools', a poem from his last published collection *High Windows* (1974), of old people 'crouching below/ Extinction's alp' and noted the premonitory signs of extinction that could be read upon their bodies: 'Ash hair, toad hands, prune face dried into lines'. The combined pity and glee to be found in this poem will be familiar to those readers who have kept company with the minor players in the Proustian social comedy. In *Le Côté de Guermantes*, for example, we encounter in the circle of Mme de Villeparisis one Alix, known in a derisive jingle as the 'marquise du quai Malaquais'. She is one of three seeming relics from the age of Marie-Antoinette who together resemble the classical Fates. The comedy of salon manners gives way in this scene to a grotesque comedy of impending death. To be unsuccessful in the art of conversation involves more than social death; it brings one suddenly closer to the real thing:

Le coup d'Alix avait raté, elle se tut, resta debout et immobile. Des couches de poudre plâtrant son visage, celui-ci avait l'air d'un visage de pierre. Et comme le profil était noble, elle semblait, sur un socle triangulaire et moussu caché par le mantelet, la déesse effritée d'un parc. (II, 497)

Alix's shot had misfired; she stood silent, erect and motionless. Plastered with layers of powder, her face had the appearance of stone. And, since the profile was noble, she seemed, on a triangular, moss-grown pedestal hidden by her cape, like a crumbling goddess in a park. (III, 225)

Alix supporta le coup sans faiblir. Elle restait de marbre. Son regard était perçant et vide, son nez noblement arqué. Mais une joue s'écaillait. Des végétations légères, étranges, vertes et roses, envahissaient le menton. Peut-être un hiver de plus la jetterait bas. (II, 499)

Alix bore the blow without flinching. She remained marble. Her gaze was piercing and blank, her nose proudly arched. But the surface of one cheek was flaking. A faint, strange vegetation, green and pink, was invading her chin. Perhaps another winter would finally lay her low. (III, 229)

In such passages, the narrative voice directs its mockery against Mme de Villeparisis and her kind, and turns the entire culture of the salon into an inflated *vanitas* emblem. Yet the malice of this hostess towards her tiresome antiquated guests is also irresistibly seductive. There is delight to be had in watching other people's faces as they shrivel and flake, or their chins being invaded by menacing vegetable growths. The narrator catches the prevailing tone of the society in which he moves and makes its cruelty his own. His language catches fire: what better fate for a Fate ('Parque') than to be parked in a park ('parc')?

A still more revealing case from among these minor characters called upon to do little else but age and die is that of Mme d'Arpajon. Although she attracts a certain amount of attention earlier in the novel as a former mistress of the duc de Guermantes, it is only in *Sodome et Gomorrhe*, and then in the final tableau of *Le Temps retrouvé*, that she comes briefly into her own. In the first episode, she is drenched by the fountain which adorns the garden of the prince de Guermantes and congratulated by the Grand Duke Vladimir on the aplomb with which she recovers from this indignity. 'Bravo, la vieille!' is the ominous form of compliment he chooses (III, 57; 'Bravo, old girl!' (IV, 67)). By the time of her reappearance in the *bal de têtes*, Mme d'Arpajon has become old indeed and, like so many of her fellow masqueraders, is at first unrecognisable to the narrator. He has to work hard to reconstruct her as she once was:

> Peu à peu pourtant, à force de regarder sa figure hésitante, incertaine comme une mémoire infidèle qui ne peut plus retenir les formes d'autrefois, j'arrivai à en retrouver quelque chose en me livrant au petit jeu d'éliminer les carrés, les hexagones que l'âge avait ajoutés à ses joues. D'ailleurs, ce qu'il mêlait à celles des femmes n'était pas toujours seulement des figures géométriques. Dans les joues restées si semblables pourtant de la duchesse de Guermantes et pourtant composites maintenant comme un nougat, je distinguai une trace de vert-de-gris, un petit morceau rose de coquillage concassé, une grosseur difficile à définir, plus petite qu'une boule de gui et moins transparente qu'une perle de verre.
>
> (IV, 515)

Yet gradually, as I studied her face, hesitant and uncertain like a failing memory which has begun to lose the images of the past, I succeeded in rediscovering something of the face which I had known, by playing a little game of eliminating the squares and the hexagons which age had added to her cheeks. For in her case the material which the years had superimposed consisted of geometrical shapes, though on the cheeks of other women it might be of quite a different character. On those, for instance, of Mme de Guermantes, in many respects so little changed and yet composite now like a bar of nougat, I could distinguish traces here and there of verdigris, a small pink patch of fragmentary shell-work, and a little growth of an indefinable character, smaller than a mistletoe berry and less transparent than a glass bead.

(VI, 308–9)

The almost characterless Mme d'Arpajon is, at this eleventh hour, on the verge of acquiring individual features, for death the geometer has made decipherable marks upon her person. But no sooner has her face been given patterning of its own than the narrator's attention is drawn to another much more familiar face – that of the duchesse de Guermantes – and to sciences less immaterial than mathematics. Mme d'Arpajon is despatched twice over: she exists as a flesh and blood creature only in so far as the narrator is prepared to calculate her back to life, and she has in any case only fleeting interest as a specimen of mortal humankind. The duchesse de Guermantes and the numerous others who follow her in Proust's ghoulish procession are more complex in their dying than this bit-player can ever be. Imminent death turns the assembled company in countless new directions: their tissues are invaded by vegetable stains, calcium deposits, micro-organisms, colonies of polyps, artefacts of glass and marble, and each of their mutations brings a new kind of science into play.

Proust's single conceit is endlessly replayed in this scene. Although death makes everybody putrid in due course, before doing so it makes people resemble all manner of non-human and often super-durable elements of the natural world. Whereas Mme d'Arpajon in the last flicker of her individuality becomes an abstract system of lines and angles, Mme de Guermantes in her facial encrustations lives out a commoner human destiny – that of becoming again, after a brief period of selfhood, indestructible matter extended in physical space. Mind goes; self and character go. And the typical preoccupations of the mental scientist, so richly cultivated by the narrator elsewhere, are abandoned in favour of a fantasmatic geology, palaeontology, zoology, botany and biochemistry. Over and over again the narrator recharges his scientific curiosity by confronting it with withering human flesh:

> Les femmes tâchaient à rester en contact avec ce qui avait été le plus individuel de leur charme, mais souvent la matière nouvelle de leur visage ne s'y prêtait plus. On était effrayé, en pensant aux périodes qui avaient dû s'écouler avant que s'accomplît une pareille révolution dans la géologie d'un visage, de voir quelles érosions s'étaient faites le long du nez, quelles énormes alluvions au bord des joues entouraient toute la figure de leurs masses opaques et réfractaires.
>
> (IV, 524)

> The women sought to remain in contact with whatever had been most individual in their charm, but often the new matter of their face no longer lent itself to this purpose. One was terrified, because it made one think of the vast periods which must have elapsed before such a revolution could be accomplished in the geology of a face, to see what erosions had taken place all the way along the nose, what huge alluvial deposits at the edge of the cheeks surrounded the whole face with their opaque and refractory masses.
>
> (VI, 317, 311-12)

The tone of the whole episode is not one of creaturely compassion but one of intellectual revelry and rage. The narrator, who had previously compared the ailing Brichot, lurking behind his thick spectacles, with 'une insignifiante bestiole agonisante' (III, 703; 'the last throes of some tiny insignificant beast' (V, 221)) in an elaborately equipped laboratory, now emerges as a tireless experimenter on living flesh. He looks beneath the skin, peers through the veil of momentary human affairs to catch a glimpse of the impersonal regularities of nature.

The cruelty of the embryonic Proustian artist is very much part of his project, rather than a set of dark grace-notes or marginalia that he happens to add to it. In order to do justice to his sense of tragedy, to his knowledge that human mortality is an irremediable fact, the narrator cannot simply report on the spectacle of other people's dying. He must deliver death inside his soliloquy, by becoming the agent of a mortal force that seems to be intrinsic not only to external nature but to the daily activities of the human mind. The narrator half-apologises for this disconcerting duty of his at a number of points in *Le Temps retrouvé*:

> On peut dire qu'il n'y avait pas, si je cherchais à ne pas en user inconsciemment mais à me rappeler ce qu'elle avait été, une seule des choses qui nous servaient en ce moment qui n'avait été une chose vivante, et vivant d'une vie personnelle pour nous, transformée ensuite à notre usage en simple matière industrielle. (IV, 608)

> But let us cease to make use of them in an unconscious way, let us try to recall what they once were in our eyes, and how often do we not find that a thing later transformed into, as it were, mere raw material for our industrial use was once alive, and alive for us with a personal life of its own. (VI, 428–9)

One cannot make books in accordance with this scheme without being prepared to imagine people dead and without from time to time becoming Burke and Hare in one's own employ. The narrator will melt down real-life characters and blend them together to produce the dramatis personae of the novel he intends to write, and in the closing stages of his vocational history he already shows inordinate enthusiasm for this industrial reprocessing of the human person. Ruthlessness is required in the manufacture of fictions. Just as Géricault in his studies of dissected limbs paints severed arms and legs in a languid embrace and bathes them in an opulent *chiaroscuro*, so Proust through the mouthpiece of his narrator creates macabre assemblages from human body-parts, and new phantom bodies from the debris of nature, while allowing an irrepressible verbal wit to play across their discontinuous surfaces. Dissection has become one of the fine arts. The writer obliges himself to stay in touch with the undertow of destruction that runs beneath his creative acts.

The savagery of Proust's writing on old age is part of a wider vehemence and disconsolateness in the book as a whole. It would be too easy to be comforted by a cult of artistic work-in-progress and by visions of the artwork itself as complete and consummated in the fullness of time, and the narrator, even as he feeds upon such visions, reminds himself of what art cannot conquer. The 'tiny planet' that Bergotte in the end resembles offers 'une image anticipée des derniers jours de la grande quand, peu à peu, la chaleur se retirera de la Terre, puis la vie' (III, 689; 'a prophetic image of the greater, when gradually heat will withdraw from the earth, then life itself' (V, 204)). The productions of the artist are powerless in the face of the second law of thermodynamics, and Bergotte's journey into oblivion is a prophetic image of the narrator's own:

> Sans doute mes livres eux aussi, comme mon être de chair, finiraient un jour par mourir. Mais il faut se résigner à mourir. On accepte la pensée que dans dix ans soi-même, dans cent ans ses livres, ne seront plus. La durée éternelle n'est pas plus promise aux œuvres qu'aux hommes.
>
> (IV, 620–21)

No doubt my books too, like my fleshly being, would in the end one day die. But death is a thing that we must resign ourselves to. We accept the thought that in ten years we ourselves, in a hundred years our books, will have ceased

to exist. Eternal duration is promised no more to men's
works than to men.   (VI, 445)

Proust's account of death in the closing stages of *Le Temps
retrouvé* is brutal and, within its own terms, exhaustive. Duchesses with sprouting chins and silted cheeks die, but then so
do moons, stars and narrative fictions. Yet although the novelist
is no exception to the general drift of things and is destined –
homme and *œuvre*, kit and caboodle – to disappear from the
scene, he has a privilege that not all construction workers
possess: he can use his knowledge of mutability as building
material for his work. He can raise a fictional edifice which is,
in part at least, held up and held together by an active sense
of its own impermanence.

Le Temps retrouvé* sets out in their largest and most emphatic
form tensions that have been insinuatingly present in the work
from a very early stage. Death in this last volume is on the one
hand made a matter of indifference by the narrator's new-found
sense of creative potency (IV, 446; VI, 218) and, on the other,
becomes deeply ingrained into his sense of selfhood: 'Cette
idée de la mort s'installa définitivement en moi comme fait un
amour' (IV, 619; 'This idea of death took up permanent residence within me in the way that love sometimes does' (VI,
444)). The work of art offers posthumous survival to its originator, yet will definitively cancel him when it too ceases to be.
The narrator's soon-to-be-written novel looks shapely and
enticing, has a youthful bloom upon it, stands out in proud
contrast against the grotesque stricken multitude that society
has become, yet it too, after a pause, faces disfigurement and
decay. And the human power of remembrance, without which
the promised work cannot be realised, is itself, in due course,
to expire.

These tensions bear so much emphasis in *Le Temps retrouvé*
that it would make sense to see a special form of *Bildungsroman*

as reaching completion there. Looking back over the novel's mighty bulk from this late vantage point, we could see the entire thing as having narrated the *Bildung*, the phased growth and development, of novel form itself rather than simply the personal history of Proust's protagonist. Early on, as the narrator sets down his first tentative written reaction to the steeples of Martinville in 'Combray' (I, 179–80; I, 217–18), the idea of a novel had first begun to crystallise, and now, so much later, and with so much imagery of fertility and ripeness still hanging in the air, the novel begins to look ahead to its own wintertime. Once upon a time the novel was not, even as an idea, and at some undateable future time it will again not be. Its little life is rounded with a sleep.

But to view the culminating power of *Le Temps retrouvé* solely in these terms would be to overlook the preoccupation with death that marks so many earlier episodes in the work, and the power that Proust ascribes in them to mortality as an immanent mental force. The narrator's mind is death-dealing when it seeks to improve upon the activities of the ageing process in humans, but more alarmingly so when it returns with quiet insistence to the fact that humans sometimes all too plainly will each other dead and that in their thoughts they wield a power of life and death over all comers. This theme, introduced in the episode of the grandmother's remembered death, rises to a pitch of true terror in the vast aftermath of the narrator's affair with Albertine; and in both episodes it raises tantalising questions about the competence of novel form.

The pathos of the narrator's situation in *Sodome et Gomorrhe*, when he finds himself involuntarily reliving his grandmother's death, is enshrined in the photograph that Saint-Loup had taken of her (III, 155–6 recapitulating II, 144; IV, 183–4 and II, 423). There she is in the photographic image – visible, characterful, a living figure – but at the same time she is not there at all: death, following in the footsteps of Saint-Loup armed with his apparatus, has dematerialised her and reduced her to a lifeless inky trace. The relationships between the photographer and his model and between the representational image and the irretrievable person lying behind it, tell the narrator something important about his grief, but they understate the puzzlement that accompanies his loss. How can it be that the spontaneous movements of my remembering and forgetting mind have such power over another life? That in dreams or daydreams I can summon up, in its phenomenal fullness, the sensation of having a living person close at hand, and then wake to find her not simply gone but deserted and allowed to die? The narrator displays, in repeatedly asking questions of this kind, an unsubduable sense of personal responsibility and intellectual anguish. Whereas earlier in the novel, the 'great mystery' of extinction and resurrection had belonged entirely to the passage of the self through time (II, 177; II, 462), it is now rediscovered in the dealings between the self and others. The narrator's phrases strike off in many directions but this same mysterious polarity exerts a fatal gravitational pull on them:

> cette contradiction si étrange de la survivance et du néant entrecroisés en moi. (III, 156)

> that contradiction of survival and annihilation, so strangely intertwined within me. (IV, 184)

> la douloureuse synthèse de la survivance et du néant.
> (III, 157)

> the painful synthesis of survival and annihilation. (IV, 184)

> cette incompréhensible contradiction du souvenir et du néant. (III, 165)

that incomprehensible contradiction between memory and non-existence. (IV, 194)

The language of this passage is richly figurative and reinvents in tiny allusive touches the fateful journey of Orpheus down into the Plutonian dark. Yet the attempt to rescue a loved one from the realm of death involves, properly speaking, no journey at all. Eurydice is lost and recovered, revived and re-killed, by operations of the mind that seem at once volitional and motiveless. Being in pursuit of her is not movement towards a goal but a drastic mental fidget, and to this the narrator's almost synonymous phrases give voice strongly. An unintelligible rhythm runs through the life of subjectivity, and although the death of a loved person provokes this rhythm in an aggravated form it does not belong to the grieving mind alone. The strange contradiction between survival and nothingness is, in Proust's account, a burden that minds bear anyway, and that is present in any relationship between a living individual and another individual alive or dead. Mourning raises to a new level of intractability a conflict that any intermeshing of subjectivities will already have produced.

One of the things that is so extraordinary about the Albertine 'episode' – if one may be allowed the term in speaking of a sequence that extends across a thousand and more pages of Proust's text – is that the story it tells so firmly refuses to be a story. In this narration the end of the affair, and its 'aftermath', as I called it a moment ago, resemble the affair itself in countless particulars. Albertine gone is uncannily similar to Albertine present and threatening to go. Albertine dead is brought back to life not simply by chance memories and associations, but by a vigorous resurrectionist tendency of the narrator's imagination: he exhumes her in order to have her die again. The whole thing is the chronicle of a loss that perpetually stops short of completion, of an absence that is never absence enough, and of a narrative structure that constantly threatens to dissolve into a plotless pattern of vanishings and reappearances.

Albertine disparue is built on a foundation of coincidences and improbable recurrences, very much in the manner of a fantastic tale. The narrator learns of Albertine's death as a civil subject by way of a telegram from her aunt, Mme Bontemps: 'MON PAUVRE AMI, NOTRE PETITE ALBERTINE N'EST PLUS . . .' (IV, 58; 'My poor friend, our little Albertine is no more' (V, 544)). But even as he reports on the previously unknown form of suffering that this news prompted in him, he is reminded of the words in which his mother had told him of his grandmother's death: 'Mon pauvre petit, ta grand-mère qui t'aimait tant ne t'embrassera plus' (IV, 59; 'My poor boy, your grandmother who was so fond of you will never kiss you again' (V, 545)). This is one of many moments in the novel where the two lost women are linked in the narrator's reverie and where words appropriate to the one are re-used of the other. The two loves were incommensurable – the one all tenderness and solace and the other causing jealous anguish – yet the deaths of the two women move him in the same way and place upon him a single responsibility for remembrance: if he stops thinking about them they will irreversibly cease to be.

A further uncanny textual repetition enhances this sense of undifferentiation between love-objects. A telegram having brought news of Albertine's death, a second telegram, from Gilberte (we learn after a period of suspense), seems to bring her back to life again: 'MON AMI VOUS ME CROYEZ MORTE, PARDONNEZ-MOI, JE SUIS TRÈS VIVANTE . . .' (IV, 220; 'My dear friend, you think me dead, forgive me, I am quite alive . . .' (V, 736)). The reader's curiosity is teased, and in due course is to be satisfied, but the narrator's immediate

commentary on the message goes a long way towards disabling
the wish for knowledge before it has fully taken hold:

> Alors il se passa d'une façon inverse la même chose que
> pour ma grand-mère: quand j'avais appris *en fait* que ma
> grand-mère était morte je n'avais d'abord eu aucun chagrin.
> Et je n'avais souffert effectivement de sa mort que quand
> des souvenirs involontaires l'avaient rendue vivante pour
> moi. Maintenant qu'Albertine dans ma pensée ne vivait plus
> pour moi, la nouvelle qu'elle était vivante ne me causa pas
> la joie que j'aurais cru. Albertine n'avait été pour moi qu'un
> faisceau de pensées, elle avait survécu à sa mort matérielle
> tant que ces pensées vivaient en moi; en revanche maintenant
> que ces pensées étaient mortes, Albertine ne ressuscitait
> nullement pour moi avec son corps.   (IV, 220)

> Then there occurred in me in reverse a process parallel to
> that which had occurred in the case of my grandmother.
> When I had learned the fact of my grandmother's death, I
> had not at first felt any grief. And I had been really grieved
> by her death only when certain involuntary memories had
> brought her alive again for me. Now that Albertine no longer
> lived for me in my thoughts, the news that she was alive
> did not cause me the joy that I might have expected.
> Albertine had been no more to me than a bundle of thoughts,
> and she had survived her physical death so long as those
> thoughts were alive in me; on the other hand, now that
> those thoughts were dead, Albertine did not rise again for
> me with the resurrection of her body.   (V, 736-7)

Again the individuality of the two women is smoothed away
in favour of a capacious theoretical claim. The dead have an
afterlife only as the creatures of a living person's thought, and
one does not even have to be dead in empirically verifiable
ways in order to enjoy the privilege. Gilberte, who is alive,
communicative and on the verge of marriage, is, by virtue of
being one of the narrator's lost loves, already entitled to join

this ghostly company. The three women merge, not as an eternal feminine or a composite Eurydice but as an instrument of the narrator's thinking. Each is a 'bundle of thoughts', but something much more organised too: a mental structure by which absence is woven into presence, and losing into having.

If this section of *Albertine disparue* belongs to the literature of 'the fantastic', it brings something quite unusual to that tradition in that it builds bridges between ancient myth and the modern communications industry. Orpheus speaks on the telephone, and messages are sent by telegram from Hades to the upper world. Coincidence is everywhere. Gilberte's telegram is strange in itself in that it seems to answer and revoke an earlier telegram of which she had no knowledge, and doubly strange in that it repeats a coincidence from earlier in the novel. In *Le Côté de Guermantes*, the narrator had found himself receiving a telephone call from someone else's grandmother, believing her for a moment to be his own (II, 436; III, 152). In both cases, error is superinduced upon error, and a faulty communications network becomes the emblem of a mental world over which the individual can exercise little authority or control. Information gets lost, misheard, misread and misinterpreted. Meaning is arbitrarily cancelled, distorted and restored. Subjectivity becomes so much centreless circuitry, an impersonal mechanism with no hard volitional core.

Speculative writing of this kind, which among its many subjects dwells on the perils of excessive speculation, has in Proust's hands a magical capacity for self-renewal, but it is marked, too, by massive levels of redundancy. In *La Prisonnière* and *Albertine disparue* the narrator has two main claims to make about Albertine as a personality, and each of them is also, and lavishly, a claim about certain features of the mental life. (Albertine acts in this novel both as a character like any other and as an especially promising entry point to an elaborate dynamic psychology.) The first claim is simply that Albertine is a void, and that if the exertions of the narrator's consciousness do not provide her with shape and substance she will return to her native blankness. The second is that, desire-driven minds abhorring a vacuum, Albertine is an inexhaustible stimulus to fantasy and the elaboration of fiction. And of course claims of this kind hold good on either side of her disappearance and subsequent death. In *La Prisonnière* she has only to leave the room for the narrator to feel 'le néant qu'elle était pour moi' (III, 538; 'how utterly meaningless she was to me' (V, 23)), and at any stage, absent or present, dead or alive, she can have *le néant* – literally 'nothingness' – thrust upon her. *Albertine disparue* recounts the narrator's endlessly frustrated attempt to create a lasting pocket of oblivion for his former partner. In the same way, he excites and torments himself with fantasies that are not governed by such matters as the material death of the beloved. During the period of her captivity Albertine was a suspect under constant surveillance, imagined by the narrator as enjoying love-play with others whenever she could briefly escape him, and imagined imagining it whenever she could not. After her death, the work of fantasy carries on unabated. The narrator is assailed by what he had already had occasion to call 'staircase jealousy' (III, 594; V, 90), a feeling which, like 'staircase wit' ('l'esprit de l'escalier'), comes too late to have any practical impact on the affairs of men and women:

> Mes curiosités jalouses de ce qu'avait pu faire Albertine étaient infinies. J'achetai combien de femmes qui ne m'apprirent rien. Si ces curiosités étaient si vivaces, c'est que l'être ne meurt pas tout de suite pour nous, il reste baigné d'une espèce d'aura de vie qui n'a rien d'une immortalité véritable mais qui fait qu'il continue à occuper nos pensées de la même manière que quand il vivait.   (IV, 92)

My jealous curiosity as to what Albertine might have done was unbounded. I suborned any number of women from whom I learned nothing. If this curiosity was so tenacious, it was because people do not die for us immediately, but remain bathed in a sort of aura of life which bears no relation to true immortality but through which they continue to occupy our thoughts in the same way as when they were alive. (V, 584)

As a story of quest and conquest playing themselves out in a mental interior, this paragraph, and others having the same underlying rhythm, are profoundly disappointing. The introspective mind presses ahead towards new discoveries, yet finds instead a time-honoured pattern and a sententious wisdom that it itself has already made commonplace. The narrator already knows that jealousy is retroactive, that mental killing and resuscitation belong to a causal order that is quite different from the one in which murders and fatal accidents occur, and that he had lived through the pain of bereavement long before being bereft. However fierce his later curiosity becomes, its earlier prototypes have forestalled it. Wherever his later journeys lead, Albertine has always arrived there before him. She is already dead before a riding accident kills her, and still alive after the burial rites have been performed. She is an insoluble conundrum, and an unstoppable supplier of current to the networks of the text.

Material of this kind is of course stubbornly resistant to the ordinary architectonic requirements of fictional narrative. Chronology, causality and any convincing sense of culmination, outcome or dialectical resolution are difficult to impose upon a closely woven tissue of abstract motifs all of which seem to be simultaneously in force. Proust is of course ingenious in holding certain aspects of the problem at bay. His haunting coincidences and sudden *coups de théâtre*, even at the expense of seeming melodramatic at times, create a real sense of shape and of temporal progression within the ramifications of a story that refuses to behave like one. And the problem of creating a coherent narrative out of a most unpromising set of introspective manoeuvres is ascribed not to the author but to the narrator. It is one of the things that makes him interesting as a character and the solution that he eventually supplies in *Le Temps retrouvé* helps Proust to end his novel on a triumphant reassertion of narrative closure. This is the successfully worked-out story of a man who, for long periods of his emotional career, finds it difficult to tell stories that end.

Yet despite these eventual architectural achievements, the Albertine episode is in itself a tumbledown narrative edifice, and has a non-narratable rhythm running through it. Proust frequently characterises this quality of recalcitrance in his material. In *Sodome et Gomorrhe*, the periodic inward destruction of the loved-one's after-image is likened to 'une douleur physique à répétition' (III, 155; IV, 182), a physical pain that has a repeater mechanism fitted to it, in the manner of a rifle or a clock. Pain has no story to tell: it is there or not, tolerable or not, increasing or declining in intensity, but of progress and argument and sense-making over time it knows nothing. At moments the text of the novel is given over to these empty rhythms of pain, and the action of the repeater becomes noisily audible:

> de même qu'on a peine à penser qu'un mort fut vivant ou que celui qui était vivant est mort aujourd'hui, il est presque aussi difficile, et du même genre de difficulté [. . .] de concevoir que celle qui fut jeune est vieille, quand l'aspect de cette vieille, juxtaposé à celui de la jeune, semble tellement l'exclure que tour à tour c'est la vieille, puis la jeune, puis la vieille encore qui vous paraissent un rêve. (IV, 519)

> just as one has difficulty in thinking that a dead person was once alive or that a person who was alive is now dead, so

> one has difficulty, almost as great and of the same kind [. . .]
> in conceiving that she who was once a girl is now an old
> woman when the juxtaposition of the two appearances, the
> old and the young, seems so totally to exclude the possibility
> of their belonging to the same person that alternately it is
> the old woman and then the girl and then again the old
> woman who seems to one to be a dream.   (VI, 312)

In this passage from *Le Temps retrouvé*, the central contrast
to be found in the final stages of the volume is reduced to an
unlovely staccato. Characters who were once young are now
old and death-threatened. The narrator has already told us
this, and he will tell us it again at enormous length. The
desperate see-sawing of *jeune* and *vieille* is not a perception
but an impediment to perception, and a mortification of the
narrative impulse. Contraries flap against each other: youth
against age, survival against extinction. Nothing else is happening.

Large sections of the Albertine episode are given over to a
looser-limbed version of this rhythm. Although Albertine herself is fleet-footed and multiform, the brooding to which she
gives rise finds the narrator returning endlessly to the scene of
his earliest separation anxieties, and to a quasi-philosophical
meditation on loss, and on death which is the hyperbolic
expression of loss, as they seep through the shifting textures
of human consciousness. Albertine is becalmed in the text,
embalmed by it, lost beneath the glistening glaze of its abstractions. Nothing can happen, and no story can be told, as the
mortician-narrator moves to and fro.

As might be expected of a writer as penetrating in his self-
awareness as Proust, exactly this tendency of the narrator's
imagination is solidified into subject-matter for the book. The
perils faced by an artistic mind that is too much in love with
concepts and categories are figured in a resolutely matter- based

language – that of sculpture in general, and of mortuary sculptural decoration in particular. Death goes to work upon the grandmother's face, first in the manner of a malevolent artisan:

> [son visage] avait tellement changé que sans doute, si elle eût eu la force de sortir, on ne l'eût reconnue qu'à la plume de son chapeau. Ses traits, comme dans des séances de modelage, semblaient s'appliquer, dans un effort qui la détournait de tout le reste, à se conformer à certain modèle que nous ne connaissions pas. Ce travail du statuaire touchait à sa fin et, si la figure de ma grand-mère avait diminué, elle avait également durci. Les veines qui la traversaient semblaient celles, non pas d'un marbre, mais d'une pierre plus rugueuse. (II, 620)

> [her face] was so altered that probably, had she been strong enough to go out, she would have been recognised only by the feather in her hat. Her features, as though during a modelling session, seemed to be straining, with an effort which distracted her from everything else, to conform to some particular model which we failed to identify. The work of the sculptor was nearing its end, and if my grandmother's face had shrunk in the process, it had at the same time hardened. The veins that traversed it seemed those not of marble, but of some more rugged stone. (III, 372)

and then in the manner of one commissioned to provide spiritual consolation:

> Un sourire semblait posé sur les lèvres de ma grand-mère. Sur ce lit funèbre, la mort, comme le sculpteur du Moyen Âge, l'avait couchée sous l'apparence d'une jeune fille. (II, 641)

> A smile seemed to be hovering on my grandmother's lips. On that funeral couch, death, like a sculptor of the Middle Ages, had laid her down in the form of a young girl. (III, 397)

The true horror of such workmanship emerges, however, when the narrator begins to realise that his task is to replicate it, and that writing a book involves creating a mausoleum for individuals who were once alive. Living substance is enmarbled and entombed by the writer's pen; the semantic commotion of a literary text gives a false air of animation to what are now only frozen simulacra of the human form.

Proust's statuary is assembled, demolished and reassembled with breathtaking virtuosity, and long-range cross-references between images abound. In 'Un Amour de Swann', Mme Verdurin, on hearing the names of certain 'bores' mentioned, turns herself into an impenetrable surface which repels inopportune conversational sallies: 'Ce n'était plus qu'une cire perdue, qu'un masque de plâtre, qu'une maquette pour un monument, qu'un buste pour le Palais de l'Industrie' (I, 255; 'She was no more than a wax cast, a plaster mask, a maquette for a monument, a bust for the Palace of Industry' (I, 311)). During the scene in *La Prisonnière* in which Vinteuil's septet is first performed, Mme Verdurin's art of striking monumental poses reaches new heights: she becomes a 'divinité qui présidait aux solennités musicales, déesse du wagnérisme et de la migraine, sorte de Norne presque tragique, évoquée par le génie au milieu de ces ennuyeux' (III, 753; 'a deity presiding over the musical rites, goddess of Wagnerism and sick-headaches, a sort of almost tragic Norn, conjured up by the spell of genius in the midst of all these "bores" ' (V, 281)), and the anatomical feature which is most plainly sculptural and best-equipped to hold bores at a distance, undergoes a corresponding amplification. The forehead which had once been merely 'bombé' or 'domed' (I, 254; I, 311), now reappears in duplex form: 'les hémisphères de son front blanc et légèrement rosé magnifiquement bombés' (III, 753; 'the twin hemispheres of her pale, slightly roseate brow magnificently bulging' (V, 280)). Similarly, Legrandin, who in 'Combray' had rhapsodised to the narrator of Balbec and spoken of its coast as 'la plus antique ossature géologique de notre sol' (I, 129; 'the most ancient bone in the geological skeleton that underlies our soil' (I, 156)), in *Le Temps retrouvé* has become a bony geological specimen in his own right:

> La suppression du rose, que je n'avais jamais soupçonné artificiel, de ses lèvres et de ses joues donnait à sa figure l'apparence grisâtre et aussi la précision sculpturale de la pierre, sculptait ses traits allongés et mornes comme ceux de certains dieux égyptiens. (IV, 513)

> The suppression of the pink, which I had never suspected of being artificial, upon his lips and his cheeks gave to his countenance the greyish tinge and also the sculptural precision of stone, so that with his long-drawn and gloomy features he was like some Egyptian god. (VI, 304)

In this closing sequence of the novel, as we have seen, death moves as a monumental mason among the assembled guests, petrifying their facial tissues and carving a premature memorial to each of them in turn. The last appearance of sculpted stone in the novel coincides with the last echo of Balbec and its coastal storms: the duc de Guermantes stands as a weather-worn block, lashed by seas of the kind that the young narrator had first discovered in Brittany and Normandy, and awaiting 'la tempête où tout va sombrer' (IV, 595; 'a supreme all-foundering storm' (VI, 411)).

By far the most sinister of these figures, however, is another stone hostess rather than a stone guest. The narrator inserts a sudden hairpin bend into his last stretch of linear narrative in order to accommodate an event taking place at 'the other end of Paris'. This is a modest tea-party given by La Berma, which runs concurrently with the Guermantes *matinée* and divides the loyalties of the single guest who appears:

> La Berma avait, comme dit le peuple, la mort sur le visage. Cette fois c'était bien d'un marbre de l'Érechtéion qu'elle

avait l'air. Ses artères durcies étant déjà à demi pétrifiées, on voyait de longs rubans sculpturaux parcourir les joues, avec une rigidité minérale. Les yeux mourants vivaient relativement, par contraste avec ce terrible masque ossifié, et brillaient faiblement comme un serpent endormi au milieu des pierres. (IV, 575-6)

Death, as the saying goes, was written all over her face, and she resembled nothing so much as one of the marble figures in the Erechtheum. Her hardened arteries were already almost petrified, so that what appeared to be long sculptural ribbons ran across her cheeks, with the rigidity of a mineral substance. The dying eyes were still relatively alive, by contrast at least with the terrible ossified mask, and glowed feebly like a snake asleep in the midst of a pile of stones. (VI, 386)

This description could have been a straightforward retreat from the printed page towards the gestural artistry of the great actress and the mute splendour of Greek sculpture. La Berma's approaching death could properly have called forth from her a last grand histrionic posture; her calm strength in the face of death could have conjured up memories of the impassivity with which the caryatids on the Erechtheum porch bear the weight of the entablature above them.

But in fact this brief visit to the Acropolis takes us on a long journey back within the novel, and speaks volumes about the powers of the printed page. The narrator's last reference to the Erechtheum and its female figures had been in *A l'ombre des jeunes filles en fleurs*, during the scene in which Mme Swann presides over a luncheon in honour of Bergotte. There the qualities of the actress's performance in Racine's *Phèdre* had been tossed to and fro in bookish conversation between Swann, Bergotte and the narrator, and a benign competition had developed between them in the deployment of information about Athens (I, 550-52; II, 155-7). La Berma's characteristic gesture of the arm in one particularly acclaimed scene had been modelled, consciously or not, on certain of the *Korai* to be found in the Acropolis Museum rather than on the caryatids themselves. Bergotte, as he makes this and other claims, dazzles the narrator with his learning, wit and sense of style. He is a critic as well as a novelist and essayist, and the author indeed of a short work on *Phèdre*; he even comes close, in the narrator's enchanted evocation of his literary prowess, to becoming the author of the celebrated 'prayer on the Acropolis' that Renan had declaimed in his *Souvenirs d'enfance et de jeunesse* (1883).

La Berma had, in short, been lost to literature in this earlier episode. And what the narrator now does at the very end of the novel, while gently correcting Bergotte and moving his reader's attention back from the museum to the temple itself ('Cette fois c'était bien d'un marbre de l'Érechtéion qu'elle avait l'air'), is re-assume and re-assert the textual imperative in his own name. La Berma is summoned up from the remote past of the novel, conjured into the narrative from the other end of Paris, in order to become a stony spectre like so many others, a further exhibit in an already overflowing museum of antiquities. Literature has claimed her again, and this time for good. She joins this statuesque company rather as Judith joins the assembled former brides of Bluebeard at the end of Bartók's opera (1911). There is of course still a great deal of play in the text at this point, a delicate lapping of image against remembered image, and a sense that literature in the end casts only a flimsy palliative film over the stark reality of human dying, but the would-be deadliness of the artistic enterprise itself is nevertheless relentlessly emphasised. A snake is asleep among the rocky surfaces of La Berma's face, and the narrator, in order to write the book he has been planning, must be prepared to become that snake and bare his teeth. Novels of worth do not emerge from the pens of those whose intentions are always virtuous and whose venom-sac has been surgically removed.

Death in Proust's novel, then, has two faces which are monumental, elaborate and inseparable from each other. On the one hand death is a transcendent power, part of an overarching natural design in which the lives of human individuals count for very little; it is visited from without upon the human body and upon consciousness. But on the other hand, death is immanent in human minds, a power that individuals seek to exercise upon others and, more selectively, upon themselves. When news reaches the narrator, early in *Le Temps retrouvé*, that Robert de Saint-Loup has been killed at the front, the narrator's report is equivocal to the point of undecidability on the question of where responsibility for this event lies. It is one more slaying in a roll-call of millions, an accidental death which has taken place inside a framework of calculated mass slaughter. Yet the power of death, both in war and in peace-time, is such that the accidents which precipitate it are no more than the 'formalities necessary for its realisation':

> Et ne serait-il pas possible que la mort accidentelle elle-même
> – comme celle de Saint-Loup, liée d'ailleurs à son caractère
> de plus de façons peut-être que je n'ai cru devoir le dire –
> fût, elle aussi, inscrite d'avance, connue seulement des dieux,
> invisible aux hommes, mais révélée par une tristesse à demi
> inconsciente, à demi consciente [. . .] particulière à celui
> qui la porte et l'aperçoit sans cesse, en lui-même, comme
> une devise, une date fatale? (IV, 429)

And may it not be possible that accidental death too – like that of Saint-Loup, which was perhaps in any case linked to his character in more ways than I have thought it necessary to describe – is somehow recorded in advance, known only to the gods, invisible to men, but revealed by a peculiar sadness, half unconscious, half conscious [. . .] to the man who bears and forever sees it within himself, as though it were some heraldic device, a fatal date? (VI, 196-7)

Saint-Loup is the part-instigator of his own going; he has heard the call of an external law and made it part of an internal necessity seeking consummation at its appointed hour.

'La mort paraît assujettie à certaines lois' (IV, 429; 'death appears to be obedient to certain laws' (VI, 196)): the narrator's extended final tribute to the law-governed action of death both in the cosmos and in the intimacy of the human affections casts an eerie retrospective light on much that has been narrated earlier in the novel. Disparate features of the work suddenly seem to be developing a new collective meaning. The narrator and Albertine had been locked in prolonged deadly combat. The narrator had been the sole instrument of survival for his dead grandmother. He had dwelt with rapt attention upon the impermanence of human selfhood, and seen each new self that the individual achieved as requiring that its predecessor self be destroyed. He had watched ruthless artists sacrificing living human beings to the requirements of their trade, and assembling their fictional characters from the *disjecta membra* of their family and friends. And he had understood, from within the dense fabric of his own abstract reflections, the impatient movement of the scientific intelligence from mere local particulars to an imposing general scheme. As the novel moves towards its close, all these different dispositions of the human mind begin to acquire the force of a single encompassing legal provision. This is 'la loi cruelle de l'art' (IV, 615; 'the cruel law of art' (VI, 438)), in the narrator's last shorthand formulation, and it had been framed in terms appropriate to the artistic workshop on numerous earlier occasions:

> Aussi fallait-il me résigner, puisque rien ne peut durer qu'en devenant général et si l'esprit meurt à soi-même, à l'idée que même les êtres qui furent le plus chers à l'écrivain n'ont

fait en fin de compte que poser pour lui comme chez les peintres. (IV, 484)

And so I had to resign myself, since nothing has the power to survive unless it can become general and since the mind's own past is dead to its present consciousness, to the idea that even the people who were once most dear to the writer have in the long run done no more than pose for him like models for a painter. (VI, 264)

But, here and elsewhere, what painters, writers and composers do in obedience to the conventions of their guild is of interest to others only because artists also grapple, beyond the tools and materials of their craft, with an inveterate tendency of the human mind. The narrator generalises boldly about the will to generalise: it is the mind seeking furtherance by way of its own extinction. Artists and scientists travel this route, but so do all thinking beings who have stumbled upon knowledge of their own mortality. All members of this community of the mind create memorials to themselves, and identify with what is expected to outlast them.

Proust, in attributing to his narrator this alertness to death as a law of nature and inviting him to address its consequences at such length, almost but not quite becomes a latterday Epicurean philosopher. The performance is impressively coherent: death is an inescapable presence in nature and in minds, which are natural products like any other and, for all their singular qualities, still subject to the general law of growth and decay. This being a work of self-conscious literary art rather than a treatise, the narrator is called upon to personify a variety of viewpoints and to give each of them their appropriate rhythm and intensity within a single protracted dramatic monologue. Embodying the viewpoint of courageous acceptance, the narrator speaks of death as Montaigne or Lucretius did, and gives it a seductive, variegated and all too human voice. Montaigne in his great essay 'Que philosopher, c'est apprendre à mourir' ('To philosophize is to learn how to die') (1580) had given to Nature itself the role of a compassionate spokeswoman for death:

> Mais nature nous y force. «Sortez, dit-elle, de ce monde, comme vous y estes entrez. Le mesme passage que vous fites de la mort à la vie, sans passion et sans frayeur, refaites le de la vie à la mort. Vostre mort est une des pieces de l'ordre de l'univers; c'est une piece de la vie du monde,
>
> > *inter se mortales mutua vivunt*
> > *Et quasi cursores vitaï lampada tradunt.*
>
> Changeray-je pas pour vous cette belle contexture des choses? C'est la condition de vostre creation, c'est une partie de vous que la mort; vous vous fuyez vous mesmes. Cettuy vostre estre, que vous joüyssez, est egalement party à la mort et à la vie. Le premier jour de vostre naissance vous achemine à mourir comme à vivre,
>
> > *Prima, quæ vitam dedit, hora carpsit.*
> > *Nascentes morimur, finisque ab origine pendet.*
>
> Tout ce que vous vivez, vous le desrobez à la vie; c'est à ses despens. Le continuel ouvrage de vostre vie, c'est bastir la mort. Vous estes en la mort pendant que vous estes en vie. Car vous estes après la mort quand vous n'estes plus en vie.

Nature drives us that way, too: 'Leave this world', she says, 'just as you entered it. That same journey from death to life, which you once made without suffering or fear, make it again from life to death. Your death is a part of the order of the universe; it is a part of the life of the world: *Mortal creatures live lives dependent on each other; like runners in a relay they pass on the torch of life.* Shall I change, just for you, this beautiful interwoven structure! Death is one of the attributes you were created with; death is a part of you; you are running away from yourself; this *being* which you enjoy is equally divided between death and life. From the day you were born your path leads to death as well as life: *Our first hour gave us life and began to devour it. As we are born we die; the end of our life is attached to its beginning.* All that you live, you have stolen from life; you live at her expense. Your life's continual task is to build your death. You are *in* death while you are *in* life: when you are no more *in* life you are after death.

Lucretius, in the main passage that Montaigne is here imitating and adapting, had similarly personified Nature, and under that alias had called humankind to account for its feebleness in the face of mortality:

> Denique si vocem rerum natura repente
> mittat et hoc alicui nostrum sic increpet ipsa:
> 'quid tibi tanto operest, mortalis, quod nimis aegris
> luctibus indulges? quid mortem congemis ac fles?'
>
> (*De rerum natura*, III, 931–4)

> Suppose that Nature herself were suddenly to find a voice and round upon one of us in these terms: 'What is your grievance, mortal, that you give yourself up to this whining and repining? Why do you weep and wail over death?'

Proust's narrator can also sound wise and comfortably cajoling on the theme of death, especially towards the end of the novel and especially when he speaks in his moralising vein. Death is part of the natural order, and need hold no terrors for the reflective intelligence. Even when it spreads as a contagion through the inner world of human subjectivity it remains law-bound, and an astute observer has no reason to panic as he watches its encroachments. The narrator is exhilarated by the languages of observational and experimental science, and often seems to suggest that a new zoology, geology or physics of the human passions, including the desire for death, is about to be unveiled. Besides, even when we remind ourselves that the narrator is 'a character' in the fullest sense rather than a passing rhetorical device after the model of Montaigne's Mother Nature, and that he can be characterfully unreliable, he often talks conspicuous good sense. So much so that it is tempting to call him 'Proust', and to include him in the great tradition of the French *moralistes*.

Yet Proust's account of the *belle contexture des choses*, the interwoven fabric of the natural world as caught in the ingenious shimmer of the narrator's soliloquy, differs from Montaigne's in one essential respect. At moments, it conspires with violence and death; for long paragraphs, it has suffering, dread, outrage and, yes, panic running through it. The narrator schools himself in cruelty, and is prepared, when it comes to the effects of death-awareness upon the mind, and of illness and ageing upon the body, to cultivate excess. He croons over disfigurement. He steals with slow delectation through his chamber of horrors, pausing before each stony death-mask. If we were looking for a point of contact between this component of the narrative voice and the sensibilities of the European Renaissance, we might well go not to the essays of Montaigne but to the plays of his English contemporary Shakespeare, and remember those moments when Elizabethan disenchantment veers towards Jacobean brutality. 'Violent sorrow seems a modern ecstasy', says Ross, describing the state into which Scotland has fallen after Macbeth's usurpation of the throne. Even when we have reminded ourselves that Shakespeare's 'modern ecstasy' may well have had a medical tinge to it – suggesting not just rapture but a possible organic lesion – the phrase is entirely appropriate to a novelist in the Proustian mould. For Proust is a writer who has a keen eye for symptoms and records them with relish, and one who looks forward in his modernity to the pestilential theatre of Artaud, and the ecstatic cruelties of Genet's *Les Bonnes* (*The Maids*, 1948) and *Le Balcon* (*The Balcony*, 1956),

Peter Weiss's *Marat/Sade* (1964), or Hubert Selby Jr's *Last Exit to Brooklyn* (1966).

These divergent views of death make the narrator yet again into an odd hybrid, or so it at first seems. He is capable of philosophic calm, yet has a mania for emblems and mementoes of death. But perhaps there is something not unusual at all about this particular relationship. It could be claimed that Proust needs his stricken Guermantes guests rather as Sir Thomas Browne needed his archaeological discoveries in the essay on Urn-Burial (1658) – as an anchorage for his general observations on mortality. Luminous maxims take on a new quality of precision and particularity, and a new curiosity-value, when they are offered to the reader in this way. New knowledge of death has been stirred into existence during the contemplation of material relics, and remains memorable by way of a continuing association with them. 'Time, which antiquates antiquities, and hath an art to make dust of all things, hath yet spared these minor monuments', wrote Browne of his captivating Norfolk urns; and Proust gathers durable curiosities into his text with a similar sense of relief, and of intellectual joy. His petrified dukes and duchesses are the minor monuments which allow the writer sufficient exemption from death to allow him to carry on writing. They are the talismanic figurines which oversee his literary labours.

Yet the novel does contain a major internal disproportion, and this is to be seen in the uneasy co-presence of Proust's generalising death-haunted textual music and what could be called the social comedy of dying. I know of nothing stranger in this strange book. By the time the end of his narrative comes into view, the narrator has long been convinced that suffering suits the purposes of his future book much better than happiness. Where the one is fertile, the other is barren. Where the one gives forward propulsion to the creative project, the other places a drag upon it. But a corollary of this view is that death begins to acquire a new prestige: 'comme on comprend que la souffrance est la meilleure chose que l'on puisse rencontrer dans la vie, on pense sans effroi, presque comme à une délivrance, à la mort' (IV, 488; 'once one understands that suffering is the best thing that one can hope to encounter in life, one thinks without terror, and almost as of a deliverance, of death' (VI, 271)). The superior epistemic status that he grants to painful over pleasurable experiences finds expression at times in macabre sentences of terrifying intensity:

> Les chagrins sont des serviteurs obscurs, détestés, contre lesquels on lutte, sous l'empire de qui on tombe de plus en plus, des serviteurs atroces, impossibles à remplacer et qui par des voies souterraines nous mènent à la vérité et à la mort. (IV, 488)

> Sorrows are servants, obscure and detested, against whom one struggles, beneath whose dominion one more and more completely falls, dire and dreadful servants whom it is impossible to replace and who by subterranean paths lead us towards truth and death. (VI, 272)

These nightmare members of the household staff are not born in a passing moment of Gothic fantasy. They are an image that suddenly distils a major tendency of the preceding narration, an extreme form of what might be called, in Heideggerian phrase, the being-towards-death (*sein zum Tode*) of Proust's novel. So much pain, so much loss, have already been dramatised in this work, that it makes a desperate kind of sense for the whole thing to be seen latterly as an *ars moriendi*. The secret destination of the narrator's quest has been a moment of combined truth-death beyond which there is silence at last. Yet if writing of this kind speaks of an intolerable but inescapable immanence of death in literary creativity, another kind of writing, running alongside it at times and intertwined with it at

others, has an entirely distinct tonality. Proust's novel contains a
sociological study of the customs and rituals associated with
death, and this is set forth as a source of unembarrassed mirth
and high spirits.

The grandmother's death-scene, which is so plaintive and
so fully stocked with clinical details, is also an occasion for
satirical comedy in the grand manner. Three separate medical
practitioners are involved, and the last of them, M. Dieulafoy,
who specialises in the last rites, offering his patients a secular-
ised sacrament of extreme unction, calls forth from the narrator:
'on se croyait chez Molière (II, 638; 'one thought one was in
a Molière play' (III, 394)). All three are proficient, yet each in
turn becomes a figure of fun. 'Le professeur', who had been
delayed in his party-going by the grandmother's stroke, is to
reappear at another party in *Sodome et Gomorrhe* and be given
Molieresque speeches of his own. Françoise is concerned that
this death should be played as a 'scene' in the true theatrical
sense, and finds the whole thing slightly disappointing and
worthy only of a provincial troupe (II, 627; III, 381); she takes
herself away from the care of her patient in order to try on the
mourning attire she has already ordered (II, 631; III, 385).
The broadest comedy is to be found in the procession of
visitors who come to pay their last respects, or who are kept
away by subsequent engagements or less important business.
These characters are recalled by the narrator in *Le Temps
retrouvé* and raised there to a new satirical power. This later
social world is one in which the multitude of the dying are
now making serious demands on other people's time, but in
which that time is readily granted. He speaks of the 'assiduité
frivole de visiteurs attirés par une curiosité de touristes ou une
confiance de pèlerins' (IV, 524; 'the frivolous attentions of
visitors, drawn to them by the curiosity of a tourist or the
pious hopes of a pilgrim' (VI, 316)).

Similar explosions of mirth, having similar long-range after-shocks, are occasioned by the simple ruthlessness with which the living may choose to ignore the dying or the dead. People have their own lives to lead as others breathe their last, and those who insist on 'business as usual' are in a way displaying good sense and a laudable instinct for self-preservation. Proust insists, however, on a large comic discrepancy: while one person faces extinction, another devotes himself with deranged intensity to his latest leisure-time pursuit. In *Le Côté de Guermantes*, Swann announces to the Guermantes couple that he is mortally ill, yet fails to detain the attention of either of them. Where the duchess is uncertain about the etiquette governing occasions of this kind, the duke chooses an easier path, which is that of denial. The doctors are wrong; Swann will outlive all his friends, and in any case the matter is of smaller signifi-cance to the duke than his wife's regrettable choice of black shoes worn with a red dress. The whole incident is constructed as a self-contained joke in a gallows-humour vein and *Le Côté de Guermantes* derives from this joke its resounding curtain-line. But the incident is not closed at this point: in *Sodome et Gomorrhe* it is to be replayed twice, when the Guermantes refuse to allow their social plans to be disturbed by the death of their cousin Amanien, marquis d'Osmond (III, 61–2, 123; IV, 71–2, 144), and in *Le Temps retrouvé* it is to be summoned up again, when, in conversation, the red dress, and the red shoes which the duchess eventually agreed to wear, reappear as long-lost memories (IV, 588–9; VI, 402). The shoes, which link all these episodes, become in a strict sense fetish objects: they supply their wearer and her consort with a feeling of social potency. They are a monument to an everyday selfishness which may become cruel and insatiable. Self-preservation is now the only law remaining in force. The social life of the *faubourg* is red in tooth, claw and shoes.

As Proust repeats his joke, meshes it with others of the same kind, and extracts new meanings from it in its passage through time, a savage gaiety seizes hold of the book. Death, from being elsewhere a metaphysical conundrum or a biological necessity, becomes a pure social construct. All deaths become public events, upheavals within the force-field of society, and nutritious conversational fodder. Individuals die not simply because their organs can no longer sustain them, but because other people have switched off the life-support systems on which they depend. Social death – being expelled from a clan, excommunicated by old friends, or ignored in the street by a passing acquaintance – is the real thing, and terrifying, in Proust's dark pantomime. 'Notre personnalité sociale est une création de la pensée des autres' (I, 19; 'our social personality is a creation of the thoughts of other people' (I, 20)), the narrator had said in the opening pages of the work, and the icy implication of this maxim is illustrated with unwavering consistency throughout the closing episode: people from whom thought is withdrawn cease to have personalities and, for the practical purposes of the collectivity, cease to exist. Just like the loved ones who are physically dead, these social corpses turn to an 'indifferent dust' in the minds of their former companions (IV, 589; VI, 403). Mortal questions of status, reputation, clan and caste continue to fascinate the *mondains* even when they have biological death at their throats, and it is one of the peculiar beauties of Proust's closing episode that this broad gallows comedy should melt gradually into the solemn lyricism of the final paragraphs. His noisy laughter at merely social entrances and exits continues to sound even as the novel's lesser characters die and its co-protagonist is finally laid to rest: 'Profonde Albertine que je voyais dormir et qui était morte' (IV, 624; 'Profound Albertine, whom I saw sleeping and who was dead' (VI, 450)).

Proust's novel, which begins with a fragile human consciousness holding out against the surrounding darkness, moves gradually, then, towards a final tableau in which that state of siege and that power of resistance are restaged in a mighty ceremony of leave-taking. A plague was there at the start, and a plague continues to rage at the end, and the book sets out, voluminously, a rescue-plan based on the exemptions and absolutions offered by the work of art. Death threatens, and the artist, the fiction-maker, steps forward not to shake his fist at providence but to put down sentences end to end. The novel begins with the adventitious constructions of consciousness, and it concludes with them too, but now externalised by way of penmanship and printer's ink. The bedtime reader who appears on page one has become a full-time writer. Fiction has at the eleventh hour assumed a responsibility which in earlier dispensations might have fallen to theology, or philosophy, or mathematics: to make sense of the world. Fiction, especially novel-writing, is an improbable candidate for this role, for it brings with it such a lumber of pseudo-fact and gratuitous fantasy. But the novelist, in Proust's account, is a heroic discoverer of order in chaos, and of beauty in the bric-à-brac of daily life. Even as he fibs, fiddles, footles and fabulates he is bringing a new sense of structure and a new truthfulness into being. Even as he loses himself in the trifling particulars of social life or the byways of introspective thought he is finding a lost key to the nature of things. And all the while, even while writing physical, social and mental mortality into his work, he is refusing death its dominion.

There would be no point in trying to deny Proust's narrator the scale and ambition of his creative project, however unfashionable these may now seem. The whole novel is haunted by the dream of art as a supremely efficacious mode of knowledge, and of story-telling as its finest flower. The big book of

death-defying stories with which Proust's novel compares itself
is not the *Decameron*, in which the spectacle of death appears
as a horrifying initial trigger to the telling of tales, but the
Thousand and One Nights, in which the story-teller's art and
guile are endlessly remobilised to achieve a further stay of
execution. 'Narrate or die', for Proust's narrator as for Scheher-
azade, is the imperative which underlies the exercise of verbal
craft. By mere sentences placed end to end, one's sentence is
commuted for a while and the end postponed.

Death in Proust is no one thing, and operates in no one
place. It is a spectrum of possibilities and inevitabilities, and
exposes the narrator, who wants to be a writer, to an infestation
of paradoxes that might seem inimical to literary art. Death is
governed by the laws of nature, yet declares itself in a procession of accidents; it transcends the reflexive activities of the
human mind, yet is ingrained in them; it causes things to fall
apart, yet unleashes the integrative force of imagination; the
long-nursed thought of death produces depressive brooding
on the one hand, but alert sentience on the other. Death is too
much with us, yet never quite with us enough; it is the overriding theme of tragedy, yet a spur to comic and satirical
invention. The experience of death, past, present or impending,
is a keyboard on which Proust plays with maniacal dexterity.
He is literature's Liszt, and his novel contains a series of gigantic
Totentänze. Where the law of death, as it acts in the natural
world, destroys individuals in favour of populations and has a
drastic dedifferentiating effect upon human bodies and personalities, the artist rises up as a defender and enhancer of difference. Where nature kills individuals in order to protect and
promote biodiversity in the longer term, the artist has an under-
standable impatience with this programme: he wants his cornucopian variety of life-forms to be revealed to him in the here
and now, in the work he produces. Even the cancelling hand

of death must be enlisted in the service of variety, encouraged to spawn curiosities and contradictions, and invited to feed these into the emerging work. Death will have its day, will have its way with the Proustian artist in due course, but before its moment of triumph comes the artist can subject death to his own law of imaginative transformation. He can turn death into a *belle contexture* of images and sonorities, a *chiaroscuro* of abstract propositions, a heady social carnival.

All this is very familiar. If we use these and no other terms to describe the Proustian artist as he finally declares himself in *Le Temps retrouvé*, he will seem an altogether companionable fellow and the upholder of a creative creed well suited to our disabused and godless times. He will be the best sort of artist we can hope for in the trying circumstances of the age. But Proust's appetite for paradox is much more powerful than this suggests, and he yokes together in the last incarnation of his narrator two violently different viewpoints.

On the one hand, he speaks in exalted Platonising tones about the benefits that art can be expected to confer upon mortal humankind. When the narrator speaks of love, beauty and truth and the immortality towards which, in their convergence, they conduce, he echoes Diotima's great sequence of speeches in Plato's *Symposium*. He shares with Diotima a language of fecundity, ripening and child-bearing with which to evoke the progress of the human individual towards the threshold of Immortality. Following in her footsteps, he speaks of this journey as a spiritual and intellectual ascent. Indeed he parts company with her in one doctrinal particular only. Where Diotima presents the beauties of Homer and Hesiod, like the beauties of the human form, as a staging-post on the rising road towards the divine sanctuary of Beauty itself, Proust's narrator offers us the work of art as the highest human destination. Whatever we can know of immortality comes from that and no other source. But the kinship between the narrator and Plato's inspired philosopher of love is nevertheless profound. In a world of motor-cars, aeroplanes and wireless telegraphy, he dares to be anachronistic and to sound an ancient European theme. While reproducing in his book the din of technological modernity, he speaks of art as a therapy for the human passions and the only path we have towards the communication of souls.

On the other hand, and even while his doctrine of immortality through art is being propounded, death as the merciless destroyer of human tissue is never forgotten. Indeed it is celebrated:

> Certains hommes boitaient dont on sentait bien que ce n'étaient pas par suite d'un accident de voiture, mais à cause d'une première attaque et parce qu'ils avaient déjà, comme on dit, un pied dans la tombe. Dans l'entrebâillement de la leur, à demi paralysées, certaines femmes semblaient ne pas pouvoir retirer complètement leur robe restée accrochée à la pierre du caveau, et elles ne pouvaient se redresser, infléchies qu'elles étaient, la tête basse, en une courbe qui était comme celle qu'elles occupaient actuellement entre la vie et la mort, avant la chute dernière. Rien ne pouvait lutter contre le mouvement de cette parabole qui les emportait et, dès qu'elles voulaient se lever, elles tremblaient et leurs doigts ne pouvaient rien retenir. (IV, 516)

> Some men walked with a limp, and one was aware that this was the result not of a motor accident but of a first stroke: they had already, as the saying is, one foot in the grave. There were women too whose graves were waiting open to receive them: half paralysed, they could not quite disentangle their dress from the tombstone in which it had got stuck, so that they were unable to stand up straight but remained bent towards the ground, with their head lowered, in a curve which seemed an apt symbol of their own position on the trajectory from life to death, with the final vertical plunge not far away. Nothing now could check the momen-

tum of this parabola upon which they were launched; they
trembled all over if they attempted to straighten themselves,
and their fingers let fall whatever they tried to grasp.

(VI, 309)

Human beings poised on the threshold of the grave can be
rendered as geometrical figures, and the shapes they make, like
the measurable tension-levels of their resistant muscles, send
the reader back to the impersonality and objectivity of natural
law. Dying is prime subject-matter for natural science, and for
the novelist who learns some of his lessons at the feet of scientists. Yet passages of this kind are insistent and over-elaborated
in a fashion that seems an affront to the much-prized objectivity
of the scientific calling. The parabola of the human spine as it
curves towards its last resting-place is caught up in an imaginative parable (*parabole*, again) of the artist's own invention.
And the movement of this parable is sustained into the last
paragraph of the work, where the ageing human body is figured
not just geometrically but in its last topological distortion: old
people are teetering stilt-walkers, hoisted upon their accumulated years and 'parfois plus hautes que des clochers' (IV, 625;
'sometimes they become taller than church steeples' (VI, 451)).

The Platonic dream of eternal life is not countermanded by
these mesmerising images of mortality at work upon the human
frame. The redemptive power of art and the vanity of art are
both to be recognised and no resolution between them is to
be sought. Being able to contemplate both in a single
encompassing gaze is the mark of an artist who has come of
age, and of an objectivity and disinterestedness that only great
artists can achieve.

Epilogue:
Starlight on Balbec beach

povero gracile universo figlio della nulla, tutto
ciò che siamo e facciamo t'assomiglia.

ITALO CALVINO, *Cosmicomiche vecchie e nuove*

poor, frail universe, born of nothing, all we are and do resembles you.

Numbers in the Dark

In *Sodome et Gomorrhe*, the narrator tells us that he and
Albertine lay together at night among the dunes of Balbec beach
and found that the sea beside them was breathing in time to
the rhythm of their pleasurable sensations. Above them, the
sky was 'parcheminé d'étoiles' (III, 408; 'all "studied" with
stars' (IV, 484)). The phrase is reported by the narrator as
one of the hotel manager's verbal near-misses. He should of
course have said 'parsemé d'étoiles' – scattered with stars –
but, as so often happens in this novel of boundless curiosity
about language, his malapropism could not be more apropos.
The sky has become a writing surface, and the stars are signs
inscribed upon it. While the embracing lovers for a moment
find that their sexual feelings have been written as a single
stable message into the book of nature, the astral world above
them is multiple and contains messages without end. Yet again,
Proust has found a way of linking the multifariousness of human
experience with the kaleidoscopic variety of his own writing.
Although the narrator of the book has among his enduring

319

ambitions the construction of 'great laws', those regulatory principles with which he might finally control the remorseless daily flux of particulars and circumstances, the very language which he holds in readiness for this task has countless hair-triggers inside it. At any moment his sentences may run riot. The 'drunkenness of things being various' may be unleashed by any plain, simple and sober-seeming word.

Proust is at home among the stars, and accustomed to their disconcerting habits. At one moment, the stars are a pure scattering of luminous points, and turn the narrator into a scatterbrain. At the next moment, they are constellations, gigantic intimations of structure. And in either event the writer has his lessons to learn from them. Starscapes are everywhere, and from the viewpoint of the writer at work, it makes little difference whether the stars in question belong to the heavens or to the entertainment industry. Proust is perfectly familiar with 'stars' in the modern popular sense, which predates Hollywood by a good half-century, and trains a merciless eye upon them as their periods of ascendancy give way to decline. Structure and its loss are as readily available in the history of a reputation or in an ordinary convivial scene as in the contemplation of the firmament. The narrator, becoming tipsy during one of his dinners at Rivebelle in *A l'ombre des jeunes filles en fleurs*, finds himself deliciously adrift in social space that is also interstellar space:

> Toute cette activité vertigineuse se fixait en une calme harmonie. Je regardais les tables rondes dont l'assemblée innombrable emplissait le restaurant, comme autant de planètes, telles que celles-ci sont figurées dans les tableaux allégoriques d'autrefois. D'ailleurs, une force d'attraction irrésistible s'exerçait entre ces astres divers et à chaque table les dîneurs n'avaient d'yeux que pour les tables où ils n'étaient pas, exception faite pour quelque riche amphitryon,

lequel ayant réussi à amener un écrivain célèbre, s'évertuait
à tirer de lui, grâce aux vertus de la table tournante, des
propos insignifiants dont les dames s'émerveillaient. L'har-
monie de ces tables astrales n'empêchait pas l'incessante
révolution des serveurs innombrables, lesquels parce qu'au
lieu d'être assis, comme les dîneurs, ils étaient debout, évo-
luaient dans une zone supérieure. Sans doute l'un courait
pour porter des hors-d'œuvre, changer le vin, ajouter des
verres. Mais malgré ces raisons particulières, leur course
perpétuelle entre les tables rondes finissait par dégager la
loi de sa circulation vertigineuse et réglée.   (II, 167 – 8)

All this dizzy activity became fixed in a quiet harmony. I
looked at the round tables whose innumerable assemblage
filled the restaurant like so many planets, as the latter are
represented in old allegorical pictures. Moreover, there
seemed to be some irresistible force of attraction at work
among these various stars, and at each table the diners had
eyes only for the tables at which they were not sitting, with
the possible exception of some wealthy Amphitryon who,
having managed to secure a famous author, was endeav-
ouring to extract from him, thanks to the magic properties
of the turning-table, a few insignificant remarks at which the
ladies marvelled. The harmony of these astral tables did not
prevent the incessant revolution of the countless waiters
who, because instead of being seated like the diners they
were on their feet, performed their gyrations in a more
exalted sphere. No doubt they were running, one to fetch
the hors d'œuvre, another to change the wine or to bring
clean glasses. But despite these special reasons, their perpetual course among the round tables yielded, after a time,
to the observer the law of its dizzy but ordered circulation.
                                                   (II, 450 – 51)

The 'famous author' installed in the middle of these planetary
orbits is not saying much, and certainly not performing as a
writer, but the necessary tension that governs his creative writing is being allegorised around him even as he sits and says

little: he must seek vertigo, yet seek to regulate it, drink himself silly with the sheer welter of things, yet establish a new calm and a new harmony among them.

This astral imagery, and the two-way pull between order and disorder that it embodies, reach their culmination as the narrator looks at the night sky over Paris in *Le Temps retrouvé*. Saint-Loup had recently extemporised with gleeful abandon on the pleasures of aerial warfare, and the narrator now, for a moment, catches that manic voice into his own:

> Après le raid de l'avant-veille, où le ciel avait été plus mouvementé que la terre, il s'était calmé comme la mer après une tempête. Mais comme la mer après une tempête, il n'avait pas encore repris son apaisement absolu. Des aéroplanes montaient encore comme des fusées rejoindre les étoiles, et des projecteurs promenaient lentement, dans le ciel sectionné, comme une pâle poussière d'astres, d'errantes voies lactées. Cependant les aéroplanes venaient s'insérer au milieu des constellations et on aurait pu se croire dans un autre hémisphère en effet, en voyant ces «étoiles nouvelles».
>
> (IV, 380)

> After the raid of two days earlier, when it had become more full of movement than the earth, the sky had become calm again as the sea becomes calm after a storm. But like the sea after a storm, it had not yet recovered absolute tranquillity. Aeroplanes were still mounting like rockets to the level of the stars, and searchlights, as they quartered the sky, swept slowly across it what looked like a pale dust of stars, of errant milky ways. Meanwhile the aeroplanes took their places among the constellations and seeing these 'new stars' one might well have supposed oneself to be in another hemisphere.
>
> (VI, 137-8)

The scene unfolds in a city, but a city resembling the open sea. Man-made searchlights travel across the sky, but create new milky ways as they go. Aircraft, man-made and steered by men, flash upwards to join the stars in their courses. All is changed on the face of nature by these intrusions of human craft and skill. Engineering takes its place among the elements, and the literary engineer makes his own immodest bid for a place among the heroes. The paragraph ends upon a brief quotation from Heredia's 'Les Conquérants' ('The Conquerors'):

> Ou penchés à l'avant des blanches caravelles,
> Ils regardaient monter en un ciel ignoré
> Du fond de l'Océan des étoiles nouvelles.

> Or, leaning forward at the prow of the white caravels, they watched as new stars arose, in an unknown sky, from the depths of the Ocean.

Whereas Heredia's sonnet is a brilliantly concentrated footnote to a lost age of heroic grandeur, a nod towards an epic vision that the modern poet can no longer share, Proust's paragraph is made of more ambitious stuff. The modern writer can indeed emerge a hero from his own gluttonous appetite for experience. The epic poet of the modern age cannot shy away from the low, the mechanical and the mundane. He must want them. He must want aeroplanes, searchlights, cars and telephones. Above all he must allow his book to become corpulent from its ceaseless voracity.

In the process of gathering its epic weight and bulk, Proust's *A la recherche du temps perdu* absorbs into itself, as we have seen, an ever-changing comic pageant of human individuals and types. Garros the air-ace, Peary the explorer, Rosita and Doodica the Siamese twins, assorted politicians and princes, a president of the Republic, a tribe of largely nameless footmen, waiters and mechanics, a bevy of minor aristocrats, many of them famous only for a moment or two, and only on the strength of a fleeting fatuity, writers and musicians by the score, heroes and villains from the four corners of European history – all of them move forward inside the text as a variegated throng. This is astral multiplicity in the human sphere. And although Proust has limitless reserves of sarcasm and derision at his disposal, and shows unerring precision in shooting his satirical darts, he also has the underlying tenderness and generosity that all the greatest comic writers share. Follies and foibles define our humanity, and must be safeguarded. Proust's narrator clings to his airy Albertine as tenaciously as Don Quixote clings, even upon his deathbed, to his delusional Dulcinea. And, in a certain light, Proust is closer to the inimitable Cervantes than to any other writer, ancient or modern. Erich Auerbach, in his *Mimesis* (1946), that great critical overview of the 'Representation of Reality in Western Literature', writes of Quixote in terms that seem already to announce the Proustian comedy: 'As God lets the sun shine and the rain fall on the just and the unjust alike, so Don Quijote's madness, in its bright equanimity, illumines everything that crosses his path and leaves it in a state of gay confusion.' In *Sodome et Gomorrhe* the narrator describes the social antics of Charlus as those of a modern-day Don Quixote tilting at windmills (III, 53; IV, 62), but the narrator himself is a still more perfect embodiment of the quixotic temperament: his bright equanimity is brought to bear not only upon the changing procession of personalities and sexualities which pass across the social stage but upon the polymorphous variety of his own 'self'. Proust's protagonist is a man with too many qualities.

This plurality of the Proustian narrator will raise a problem for many readers. He catalogues his own follies and misperceptions with lucid discriminating intelligence, but he is also a social, political and moral chameleon whose many colourings will at times make his intelligence seem simply promiscuous. Equanimity is all very well, Proust's reader may find himself or herself protesting, but certain kinds of company should not be kept, and certain forms of conduct should not, even in a spirit of disinterested intellectual experimentation, be tolerated. Homophobia, antisemitism and paedophilia are handled, many will feel, with an excess of empathising generosity, and with a fixated imaginative engagement that is alien to the broader comic vision of the book.

There is a real cause for anxiety here, and all new readers of Proust should expect to be embarrassed or offended at times as their journey through the book proceeds. But two of the book's other qualities could be remembered at this point, and may go a long way towards restoring if not peace of mind then something approaching the calm vertigo of which the narrator speaks. The first quality that I have in mind is the overt and relentless desire-drivenness of the novel. It is a bacchanal that summons up, and recruits to its own purposes, an astonishing range of desiring styles and gambits. And Proust's writing has a headlong, flyaway pace to it, and one which blends and fuses into a single animated process obsessions, 'sexual orientations', appetites and phobias that could easily, in other hands, have been allowed to accumulate as so much inert case-material. Proust's book is a tribute to the waywardness and improbability of desire, and places upon itself, as a matter of principle, the requirement that it shock and provoke. Even *Le Temps retrouvé*, which spends so much time reviewing and reweaving materials from earlier in the novel, has, in the field of sexual desire, its major surprise: it eroticises the spectacle of impending death. Proust is to sexuality what Talleyrand is to diplomacy and statesmanship. He is a dextrous negotiator, makes pliability and plasticity into art forms, and relishes the passage from one tight corner to the next.

My second quality is related to the first, but is by no means always to be found among literary experimentalists upon human desire. It is the quality that the young narrator finds in Bergotte's prose, and that the dying Bergotte finds in Vermeer's *View of Delft*. The novel is built from a multitude of different layers or levels, and the ready communication between layers that is encouraged by Proust's writing creates an astonishing sensation of semantic depth and resonance. Desire, given voice in prose of this kind, far from running a merely unilinear forward course, begins to develop echoes and harmonics. Desire is greedy, but at the same time full of shades and gradations; it flings itself forward in time yet constantly remembers its own past. It is the elaborate polyphonic texture of Proust's prose, and its power of self-remembrance, that allows his reader to achieve a special ecstasy by way of the printed page. The cruel extremities of desire, together with the torments of the jealous imagination and the ill-adaptation of lover to lover, begin to dance with a new sense of openness and possibility.

And this quality is, of course, what makes Balbec beach for ever dissimilar to the beach at Cabourg, however prodigal that resort may become with its salt, its sand and its breezes. Balbec is not to be found on any map, for it migrates and mutates. The narrator may glimpse it for a moment in the Bois de Boulogne, as in this moment from *Le Côté de Guermantes*:

Nous fîmes quelques pas à pied, sous la grotte verdâtre, quasi sous-marine, d'une épaisse futaie sur le dôme de laquelle nous entendions déferler le vent et éclabousser la pluie. J'écrasais par terre des feuilles mortes qui s'enfonçaient dans le sol comme des coquillages et je poussais de ma canne des châtaignes, piquantes comme des oursins.

(II, 683)

We went a little way on foot into the greenish, almost submarine grotto of a dense grove on the dome of which we heard the wind howl and the rain splash. I trod underfoot

dead leaves which sank into the soil like sea-shells, and
poked with my stick at fallen chestnuts prickly as sea-
urchins. (III, 449)

Suddenly, while strolling in their urban pleasure-ground,
Albertine and the narrator are back upon a Northern shore,
treading on ghostly shells and sea-urchins; from a single point
in the history of their love, a long vista opens up in geological
time. Or again, the narrator may catch sight of the Balbec shore
in the indoor domain of Albertine's captivity:

> Je pouvais bien prendre Albertine sur mes genoux, tenir sa
> tête dans mes mains, je pouvais la caresser, passer longue-
> ment mes mains sur elle, mais, comme si j'eusse manié une
> pierre qui enferme la salure des océans immémoriaux ou
> le rayon d'une étoile, je sentais que je touchais seulement
> l'enveloppe close d'un être qui par l'intérieur accédait à
> l'infini. (III, 888)

> I could, if I chose, take Albertine on my knee, hold her
> head in my hands, I could caress her, run my hands slowly
> over her, but, just as if I had been handling a stone which
> encloses the salt of immemorial oceans or the light of a star,
> I felt that I was touching no more than the sealed envelope
> of a person who inwardly reached to infinity. (V, 441)

Beyond geological time and astronomical distance lies the
inscrutable inwardness of human desire, which Proust maps
endlessly. Balbec beach is a portion of that desire-map, and
sustained in being by textual artifice and rhetorical cunning.
But if Balbec beach in the end is a text and nothing more, it
has the peculiarity of straining always to rejoin the real world.
Writing as fine as this can be expected only from an author
who has held stones in his hand, tasted salt on his tongue,
and, even as his mental constellations dance within him, opened
his eyes to the light of real stars.

NOTES

---

v   LICHTENBERG: *Gedankenbücher*, ed. Franz H. Mautner (Frankfurt-am-Main: Fischer, 1963), 238; *Aphorisms*, trans. R. J. Hollingdale (London: Penguin, 1990), 189.

v   EMERSON: *The Essays*, ed. Alfred R. Ferguson and Jean Ferguson Carr (Cambridge, Mass., and London: Harvard University Press, 1987), 126.

v   KHLEBNIKOV: *Collected Works*, vol. 1, trans. Paul Schmidt, ed. Charlotte Douglas (Cambridge, Mass., and London: Harvard University Press, 1987), 321.

Preface

xi   PROUST: III, 762; V, 291.

xv   'MYSTERIOUS THREADS': the poet concerned is Hugo in his celebrated 'Tristesse d'Olympio'.

xvii   SHAKESPEARE: *Troilus and Cressida*, III.ii.80.

I : *Self*

1   KALEVALA: text and translation are quoted from the liner-notes to Mari Anne Häggander's recording of Sibelius's orchestral song *Luonnotar* (BIS CD-270).

1   AUSTEN: for *imaginist*, see *Emma* (1815), ed. James Kinsley (Oxford: Oxford University Press, 1971; reissued in 'World's Classics', 1980), 302.

2   ALBERTINE: as nebula III, 874; V, 425; constellation: II, 180; II, 465; Milky Way: II, 472; III, 196; exploding star: IV, 568; VI, 376. Where I have listed these terms separately, Proust often uses them together. Rachel's face, for example, is both a nebula and a milky way.

2   COMPUTATIONAL SCHOLARSHIP: my figure is based on data supplied by Etienne Brunet in his invaluable concordance *Le Vocabulaire de Proust*, 3 vols (Genève–Paris: Slatkine–Champion, 1983).

9   COMME ÇA: on the temporal mechanism that this discovery reveals, see below 54–55.

9   IN MANY EDITIONS OF THE NOVEL: on the problem of locating the exact dividing line between *Albertine disparue* and *Le Temps retrouvé*, see Tadié's introduction to the new Pléiade edition (I, xc) and Jean Milly's introduction to the Garnier–Flammarion edition of *La Fugitive* (= *Albertine disparue*) (1986), 34–6.

10   TENNYSON: these lines are the first stanza of one of the songs from *The Princess* (*Poems and Plays*, Oxford: Oxford University Press, 1965), 173.

10   LACRIMAE RERUM: Virgil, *Aeneid*, I, 462.

12   MME VERDURIN: this passage is quoted below, 299.

16   SPITZER: 'L'Etymologie d'un «cri de Paris»', in *Etudes de style* (Paris: Gallimard, 1970), 474–81. This volume also contains Spitzer's great essay 'Le style de Marcel Proust' (397–473).

21   KEATS: *Letters of John Keats*, ed. Robert Gittings (Oxford: Oxford University Press, 1970), 326. The phrase is from Keats's long letter to George and Georgiana Keats of 17–27 September 1819.

21   MORALLY RESOLVED ARTIST: for a more detailed account of the novel's bold moral resolution, see below 199–208.

21–22   RYLE: *Collected Papers*, I (*Critical Essays*) (London: Hutchinson, 1971), 284.

23   GLORIOUS LIE: the phrase 'glorieux mensonges' is used by Mallarmé in his letter to Henri Cazalis of 28 April 1866 (*Correspondance*, ed. Bertrand Marchal, Paris: Gallimard/Folio, 1995, 298).

23   LE MENSONGE: for further comment on this passage, and a fuller quotation, see below 181–83.

25   LES ECOSSAIS: kilted soldiers reappear, in a more detailed erotic landscape, on pp. 152–7 below.

26   BUSONI: Ferruccio Busoni's essay is to be found in *Three Classics in the Aesthetic of Music* (New York: Dover, 1962), and this quotation on p. 89.

II : *Time*

30   SZYMBORSKA: *Wielka Liczba* (Warsaw: Czytelnik, 1976), 31; *View with a Grain of Sand*, selected poems trans. Stanisław Barańczak and Clare Cavanagh (London: Faber and Faber, 1996), 119 ('Warning').

32–33   ADORNO: *Notes to Literature*, I, ed. Rolf Tiedemann, trans. Shierry

Weber Nicholsen (New York: Columbia University Press, 1991), 174–5.

44   FREUD: Freud speaks in these terms on numerous occasions; see, for example, *Three Essays on the Theory of Sexuality* (1905) (Standard Edition of the Complete Psychological Works, ed. James Strachey: Hogarth Press and Institute of Psycho-Analysis, 1953–74), VII, 194.

45   MISS SACRIPANT: see also pp. 184–85 below.

57   EMILY DICKINSON: I refer to poem 258 ('There's a certain Slant of light') in Thomas H. Johnson's edition (*The Complete Poems*, London: Faber and Faber, 1970, 118).

57   MONTJOUVAIN: the three episodes to which I refer begin on I, 157, 23 and 44 respectively (I, 190, I, 25, I, 51).

III : *Art*

68   ACTS OF JOHN: *The Apocryphal New Testament*, ed. J. K. Elliott (Oxford: Clarendon Press, 1993), 319.

68   MARY MCCARTHY: 'The Fact in Fiction', *On the Contrary* (London: Heinemann, 1962), 259.

68   WALTER PATER: *The Renaissance. Studies in Art and Poetry*. The 1893 text, ed. Donald L. Hill (Berkeley, Los Angeles and London: University of California Press, 1980), 189.

73   LAVIGNAC: *Le Voyage artistique à Bayreuth* (Paris: Delagrave, 1897).

82   PATER: *The Renaissance*, 188.

84   BARTHES: 'La cuisine du sens', *L'Aventure sémiologique* (Paris: Seuil, 1985), 227–9.

90   LAON CATHEDRAL: a much fuller account of the Laon oxen is to be found in Proust's essay 'La Mort des cathédrales' (1904), reprinted in *Contre Sainte-Beuve* précédé de *Pastiches et mélanges* et suivi de *Essais et articles*, ed. Pierre Clarac (Paris: Bibliothèque de la Pléiade, Gallimard, 1971), 148–9.

93   BORGES: Jorge Luis Borges, 'Pierre Menard, Author of the *Quixote*', in *Labyrinths*, ed. Donald A. Yates and James E. Irby (Harmondsworth: Penguin, 1970), 71.

98   ODYSSEY: my translations here and elsewhere are taken from Robert Fagles's magnificent new version (New York: Viking Penguin, 1996). This description of Aeolus appears on p. 231.

98   CIMMERIANS: Fagles, 250.

99   'JE M'EFFORÇAIS ...': for other references to the Cimmerians in Proust's novel see II, 55; II, 316 and II, 251; II, 551.

102 IN REMEMBERING THESE LINES FROM THE *ODYSSEY*: Fagles, 256.

104 PENELOPE: Fagles, 465.

106 ALDOUS HUXLEY: 'Tragedy and the Whole Truth' (1931), *Music at Night and Other Essays* (London: Phoenix Library, Chatto and Windus, 1932), 3–18. Huxley's list of representative Whole-Truth novelists contains the names of Lawrence, Gide, Kafka, Proust and Hemingway.

107 MAHLER: I am indebted to Deryck Cooke's *Gustav Mahler. An Introduction to His Music* (London: Faber and Faber, 1980), 15–18, for my references to Huxley and to Mahler. Cooke uses Huxley's essay as a guide to Mahlerian 'impurity'.

109 WALLACE STEVENS: 'An Ordinary Evening in New Haven', *Collected Poems* (London: Faber and Faber, 1955), 465–89 (see 488–89).

113 'SOMETHING FAR MORE DEEPLY INTERFUSED': the phrase is from Wordsworth's 'Tintern Abbey'.

120–21 STEVENS: 'The Man on the Dump', *Collected Poems*, 202.

122 *AENEID*: the quotations in English are from Robert Fitzgerald's translation (New York: Random House, 1983), 175, 171.

IV : *Politics*

133 MUSIL: *The Man Without Qualities*, trans. Eithne Wilkins and Ernst Kaiser (London: Secker and Warburg, 1954), I, 126.

146 WAGNER: In 'Judaism and Music', Wagner writes: 'As long as the separate art of music possessed a really organic need for life, up until the time of Mozart and Beethoven, there were no Jewish composers to be found: it was impossible for an element completely foreign to this living organism to take any part in its growth. Only when a body's inner death is evident can outside elements gain entry, and then only to destroy it. Then the flesh of that body is transformed into a swarming colony of worms. But who, looking at it, could imagine such a body to be alive? The true life, in other words the spirit, has fled elsewhere. This is what life is about. Only in true life can we too find the spirit of art again: not within its worm-infested corpse.' Richard Wagner, *Stories and Essays*, ed. Charles Osborne (London: Peter Owen, 1973), 38–9.

156 ELUARD: Paul Eluard (1895–1952) had given one of his collections the title *Le dur désir de durer* (*The Hard Desire to Last*, 1946).

159 LITERARY PASTICHES: these four authors are among Proust's

targets in *Pastiches et Mélanges* (1919). A further imitation of the Goncourts appears in *Le Temps retrouvé*, in pages where the art of parody reaches its *nec plus ultra* (IV, 287–95; VI, 23–32).

168   FALSTAFF: *Henry IV* (Part II), V.v.48.

173   MOSCA: in *La Chartreuse de Parme* (*The Charterhouse of Parma*, 1839).

V : *Morality*

175   POPE: *The Poems of Alexander Pope*, ed. John Butt (London: Methuen, 1963), 513–14.

175   FRAGMENT OF THE REAL WORLD: Charity and Envy are a contrasting pair in Proust's paragraph as they are in Giotto's design. Both panels are reproduced in Giuseppe Basile's *Giotto: the Arena Chapel Frescoes* (London: Thames and Hudson, 1993), 323 and 340, 325 and 347. Close inspection of the *Caritas* panel shows that Giotto is even more material, and less allegorical, than Proust's narrator suggests: the figure passes upwards not an inflamed heart, but a fruit or, possibly, a purse.

176   URIAH HEEP: *David Copperfield* (London: Oxford University Press, 1948), 234–5.

177   TOUT ÊTRE SUIT SON PLAISIR: this is an almost literal translation of Virgil's 'trahit sua quemque voluptas' ('Each is drawn on by what delights him most'; *Eclogues*, II, 65). Proust's allusion to Virgil's homosexual love-scene – 'The Passionate Shepherd to his Love' – is of course appropriate to the courtship of Charlus and Jupien, which provides the context for this maxim (*The Pastoral Poems*, trans. E. V. Rieu, Harmondsworth: Penguin, 1954, 34–5).

181   MONTAIGNE: 'il ne se trouva jamais aucune opinion si desreglée qui excusat la trahison, la desloyauté, la tyrannie, la cruauté, qui sont nos fautes ordinaires' (*Œuvres complètes*, ed. Albert Thibaudet et Maurice Rat (Paris: Bibliothèque de la Pléiade, Gallimard, 1962, 208); 'no opinion has ever been so unruly as to justify treachery, disloyalty, tyranny and cruelty, which are everyday vices in us' (*The Complete Essays*, trans. M. A. Screech (London: Allen Lane, The Penguin Press, 1991), 236).

181   SHKLAR: *Ordinary Vices* (Cambridge, Mass.: Harvard University Press, 1984).

181   KIERKEGAARD: In *Either/Or*, trans. David F. Swenson and Lillian Marvin Swenson, rev. Howard A. Johnson (Princeton: Princeton University Press, 1959), I, 83–134, and elsewhere.

187 MONADOLOGY: *The Monadology and Other Philosophical Writings*, trans. Robert Latta (Oxford: Oxford University Press, 1898), 256.

187 'NOT ONLY, I SAY': Quoted by Arthur O. Lovejoy in *The Great Chain of Being* (Cambridge, Mass.: Harvard University Press, 1936), 145.

189 FORSTER: *Aspects of the Novel*, ed. Oliver Stallybrass (London: Penguin, 1990), 146.

190 'ET DEPUIS . . .': *'elles* rinçaient' refers to the Larivière wife and her maid.

197 SEZNEC: *La Survivance des dieux antiques. Essai sur le rôle de la tradition mythologique dans l'humanisme et dans l'art de la Renaissance* (Paris: Flammarion, 1980). On euhemerism, see pp. 17ff.

198 PEARY: Proust, however, seems not to have been able to remember Peary's name, and left a blank in the manuscript at this point. On Peary's reinstatement by the second Pléiade team, see III, 1770 n.

198 ABSTRACT LAWS: On Proust's sententiousness, and on his scientific modelling, I have benefited greatly from conversations with Nicola Luckhurst, whose doctoral dissertation is devoted to the co-presence of maxim and metaphor in *A la recherche*. Among many graduate students to whom my thanks are also due, I should like to mention particularly Ingrid Wassenaar and Paul Rickett.

200 NUSSBAUM: *Love's Knowledge. Essays on Philosophy and Literature* (New York and Oxford: Oxford University Press, 1990), 48.

201–2 MME DE GUERMANTES: Mme de Guermantes has already appeared in the novel as a discriminating admirer of Hugo. In *Le Côté de Guermantes* she had triggered in the narrator a brilliant critical excursus on the differences between early Hugo and late (II, 837–8; III, 635–6). This is one of many passages in which the narrator reflects on the role of abstract ideas in works of art.

202 'QUE SUR TOUTE EXISTENCE . . .': *Œuvres poétiques*, ed. Pierre Albouy (Paris: Bibliothèque de la Pléiade, Gallimard, 1967), II, 832.

203–4 BEETHOVEN: the Kyrie of the Missa Solemnis bears this injunction in addition to the customary tempo marking.

204 OUBLIEUSE MÉMOIRE: 'forgetful memory'. This is the title of a collection of poems by Jules Supervielle (1884–1960).

204 *LES CONTEMPLATIONS*: *Œuvres poétiques*, II, 482.

205 EDMUND WILSON: *Axel's Castle. A Study in the Imaginative Literature of 1870–1930* (London: Penguin, 1993), 143–4.

206 POEM OF REDEMPTION: Alastair Smart speaks of the Arena Chapel as 'Giotto's great poem of the Redemption' in his *The Dawn of Italian Painting 1250–1400* (Oxford: Phaidon, 1978), 49.

206 IRIDESCENT: on moral 'iridescence' see Gilbert Ryle, quoted above, 22.

208 OBLIVION: on the destructibility of books and their authors, see below 286–7.

VI : Sex

209 MALLARMÉ: *Correspondance*, ed. Bertrand Marchal (Paris: Gallimard/Folio, 1995), 206–7.

214 SALOME AND LULU: Oscar Wilde's *Salome* (1894) provided the basis for Richard Strauss's opera of the same name (1905); Alban Berg's *Lulu* (1935) was based on Frank Wedekind's *Erdgeist* (1895) and *Die Büchse der Pandora* (1901).

222 PHILOLOGICAL EXERCISE: on Albertine's speech, see above 195.

227 WALTER PATER: *Appreciations* (London: Macmillan, 1899), 19–20.

229 VORACIOUS ARTIST: on the narrator's admiration for Charlus as a verbal performer, and his eventual dismissal of Charlus, see above 162–68.

231 EXPLOITATION OF CHILDREN: I am particularly grateful to my former research student John Williams for drawing my attention to the passages which I now discuss.

232 OVID: the text of the *Amores* is quoted from the first volume of the Loeb Classical Library edition of Ovid (second edition, revised by G. P. Goold, Cambridge, Mass.: Harvard University Press, 1977, 392) and the translation, slightly modified, from *The Erotic Poems*, trans. Peter Green (Harmondsworth: Penguin, 1982), 116.

236 'MELODY OF CHILDREN AT PLAY': *Lolita* (London: Penguin, 1995), 308.

237 GOETHE: Goethe's celebrated 'Erlkönig' dates from *c.*1782. Text and translation by Christopher Middleton are to be found in *The Collected Works*, I (*Selected Poems*), ed. Christopher Middleton (Princeton: Princeton University Press, 1994), 86–7.

238 'HOMO SUM': Terence's celebrated slogan 'Homo sum; humani nil a me alienum puto' ('I am a man; I count nothing human foreign to me') is to be found in his play *Heauton Timorumenos* (163 BC).

239 FREUD: Freud discusses those 'wrecked by success' in his 'Some Character-types Met With in Psycho-Analytic Work' (Standard Edition of the Complete Psychological Works, ed. James Strachey: Hogarth Press and Institute of Psycho-Analysis, 1953–74), XIV, 316–31.

247 SEA-URCHINS: for Proust sea-urchins clearly represent the degree zero of animal desire; see also I, 552; II, 157 and II, 683; III, 449 (quoted below, pp. 326–27).

250 BUNYAN: *Grace Abounding to the Chief of Sinners* (London: Penguin, 1987), 15.

250 DICKENS: *Dombey and Son* (London: Oxford University Press, 1950), 764.

250 JAMES: *The Golden Bowl* (London: Penguin, 1966), 463.

256 PETRARCH: text and translation are quoted from *Petrarch's Lyric Poems* trans., ed. Robert M. Durling (Cambridge, Mass.: Harvard University Press, 1976), 246–7.

259 HARDY: *The Complete Poems*, ed. James Gibson (London: Macmillan, 1976), 349.

262–62 OVID: text and translation are quoted from the first volume of the Loeb Classical Library edition of Ovid (second edition, revised by G. P. Goold, Cambridge, Mass.: Harvard University Press, 1977, 498–9).

265 MARVELL: 'Magnanimous Despair alone/ Could show me so divine a thing,/ Where feeble Hope could ne'er have flown/ But vainly flapped its tinsel wing.' (*Andrew Marvell*, The Oxford Authors, ed. Frank Kermode and Keith Walker, Oxford: Oxford University Press, 1990, 35).

VII : *Death*

268 'LITTLE TO SAY ABOUT EPIDEMIC DISEASE': epidemic disease was, however, the speciality of Proust's father and it was to Adrien Proust's study of the plague that Camus turned when preparing *La Peste* (see Jean-Yves Tadié, *Marcel Proust*, Paris: Gallimard, 1996, 45–56).

271 YEATS: the sentence 'Mad Ireland hurt you into poetry' occurs in W. H. Auden's 'In Memory of W. B. Yeats' (*Collected Poems*, ed. Edward Mendelson, London: Faber, 1991, 248).

271 HOFMANNSTHAL: text and translation of Hofmannsthal's 'Manche freilich . . .' ('Many truly . . .') are quoted from Leonard Forster's *Penguin Book of German Verse* (Harmondsworth: Penguin, 1957), 396. 'Ein Brief' ('A Letter') is available, in English translation by Michael Hofmann, in the Syrens series (London: Penguin, 1995).

276 MONTAIGNE: *Œuvres complètes*, ed. Albert Thibaudet et Maurice Rat (Paris: Bibliothèque de la Pléiade, Gallimard, 1962), 186–87;

The Complete Essays, trans. M. A. Screech (London: Allen Lane The Penguin Press, 1991), 212.

277 'EXAGGERATION AND EXCESS': on the role of 'exaggeration' in the emotion of pity, see above 200–1.

280 'JE NE SAIS QUOI': Bossuet (1627–1704) used this phrase to describe human flesh *post mortem* (*Oraisons funèbres*, ed. Jacques Truchet, Paris: Garnier, 1961, 173–4).

280 LARKIN: *Collected Poems*, ed. Anthony Thwaite (London: The Marvell Press and Faber, 1988), 196.

285 'BUT LET US CEASE': this is one of the many points towards the end of the novel where the revised English translation has not been brought fully into line with the text of Tadié's new Pléiade edition.

285–86 GÉRICAULT: two of these oil studies are reproduced in Lorenz E. A. Eitner's *Géricault: His Life and Work* (London: Orbis, 1982), 182–3.

299 'PROUST'S STATUARY': this is surveyed in detail by Jonathan Murphy, in his Ph.D. thesis *Sight or Cite? Aspects of the Visual in Proust* (Cambridge, 1994), to which I am indebted.

304 'THE IMPERMANENCE OF HUMAN SELFHOOD': at the end of the novel, summarising this element of his narrative, the protagonist says 'je comprenais que mourir n'était pas quelque chose de nouveau, mais qu'au contraire depuis mon enfance j'étais déjà mort bien des fois' (IV, 615; 'I realised that dying was not something new, but that on the contrary since my childhood I had already died many times' (VI, 437–8).

305–6 MONTAIGNE: *Œuvres complètes*, 91; *The Complete Essays*, 103.

307 LUCRETIUS: the text is quoted from the Loeb Classical Library edition of *De rerum natura*, ed. Martin Ferguson Smith (Cambridge, Mass.: Harvard University Press, 1975, 260) and the translation from *The Nature of the Universe*, trans. R. E. Latham (Harmondsworth: Penguin, 1951), 124.

308 SHAKESPEARE: *Macbeth*, IV.iii.170–71.

309 BROWNE: *Religio Medici, Hydriotaphia* and *The Garden of Cyrus*, ed. Robin Robbins (Oxford: Clarendon Press, 1972), 126.

310 'COMME ON COMPREND . . .': on the superiority of suffering over happiness, for the purposes of artistic creation, see also above 259.

310 HEIDEGGER: on 'being-towards-death', see *Being and Time* (1927), trans. John Macquarrie and Edward Robinson (Oxford: Basil Blackwell, 1962), 306ff.

319 CALVINO: *Cosmicomiche vecchie e nuove* (Milan: Garzanti, 1984), 215; *Numbers in the Dark and Other Stories*, trans. Tim Parks (London: Jonathan Cape, 1995), 272.

320 'THE DRUNKENNESS OF THINGS BEING VARIOUS': Louis Macneice's celebrated phrase is from his early poem 'Snow' (*Collected Poems*, London: Faber and Faber, 1979, 30).

322 SAINT-LOUP: this passage is quoted on pp. 26–27, above.

323 HEREDIA: José-Maria de Heredia, *Les Trophées* (1893) (Paris: Lemerre, 1947), 111.

324 AUERBACH: *Mimesis. The Representation of Reality in Western Literature* (1946), trans. Willard R. Trask (Princeton: Princeton University Press, 1968), 352.

ACKNOWLEDGEMENTS

The extent of my debt to previous writers on Proust will at once be plain to those who are familiar with the critical literature on this much-studied author. In an introductory volume aimed principally at general readers rather than Proust scholars, I have not thought it appropriate to acknowledge this debt in detail and so give the work an 'apparatus.' This does not mean that I am ungrateful for all the help I have had, and it gives me great pleasure to acknowledge it here. Four of my chapters have appeared in earlier forms elsewhere: Chapter 1 in *Moy qui me voy: The Writer and the Self from Montaigne to Leiris*, ed. George Craig and Margaret McGowan (Oxford: Clarendon Press, 1989), Chapter 2 in *Word in Time: Poetry, Narrative, Translation. Essays for Arthur Terry on the Occasion of his 70th Birthday*, ed. Leon Burnett (Colchester: Essex University Department of Literature and British Comparative Literature Association, 1997), Chapter 4 in *Narrative Voices in Modern French Fiction. Studies in Honour of Valerie Minogue on the Occasion of her Retirement*, ed. Michael Cardy, George Evans and Gabriel Jacobs (Cardiff: University of Wales Press, 1997), and Chapter 5 as *The Morality of Proust: an Inaugural Lecture delivered before the University of Oxford on 25th November 1993* (Oxford: Clarendon Press, 1994). I am grateful to all the editors and publishers concerned for permission to reproduce this material in the present volume.

FURTHER READING

Those who have read Proust's novel once could not do better than to read it again. They could reread it complete, from the top, or they could dip and skip and skim, taking their pleasures lightly and, it is to be hoped, stumbling upon half-remembered marvels at every turn. A next destination might be those prose writers among Proust's contemporaries and successors who share with him a magical power of fantasy and an infinity of stylistic invention: James, Musil, Joyce, Woolf, Borges, Beckett, Nabokov, Calvino. In due course, Proust's early works – including *Les Plaisirs et les Jours, Contre Sainte-Beuve, Jean Santeuil* and *Pastiches et Mélanges* – might be sampled, together with his voluminous correspondence and the drafts and cancelled passages that are printed as appendices to the new Pléiade edition. Proust has been fortunate in his biographers: André Maurois's *A la recherche de Marcel Proust* (Paris: Hachette, 1949) and George Painter's *Marcel Proust* (London: Chatto and Windus, 1959, 1965) both exist in French and English versions, while Ronald Hayman's *Proust: a Biography* (London: Heinemann, 1990) and Roger Duchêne's *L'Impossible Marcel Proust* (Paris: Laffont, 1994) provide stimulating and streamlined modern portraits. For the foreseeable future Jean-Yves Tadié's 958-page *Marcel Proust: biographie* (Paris: Gallimard, 1996) is likely to remain the standard work of reference. Tadié refuses to offer a 'novelised' biography in the wake of his many predecessors, and provides instead a magnificent and necessarily disparate dossier of Proustian raw materials. To this work all Proust admirers will now turn with gratitude as they pursue their individual enthusiasms. Among critical studies, Roger Shattuck's *Proust* (Glasgow: Collins/Fontana, 1974) and John Cocking's *Proust: Collected Essays on the Writer and his Art* (Cambridge: Cambridge University Press, 1982) are admirably trenchant introductions, while Leo Bersani's *Marcel Proust: the Fictions of Life and Art* (New York and London: Oxford University Press, 1965), Gilles Deleuze's *Proust et les signes* (Paris: Presses universitaires de France, 1964), Gérard Genette's *Figures III* (Paris, Seuil, 1972), Jean-Pierre Richard's *Proust et le monde sensible*

(Paris: Seuil, 1974) and Julia Kristeva's *Le Temps sensible: Proust et l'expérience littéraire* (Paris: Gallimard, 1994) are highly individualised works of critical analysis. Unforgettable short accounts of Proust have been written by Samuel Beckett (*Proust* (1931), London: Calder and Boyars, 1965), Theodor Adorno (see above, 330), Walter Benjamin ('The Image of Proust', in *Illuminations*, ed. Hannah Arendt, trans. Harry Zohn, London: Collins/Fontana, 1973, 203–17), and Edmund Wilson (see above, 334). Those who wish to find out more about the planning, composition and publication of Proust's great novel are referred to Alison Winton's *Proust Additions: The Making of 'A la recherche du temps perdu'* (Cambridge: Cambridge University Press, 1977), Richard Bales's *Bricquebec: Prototype d' 'A l'ombre des jeunes filles en fleurs'* (Oxford: Clarendon Press, 1989) and the editor's general introduction to the new Pléiade text. Close study of the French text of the novel has been hugely facilitated in recent years by Etienne Brunet's concordance *Le Vocabulaire de Proust* (3 vols, Paris–Genève: Slatkine–Champion, 1983), and by the copious end-notes in the new Pléiade edition. Readers of Proust in English will find a useful *Guide to Proust* by Terence Kilmartin in the final volume of the Scott Moncrieff/Kilmartin/Enright translation.

INDEX

'A celle qui est restée en France' (Hugo) 202–3

A l'ombre des jeunes filles en fleurs 208; antisemitism in 141–45; aristocracy in 158; astral imagery in 320–22; cross-referenced 301; Dreyfus affair in 138–39; Elstir's paintings 45–52, 60, 76–78; 'glorious lie' in 23; jealousy in 252; literary references in 99; plenitude in 187; political comedy in 135–6; retroaction in 55–56; sexuality in 45, 47–49, 52, 184, 219–21, 240–41, 254; time in 45–49

'A Villequier' (Hugo) 202

Adorno, Theodor 32–33, 35, 340

Aeneid (Virgil) 122–23

aesthetics 68, 70, 92, 105, 116, 173, 200

'After a Journey' (Hardy) 259

Albertine disparue 175; artistic references in 102; death in 291–94; desire in 229; despair in 265–66; homosexuality in 8–10, 54–55; maternal theme of 95–96, 102; paedophilia in 233–34; sexuality in 263; time in 53

altruism 21, 199–200, 204–5

Amores (Ovid) 232, 261

'Un Amour de Swann' 299; fashion in 74–75; pain in 208; prefiguration in 57; self in 20–21; sexuality in 215–17, 252; statuary imagery in 299

anatomical deficiency 246–49

anticipation 34, 58–59

antisemitism 130–31, 139, 141–47, 174, 325, 332n

appeasement 257, 261

architecture 90, 91, 96

aristocracy 127–30, 133–34, 150–51, 157–65, 168–69, 174

Aristotle 22

art 68–125, 189, 318–19; angels in 88–89; art market 69–73, 106; of artisan 87–88; artistic qualities 166–68; and communication 203–4; construction work of 109, 285–86; and death 273, 286–87, 304–5, 314–16; and history 270–72; imaginary works 76–78, 116; immortality through 317; self in 3, 110–12; and sex 218; Whole Truth artists 106–8; *see also* painting

Artaud, Antonin 267, 272, 309

artisans 87–88, 90, 109, 124–25

astral imagery v, xi, 1, 2, 18–19, 27–28, 30, 126, 175, 198, 209, 267, 271, 320–24, 328

Auden, W.H. 336n

Auerbach, Erich 324

Austen, Jane 1, 21

Axel's Castle (Wilson) 205, 340

Bacon, Francis (writer) 271

Bacon, Francis (painter) 272

Bagatelles pour un massacre (Céline) 144

Le Balcon (Genet) 152, 309

Balzac, Honoré de 159, 236

Barbey d'Aurevilly, Jules 91

Barthes, Roland 84

Voyage artistique à Bayreuth
(Lavignac) 73–74
voyeurism 23–24

Wagner, Richard 107–8, 109, 146,
332n
ar 126, 131, 156, 160–61, 165, 303
Wilson, Edmund 205, 340
working class 148–51, 153–54, 157,
169, 174

World War I 25, 126, 131, 152,
155–56, 268
writers 90

xenophobia 144

Yeats, William Butler 271

Zola, Emile 100, 103, 104–5, 141
zoophytes 186–87, 206